DIVORCING A NARCISSIST AND CO-PARENTING

HOW TO GET OUT OF AN EMOTIONALLY DESTRUCTIVE MARRIAGE AND DEFEND YOUR KIDS. TOP ADVICE FOR SPLITTING UP AND HEALING FROM NARCISSISTIC ABUSE IN A TOXIC DIVORCE.

Jessica Allen & Robert Mayer

Table of Contents

PART 1: DIVORCING A NARCISSIST

PART 2: CO-PARENTING

11

Part 1
Divorcing a Narcissist

NARCISSISM

Many of us who work in mental health have turned narcissism into an abominable monster, which must be destroyed for people to live better. Perhaps we think about it from the essentialist conviction that the capacity for intimacy is the most significant expression of emotional development, the antidote to all suffering.

How much capacity a person has to care for and care about others is one of the elements to diagnose narcissistic traits. Still, the bias of the therapist, who has preconceived ideas - theoretical and life history - about a should not be left aside, what others should aspire to, what they should value, what exchanges they should have.

Like when a patient speaks with the remarkable coldness of the relationships with his parents and siblings and tells me not to need them. He even confesses that any contact with them is the product of guilt, that he calms with a call or a two-hour visit, but that they do not mean anything in his inner world.

On the planet of the obvious, the therapist should insist that she approach them because it is recommended from the theory: make peace with her parents, stop hating siblings. But from the perspective of the unrepeatable of people. It would be necessary to understand the path that the patient has traveled until he becomes a self-centered man, who escapes from situations that, instead of being nutritious, become suffocating atmospheres that remind him parts of himself that he wants to forget.

We all have narcissistic traits to a greater or lesser extent, translated as a flight to the inner world, to protect ourselves from dependency. It is common to understand relationships from two narcissistic poles:

15

entrapment independence or the need to escape it.

According to Laplanche, the narcissist unknowingly runs away from the "enigmatic and traumatizing" messages that were unconsciously communicated to him by his parents and also maintains that we are always "translating a translation," so there are no standardized meanings, but they are still constructed. Why the parents said or did one thing or another does not have a universal answer; it is only possible to create coherent narratives for whoever asks the question.

Sometimes or almost always, therapists try to teach the patient that he is avoiding something central to life. Learning to depend, face conflict, moderate the sense of personal grandeur, stop escaping from himself; however, the patient sometimes does not agree with our ideas about the essential, and wants something different. The narcissist or someone who is going through a narcissistic state of mind believes that hell is needing others and needing it fills him with concern.

Adam Phillips explains: "Teaching the benefits of needing and being needed is our myth of secular redemption." I have seen faces and looks of amazement and incomprehension when I have transmitted the myth. The reality of many and many is that they are not fit for closeness or had or have relationships of coldness or aggression with their father or mother and do not see why it is appropriate to change. Rather than telling patients what they should want, according to our health standards, we could help them translate the traumatizing messages that made them fundamentalists of themselves, convinced that they don't need or want to need anyone.

Narcissism can be a painful condition because it is opposed to growth: to breaking the fantasy of omnipotence to face reality.

Some authors speak of the "narcissistic option," as an emerging choice: as a phobic response, to flee from destructiveness projected inside and out (the world, me and the others, are bad and dangerous) and as a response to trauma (for handle environmental deprivations, insults, military orders).

The best indicator that narcissistic traits are hurting is the feeling of not having the life you want and of hating all relationships equally. Treatment should focus on helping the patient to reconstruct the history of herself, to understand why the need of others is lived as tyranny, and to avoid imposing ideas about what is valuable in life. Narcissism is a shield, and a weapon has to be understood, without trying the quick conversion of the

16

patient to the religion of love for others.

THE FACETS OF NARCISSISM

The study of narcissism has undergone a facelift in the last two years. This personality trait is now considered to have two distinct facets: the search for admiration and rivalry. Further studies, including a recent examination of actors and actresses, have provided a more nuanced portrait of this personality. Actors, for example, crave admiration more than most people but instead tend to be less competitive than anyone else's grey. Artists want the light of the candlestick, but to be in the spotlight, they don't necessarily push others away.

This new way of understanding narcissism began in 2013, with an article in the Journal of Personality and Social Psychology that identified the two dimensions of narcissism. Mitja Back, from the University of Munster and lead author of the study, explains. Until then, measures and theories about narcissism treated this trait as a unitary construct, mixing agonist aspects (assertiveness, dominance, charm) with antagonistic elements, such as aggressiveness or demerit of others. By stacking both aspects into one, narcissistic behavior was confusing.

Back's team studied hundreds of healthy individuals and found that narcissism-related traits were grouped into two categories, both of which support a positive self-image. In praise itself, praise is sought; the defense to avoid criticism consists in lowering others. The search for admiration and rivalry each have different effects on body language, the health of personal relationships, and one's personality.

In an article in Social Psychology and Personality, actors and acting students were assessed, subjectively (by themselves and by other people), to determine if they depended on the admiration of others more than the rest of the mortals. Although achieving leading roles requires competing with other professionals, working with them involves collaboration, an aspect that is also attractive to people in the entertainment world. It was observed that they fight less than non-actors. The research was led by Michael Dufner of the University of Leipzig, who collaborated with Back on both articles.

Being aware of the duality of narcissism is profitable. Although narcissists display that bright and charming facet, it is often only a matter of time before storm clouds appear except maybe on Broadway.

TYPES OF NARCISSISTS

The term "narcissistic" refers to the person who organizes his personality about maintaining his self-esteem by achieving the affirmation from outside himself. Although we all have vulnerabilities in this area, and we are influenced by the approval or rejection of our significant people, in narcissistic people, this motivation outshines others. McWilliams points out that from the beginning of psychoanalysis, it saw that people have problems with their self-esteem that can hardly be understood in terms of unconscious impulses and conflicts. Therefore, cannot be treated with the model of therapy based on disagreement, but with the deficit model.

People organized as narcissists may feel false and loveless in private, and it took time for areas of dynamic psychology that Freud barely touched on developing to help them build self-acceptance and the capacity for deep relationships. From here, the author cites a great diversity of authors who produced contributions to the understanding of this dimension of the psyche, dwelling on the impact of the theory of object relations. In contrast, the authors questioned Freud's idea of primary narcissism since they advocate a primary relationship, narcissistic pathology being understood not as a fixation on a typical childhood grandiosity, but as compensation for an early disappointment in the relationship. He also cites the authors who highlighted the maternal function of containment.

With this development of ideas, it became clear that the openly grandiose personality was only a form of "self-disorder," and many and different manifestations of difficulty with identity and self-esteem are now recognized. The clinical literature has distinguished between two versions of narcissism: "alien" versus "hypervigilant" type; open versus covert or "shy," exhibitionist versus "closed," and the one that the author points out as her favorite, the "thin-skinned" narcissist versus "thick-skinned" (Rosenfeld, 1987). What all narcissistic people seem to have in common is an inner sense, and a terror, of inadequacy, shame, weakness, and inferiority. Their compensatory behaviors can be diverse, but they reveal similar concerns.

Drive, Affect and Temperament in Narcissism

Narcissistic people are very diverse and often subtle in their pathology; they do not always show apparent suffering. The successful narcissist (economically, socially, politically, militarily) can be admired. Still, the internal cost of the narcissistic craving for recognition is rarely visible from the outside, and the harm done to others when they pursue their goals is

19

usually rationalized as trivial or necessary.

Regarding the etiology of the narcissistic character, we still have only hypotheses, such as being more sensitive than others to non-verbal messages, or a natural disposition to adapt to the affections and expectations of others. Miller (1975) spoke of families in which caregivers exploit their children's talents to maintain their self-esteem, treating them as "narcissistic extensions" of themselves. Kernberg (1970) suggested a strong innate aggressive drive and a constitutional lack of tolerance for anxiety in the face of aggressive impulses. The primary emotions associated with the organization of narcissistic personality, shame, and envy are the most highlighted in the literature. McWilliams notes that young analysts underestimate the power of the emotional state of shame, and mistake it for guilt, intervening with interpretations that are not empathetic. Guilt is the conviction that one is in sin or has committed a wrong act; it is conceptualized as an internal criticism of the superego and connotes a sense of active potential for evil. Shame is the feeling of being seen as wrong or inappropriate, the audience is here outside of the self, and it has connotations of helplessness, ugliness, and helplessness.

Vulnerability to envy is a phenomenon highlighted by M. Klein (Segal, 1997). It consists of having the internal conviction that something is lacking and that one's inadequacy is in constant risk of exposure, so one becomes envious towards those who seem happy or have what one thinks they lack. Envy may be the root of the criticism that narcissistic personalities show, with themselves and with others: if I feel deficient and I perceive you as having everything, I try to destroy what you have by denigrating, despising, or ridiculing it.

Defensive and Adaptive Processes in Narcissism

Although they can use some defenses, the most common are idealization and devaluation. These are complementary processes, the self is idealized, and the others are devalued and vice versa. The grandiose self (Kohut, 1971) can be felt internally, or it can be projected. Narcissistic people confront any issue by processing it as a competition "Who is the best doctor? What is the best school?" All that matters is comparative prestige, and the advantages and disadvantages are nullified, all other concerns being subordinated to the general theme of valuation and devaluation. McWilliams gives the example of a patient university student with an artistic and literary sensibility, whose great father had told him that he would support him to become a doctor or lawyer, but nothing more. Since he had been treated as a narcissistic extension of his parents, he saw nothing strange in this position; Another natural defense is perfectionism.

20

Narcissistic subjects hold unrealistic ideals, convince themselves that they can achieve them, or respond to their failure by feeling inherently inadequate rather than forgivable human beings, with depressive results. In therapy, they may have selfish expectations of achieving a perfect self rather than tolerating failure and seeking more effective ways of managing their needs. The demands for perfection are expressed in chronic criticism of the person or others (the devalued person is projected or not). They may be unable to find enjoyment among the ambiguities of existence. They can try to solve their self-esteem problem by joining someone they inflate and creating an identification with that person, who then collapses when the flaw appears. So,

Relational Patterns in Narcissism

It is not uncommon, McWilliams argues, that sooner or later. The narcissistic subject becomes aware that something is wrong in his interaction with others and goes to therapy for it as the patient does not understand what it means to accept a person without judging or exploiting them. To love others as they are without idealizing them, and to express genuine feelings without shame, the only way to transmit it to them will be through the acceptance of the analyst himself, who it can become a prototype for your emotional understanding of intimacy.

The term "self-object" was proposed from the psychology of the self for people who sustain our self-esteem through affirmation, admiration, and approval reflects the fact individuals in that role function as external objects of the self and also as parts of self-definition. We all need self-objects, but reality and morality require that we also establish with others a relationship of recognition of who they are and what they need (Benjamin, 1988), not just what they do for us. Narcissistic people need their self-objects so much that the other aspects of the relationship pale or may not even be imaginable to them. Therefore, the most damaging thing in the narcissistic personality is the capacity to love. They give confusing messages to others,

Some theorize that these people have been used as narcissistic appendages themselves. They may have been vitally important to their parents, not because of who they are but because of the role they played for them. The child receives a confusing message; on the one hand, he is valued. But only in that particular role, which makes him fear that if his real feelings, especially the hostile or selfish ones, are visible, rejection or humiliation will come, thus developing the "False self" (Winnicott, 1960). McWilliams argues that a crucial difference between psychopathic and narcissistic disorder may be that while psychopathy stems from abuse and neglect,

21

(pathological) narcissism comes from a particular type of care in which support is given on the condition that the child cooperates with the parent's narcissistic agenda. It is understood that all parents look at their children with a mixture of genuine empathy and narcissistic needs, the issue is a matter of degree and balance, of whether the child also gets attention unrelated to meeting the parents' goals.

An aspect related to people who become narcissists is the familiar atmosphere of constant evaluation. The father has a plan for his son, which is vital to his self-esteem and, therefore, whenever the son disappoints him, he will be implicitly or explicitly critical. An evaluative atmosphere that shows continuous pride and applause also damages the development of realistic self-esteem because the child is always aware of being judged. Even with a favorable verdict, he knows at some level that there is something false in the constant admiration, and this will create the feeling of being a fraud, of not deserving of respect, which seems not to relate to who it is. The author cites authors who have argued that overindulgence is the leading cause of narcissistic pathology or others who support different versions of parenting in childhood: the embarrassed child, the spoiled child, and the individual child,

But the parent of a child with disturbing narcissism need not have been narcissistic himself. He may have had narcissistic needs toward a particular child, creating a setting in which the child could not discriminate between his or her genuine feelings and wishes to please or impress others. As an example, the author refers to an article by Marta Wolfenstein from 1951 in which she shows that, having grown up in hard times. No matter how liberal post-war New York was, parents gave their children the message that if they were not happy, they must feel bad about themselves. People who have experienced disaster or persecution convey to their children that they should live the life they have not lived, and the children of traumatized parents grow up with identity confusion and vague feelings of shame and emptiness.

The Narcissistic Self

It includes a vague sense of falsehood, shame, envy, emptiness or incompleteness, ugliness, and inferiority, or the compensatory counterparts. You are feeling entitled, pride, contempt, defensive self-sufficiency, vanity, and superiority. The sense of being "good enough" does not come into them.

At some level, they are aware of their psychological fragility, fear being excluded, or suddenly losing their self-esteem or self-consistency if criticized, and suddenly feeling that they are not someone. They often shift their fear of fragmentation of their inner self into concerns about their physical health and are vulnerable to hypochondriacal fears.

As a result of their perfectionism, they avoid feelings and actions that express awareness of their fallibility or their dependence on others. Gratitude and regret tend to be denied, because your sense of self is built on the illusion of having no flaws or needs and admitting them would fill you with shame.

By definition, the evaluation of the narcissistic organization of the personality implies that the patient needs external affirmation to feel internal validity. Theorists diverge from an emphasis on the theatrical or deficit side of the narcissistic self-experience. Here McWilliams refers (and returns to it later) to the central disagreement between Kernberg and Kohut about how to understand and treat narcissistic characters. The controversy came first in the evolution of pathological narcissism, whether it was the grandiose state of the self or the deficit and ashamed, is like the opposition between whether the chicken or the egg came first. Phenomenologically, these different ego states are intimately connected, like depression and mania; they are two sides of the same coin.

Transfer and Countertransference with Narcissistic Patients

Even the highest functioning patient, the person with a narcissistic character, contributes to creating an environment in the link that contrasts with the one that emerges with other personality types. Typically, the therapist first notes that the patient has no interest in exploring the therapeutic relationship. The exploration of how the patient feels towards the clinician can be seen by him as irrelevant to his concerns, or annoying. She may conclude that the therapist explores this out of her own need for reassurance (which may be a projection, even if it is true), but the patient does not usually verbalize it. It does not mean that you do not feel strong reactions towards the therapist, you can devalue him or intensely idealize him, but curiously he is not interested in the meaning of those reactions and is confused if the therapist asks about them. Your transfers can be as self-evocative as they are inaccessible to exploration. Thus, a patient may believe that he devalues the therapist because he is objectively second-rate, or that he idealizes him because he is objectively fantastic. The efforts at the beginning of therapy to analyze those reactions are unsuccessful, because the denigrated therapist will be experienced as defensive, or idealized as including admirable humility.

23

McWilliams maintains the situation of being devalued and that of being idealized are frustrating for the therapist, who feels that his existence as a human being with emotional intelligence who tries to help is extinguished. Its countertransference of making himself invisible as a real person is a signal for the diagnosis of probable narcissistic dynamics in the patient.

In connection with these phenomena, there are countertransferences of boredom, irritability, sleep, and a vague sense that nothing is happening in the treatment. The feeling that one does not exist in the consultation room is shared. Extreme drowsiness is frequent, and the author comments that when she feels it, she finds herself generating explanations such as "I have not slept enough" or "I had too much dinner," however when the patient leaves. Another enters, she returns to be upbeat and interested. Occasionally grandiose expansion countertransference may also be felt, but unless the therapist is herself a narcissistic personality, those reactions do not last long.

It relates to the particular kind of transfer characteristic of narcissistic people than projecting an internal object such as a parent onto the therapist, and they externalize an aspect of themselves, either the significant part or the devalued part of their self. The therapist is a self-object, not an entirely separate person who feels the patient as a well-delineated figure from the past.

However, most therapists can tolerate these transfers and develop empathy from these internal reactions once they understand them as expected features of working with such patients. What the therapist feels is an inevitable reflection of the patient's concerns about his self-esteem. The author advises reading Kohut and subsequent self-psychologists to learn more about the complex theories about the experience with these patients.

Therapeutic Implications of The Diagnosis of Narcissism

A general goal, according to McWilliams in these cases, is to help the patient find self-acceptance without inflating the self or devaluing others. The first requirement is patience here, especially necessary because of the boredom and demoralization that can accompany long psychotherapy with these countertransferences.

The author summarizes the two different psychodynamic views on narcissistic disorders, Kohut, and Kernberg. The essential thing for her is that Kohut (1971, 1977, 1984) saw the cause in the development of

24

pathological narcissism when facing normal maturation with difficulties in solving the everyday needs of idealizing and de-idealizing. On the other hand, Kernberg (1975, 1976, 1984) saw it as structural, that is, something that very early is twisted, leaving the person limited to primitive defenses that are different in type, rather than in degree, from those frequently used. If Kohut's conception can be seen as a plant whose root is stunted by receiving little water and sun, Kernberg's could be like a plant that has mutated into a hybrid.

As a consequence, there are different approaches to the disorder, Kohut's (e.g., 1971, 1977) recommends acceptance of idealization and devaluation, empathy with the patient's experience, and staying close to the patient's subjective experience. On the other hand, Kernberg (e.g., 1975, 1976) advocates confronting tactfully but insistently the greatness of the patient, whether of himself or projected, and systematically interpreting the defenses against envy and greed, and as a theorist of Object relations, oscillate between adopting the external and internal position. In general, the author, the Kohut approach, considered by many analysts to be for the most severe patients, of the limit-psychotic range.

After showing this controversy between authors and followers, McWilliams offers his suggestions for treatment:

- Patience and acceptance of the human imperfections that make therapeutic progress tedious in this case, because this will contrast with what the narcissistic person has internalized. Have a realistic and social attitude, more than critical and omnipotent. Humility is especially necessary for treating a narcissistic patient so that he incorporates a practical, non-judgmental approach toward his frailties.
- Pay attention to the recognition of errors by the therapist, especially empathy errors that inevitably are made. Apologizing, at the same time, confirms the patient's perception of abuse (validating their feeling) and gives an example of maintaining self-esteem while faults are admitted.
- Do not be excessively self-critical when errors are recognized. Because if the patient sees the therapist with much remorse, the message received is that mistakes are rare and require rigid self-censorship, which coincides with narcissistic psychology itself. McWilliams considers the contribution of Kohut (1984) on continuous processes of "break and repair" in therapy essential.
- Constant mindfulness of the patient's latent self-state, no matter how overwhelming it may be. Since even the most

25

arrogant narcissist will be embarrassed by criticism, the therapist must be careful to intervene sensitively.

- Discriminate between shame and guilt. Having very fragile self-esteem can be challenging for the patient to recognize their role in something negative, hiding their mistakes and hiding from those who discover them. It may induce in the therapist an attitude of non-empathic confrontation of his contribution to his difficulties, or a tendency to join the patient's lament about the poor treatment he receives from others. Neither position is therapeutic, although the second may be temporarily palliative for someone very mortified.

- When the devastation by imperfections is visible, the patient tends to justify himself. The therapist is then faced with the task of expanding the patient's narcissistic awareness, without, on the other hand, overly stimulating shame to stop treatment or withdraw emotionally. Sometimes it is necessary to instruct the patient on the need to articulate their own needs to others, because the patient regrets not being cared for, but does not realize that, when considering embarrassing to ask, he loses opportunities to have new experiences about the human interdependence.

- In these cases, it is often difficult for the therapist to know which character in the patient's life is relating to him, as it is an object-self transfer. It is necessary, then, for the patient to know that despite the countertransference feeling that one does not mean anything to the patient, the narcissistic subject often needs it more than people without self-esteem deficits. Even the most arrogant patient betrays more dependency on the therapist for his vulnerability when he is insensitive.

Differential Diagnosis

McWilliams argues that narcissistic disorder is overdiagnosed. Especially by psychodynamic clinicians, because any personality type may temporarily behave as a narcissistic character. Hence, the first necessary differentiation is between narcissistic personality versus narcissistic reactions. Any non-narcissistic person of integrity can have a narcissistic response because narcissism is ubiquitous. It is what Kohut and Wolf (1978) called "secondary narcissistic disturbances," or Kernberg (e.g., 1984), has called "narcissistic defenses." when suffering from narcissistic themes in certain situations. To distinguish this is the data of history and sentiment in the transfer.

Faced with narcissistic personalities, psychopathic women do not respond

26

to the empathic relationship, because they do not understand compassion and despise it as a sign of weakness. Therefore, they will not react to Kohut's approach. Kernberg's (e.g., 1984), centered on the confrontation of the grandiose self, can be assimilated by a psychopathic personality and is recommended by some therapists who work with them.

If a narcissistic personality is depressive, it can be misunderstood as a depressive personality. The difference is that depressed, narcissistic people feel empty while depressive people with introjective psychology, the guilty type, are subjectively full of aggressive and critical internalizations. The depressed narcissist feels without a substantial self, and the melancholic depressive feels that his person is real but hopelessly inadequate.

Confusing a narcissistic personality with an obsessive-compulsive one is easy because of the attention to detail that can be part of perfectionism. Narcissistic patients feel empty rather than angry, and they do not make much progress in therapy focused on the fight for control and blame on aggressiveness. They feel misunderstood and criticized if the therapist addresses issues that are not central to them.

Hysterical personalities, compared to narcissistic ones, are much more common in women. Hysterically organized women use narcissistic defenses, such as exhibitionism and idealization, in their relationship with men that quickly changes to devaluation and can be misinterpreted as narcissistic personalities. But their self-concerns are gender-specific and anxiety-provoking rather than embarrassing, and aside from their conflict areas, they can be warm, loving, and in no way empty. It is essential to differentiate the therapeutic requirements of both groups: hysterical patients improve with attention to object transfers, while narcissists require an appreciation of object-self phenomena.

Finally, as a personal comment on McWilliams' approach to narcissism, I highlight the sensitivity and sharpness that he transmits in his proposals for treatment and differential diagnosis. On the one hand, it seemed to be a very illuminating perspective on the consideration of narcissism as a matter that always has two poles. Because the deficit usually involves defenses, so it is typical for high states and decidedly shortage states to be shown in the same subject. On the other hand, it seems to me, however, that in Kernberg and Kohut's position controversy, he does not adopt a definite position, preferably as is characteristic of his over-inclusive area; he accepts all the approaches as useful. He includes them in the theoretical acquis without elaboration that brings coherence. However, it seems evident that people in addition to being narcissistic, can identify themselves as predominantly deficient or as mainly high, and that this does not depend on whether their disorder is more or less severe but on the type of structure of their narcissistic system. Not to recognize the two high and low faces of the narcissistic disorder, it is necessary to stop acknowledging that in many of the patients with this disorder, both fronts do not have the same weight.

THE MANUAL OF THE WICKED NARCISSIST

Since the 1980s, French psychiatrists have analyzed the figure of the wicked narcissist, who freely practices so-called moral harassment in social and work settings. Through hoax, lies, and humiliation, these types of people falsify situations to destroy the image of their target (a family member, partner, or coworker) and elevate their own at the same time. "They seek to feed their glory at the cost of the defeat of others, believing that, for each foot they crush, they gain one foot in height," defined psychiatrist Paul-Claude Racamier, creator of the term, 30 years ago.

1. Why Do They Harass?

They are very popular and appear to have it all, but "the perverse narcissists feel very intense envy towards those who seem to possess things that they do not possess or towards those who simply enjoy life," explains Marie-France Hirigoyen in a crucial essay to understand this figure: the harassment more. One of her goals is to vampirize that energy and take away her passions or, in the workplace, her professional capacity. Her obsession is not limited to one person and is repeated as a pattern in various areas of her life.

"The goods to which we refer are seldom material. They are moral qualities difficult to steal: the joy of living, sensitivity, communication, creativity", lists the French in her book. The aggressor seeks to destroy those virtues causing anxiety and depression in his victim. That the attacked man commits suicide is one of the great victories of the perverse narcissist, warns Hirigoyen. On many occasions, if he detects that his target survives and advances despite his attacks, he will make an appearance directly or indirectly in his life.

2. What Does the Perverse + Narcissistic Equation Mean?

The writer Javier Cercas carried out in The Imposter a microscopic analysis of the figure Enric Marco, a narcissist (although not perverse) who invented being a Holocaust survivor. He uses in his pages the story of the Roman poet Ovid to explain that Narcissus does not fall in love with himself. He hates himself, horrifies himself. He makes, based on self-promotion, a flattering fantasy, a lie through which he camouflages himself and hides his reality, the absolute filth of his life, his mediocrity and vileness, Cercas points out.

"The narcissistic pervert has a great narcissistic flaw; what protects him is his image. Behind his appearance of omnipotence, he is someone extremely fragile", highlights Jean Charles Bouchoux in his new book, The Perverse Narcissists (Harp editors), who has just published in Spain. What differentiates him from a narcissist is his perverse component, which generates the need to destroy the image of another while trying to improve his own.

3. Is He Who Supports A Perverse Narcissist in His Harassment-Free of Danger?

"They are directly dangerous for their victims, but also their circle of relationships," warns Hirigoyen, who recalls that one of the most common habits of these aggressors is to provoke conflicts between third parties, usually between one of their allies and their object of aggression.

Jean Charles Bouchoux agrees on this idea. The Frenchman remembers that people close to the wicked are involved in his manipulations, although he also recalled that they could act not even to become their victims.

It is not convenient to fear or glamorize these empty daffodils, which adopt the identity that is necessary for them at all times. All the images they project are false and seek to gain followers through admiration or fear.

4. How Does Your Bullying Work?

An example of the harassment of the perverse narcissist is found in Lolo, Julie Delpy's comedy premiered this summer in Spanish theatres.

Phase 1: It Is as Masochistic as It Is Sadistic

He first establishes a close relationship with his target to destabilize him without there being any witnesses. "Hints, malicious allusions, double meanings, lies, and humiliations" are the Bible of this stalker, highlights Marie-France Hirigoyen.

29

These attacks serve to discover a sadist or a masochist in their victim. If in the face of this hidden harassment, you decide to act submissively, a mistreatment relationship widely treated by psychology will continue over time. When the attacked person, on the other hand, does not tolerate the attacks, they intensify.

And then the perverse aggressor, like an excellent empty daffodil, adopts the opposite role of a masochist, maintaining attacks to provoke reactions in the other. He thus resorts again to the game of appearances and presents himself as the attacked, someone who is the victim of his charisma in the face of the envy of others: "The important thing for him is that his goal to beat seems responsible for what happens to him," says Marie. -France Hirigoyen.

Phase 2: The Black Swan Wakes Up

As the line between the aggressor and the victim is blurred, his black swan appears in the victim. What has allowed him to survive also kills him inside? And it is now that high levels of anger are reached when the wicked narcissist departs, even geographically, and hopes that his support will perpetuate the conflict, without reporting the high levels of violence to which he has subjected the victim.

The perverse wishes that both their ally and their objective end badly. "For a perverse, the supreme pleasure consists in achieving the destruction of an individual by another and in witnessing that combat which both will be weakened, and it will reinforce their omnipotence," relates the essay El harassment.

We repeat that the wicked is only dangerous if others allow it: He proposes, and his allies dispose of it. "His most significant failure is that of failing to attract others to the register of violence. It is the only way to stop his intentions "and that those who support him are not involved in them, as he seeks.

5. Why Do We Fall for The Manipulations of a Perverse Narcissist?

The most excellent resource of a perverse narcissist is based on false appearances. Societies are built through clichés, and every narcissist knows how to manage them to obtain the applause of others and, with it, social and professional success even more in a frantic society, in which we build judgments from superficial relationships. Therefore, we can find that we collaborate in the harassment of one of these aggressors.

Thanks to the simplification of topics, our day-to-day runs as quickly and efficiently as possible. An example of this is the scientific principle of Ockham's Razor, which determines that we tend to keep the least complicated option reasonable. "The simplest and most sufficient explanation would be the most probable, but not necessarily the true one," he defends.

The truth is that we are susceptible to all kinds of deception, not for lack of intelligence, but the real biological economy, according to Ockham's theory. We believed Enric Marco for decades because thinking that his approach was false was the most complicated option. The same was true for Rachel Dolezal, head of the National Association for the Advancement of Colored People posing as black for years when she was white. Both are examples of narcissists, although there is no perverse ingredient in them.

6. What Effects Does Such Isolation Produce on The Victim?

Faced with the game of false appearances, the victim loses many allies in the process. "It is important that I be able to communicate what happens when I am ready to do it," says French psychologist Jean Charles Bouchoux.

The victim knows that his truth is the option that, because it is complicated, is usually rejected. Can any other victim denounce this type of moral harassment, based on underground and permanent attacks by someone who appears to enjoy a life full of incentives, without being paranoid, self-centered or envious in the eyes of others?

In the conflict between the aggressor and the attacked, we tend to think that a person who always appears to be resolute and fun is more stable and dependable than someone who, on occasions, is frustrated, depressed or angry as a result of the situation they are already experiencing provoked by his attacker. In reality, it is normal for a mentally healthy person to develop a wide range of emotions and not just demonstrate positive ones.

The game of appearances is enlarged when the consequences of prolonged facing the anxiety and depression that this bullying generates become evident. The assaulted live with the permanent tension of thinking that, wherever they go, the hoaxes caused by their aggressor will have arrived sooner. "To resist psychologically, it is essential to receive some kind of support. Sometimes, it is enough for a single person to know how to express the victim's self-confidence, "says Hirigoyen.

31

WHAT IS GASLIGHTING AND WHY IT IS THE NARCISSISTS' PRIMARY MANIPULATION TOOL

What is Gaslighting?

Have you ever heard these phrases from your partner/father and mother/friends that have made you question yourself? If so, it is more than likely that you are a victim of Gaslighting, a form of emotional and psychological abuse that makes the person who is the subject of it question their feelings, instincts, thoughts, and mental health, giving the abusive person (usually a narcissistic) power and control.

The term has its origin in the British film "Gaslight" 1940, directed by Thorold Dickinson, based on the play "Gas Light" (known as "Angel Street" in the USA), 1938, written by Patrick Hamilton. In the film, a man manipulates his wife to convince her that she is crazy and thus be able to steal a fortune that she has hidden. He hides things like paintings, jewelry, making him think that he is responsible for those losses but does not remember it. The term refers to the gas lights that the husband uses in the attic while searching for the hidden fortune. The wife sees the lights, but the husband insists that he is raving.

Once the narcissist (or another abusive person) has used "gaslighting" to break the victim's ability to trust their perceptions and beliefs. The victim is more likely to stay in an abusive relationship Because he/she will begin to believe that he/she cannot live without the narcissist (or another type of rude person).

Gaslighting usually occurs in a relationship gradually - so much so that at first, the actions of the narcissist (or another abusive person) will seem harmless. With time, the victim ends up suffering anxiety, isolation, confusion, depression, losing a whole notion of what is happening.

Gaslighting is one of the most abusive and aggressive forms of emotional and psychological abuse. Being exposed to it over a long period can be psychologically devastating for the victim, destroying her self-esteem and making her doubt her sanity.

10 Signs They Are Gaslighting You

As for you, there are signs in your body and your head that warn you that something is not right. According to author and psychoanalyst Robert

Stern, the following are signs that they are gaslighting you:

1. You always question yourself.
2. You start to wonder if you are too sensitive.
3. You feel confused most of the time, and you have a hard time making decisions, even if they are straightforward.
4. You spend the day apologizing to that person.
5. You cannot understand why most of the time, you are sad.
6. You often apologize to others for that person's behavior.
7. You feel like you can't do anything right.
8. You feel like you are not "good enough" for other people.
9. You have the feeling that before this relationship, you were a person with more self-confidence, more relaxed, and happier.
10. You hide information from your friends and family, so you don't have to explain what happens to this person.

Actions Related to Gaslighting

Retention: the narcissist (or another type of abusive person) pretends that he does not understand you or radically refuses to listen to you. It may say something like, "I don't want to hear anything about this anymore."

Opposition: the narcissist (or another type of abusive person) questions your memory, even if you are very sure of what has happened. They tell you things like "You are wrong, you never remember things well" or "You are a liar, that has never happened" or "You are making it up, sometimes I think you are crazy."

Blocking / Detour: the narcissist (or another type of abusive person) changes the topic of conversation to silence you or to question you, saying phrases like "It's another crazy/unfortunate/insane idea of your (friend/family member).

Trivialization: The narcissist (or other types of abusive person) minimizes your needs or feelings, continually telling you that you are too sensitive or a difficult person or phrases like "Are you going to be angry about nonsense like that? But it was a joke! ».

Denial / Forgetfulness: The narcissist (or another abusive person) pretends to have forgotten what has really happened or blatantly denies the promises he has made to you. Its effects can be very harmful to you, and you do not have to tolerate this kind of behavior. Do whatever it takes to stay mentally and safe from the narcissist (or another abusive person).

Ways to Understand Narcissism

The world of narcissists is complex. The disorder they suffer confuses people about what is going on. The behavior they develop is so particular that there is a specific vocabulary to understand it and be forewarned. Here are six terms to understand the particular "Narcissus language."

Word Salad

It is a series of words that have no connection between them within the context of the phrase or speech and that have no meaning with the question or the conversation from which they come. The origin of the term is in psychiatry, baptizing the way of speaking of people with schizophrenia. They were trying to make sentences to express themselves and make themselves understood, but their brain was not able to process and correctly apply the syntax.

Narcissists use it, among other reasons, to make it appear that they have answered the question. I speak, you speak. Although they don't know the answer, so they say the last word. It is hypercompetitive. Narcissists can turn practically everything into a competition. It's like playing ping pong, not two adults having a conversation.

Flying Monkeys

The term comes from a scene in the movie "The Wizard of Oz," where the evil witch sends flying monkeys to annoy Dorothy.

Flying monkeys are those persons used by the narcissist as if they were objects to achieve their goals. If, for example, what the narcissist wants is to launch a smear campaign against the victim (something that sooner or later it is very likely to do), he will manipulate the flying monkeys to do the dirty work for him/her as telling lies about the victim, slander, harass, bully, isolate,

There are two types of flying monkeys: the one who is naive and blindly believes the lies of the narcissist and the cynic who plans to make some profit from the narcissist. They are usually family, friends, or acquaintances of the narcissist.

34

Cognitive Dissonance

The psychologist Leon Festinger was the one who gave the name to this term. It means the perception of incompatibility between two simultaneous thoughts that can negatively impact attitudes or behaviors. Victims experience permanent strain on their brains from receiving two messages at the same time that they are contradictory to each other. On the one hand, the emotional part of the brain (previously intoxicated by the narcissist with an overdose of oxytocin with the tactic of love bombardment) says that a narcissist is a right person, kind and worthy of love. On the other hand, a series of facts make the person reason (with the left part of the brain) that the narcissist is lying, deceiving, manipulating, and humiliating them.

The consequences of cognitive dissonance are usually stressed, anxiety, guilt, anger, frustration, and shame. Many times, victims end up deceiving themselves to stop feeling that tension. The higher the investment in time and feelings with the narcissist (for example, let's say the victim is married and has a child with the narcissist), the more prone the victim is to self-deception to justify their behavior and stop the cognitive dissonance. What they will do is unconsciously generate new thoughts (lies to themselves) to compensate for those that impede to continue the relationship with the narcissist.

The Scapegoat and The Golden Boy

Narcissistic fathers and mothers do not see their children as independent beings who must develop their personalities. They see them as extensions of themselves, and they end up being "reified" to satisfy the emotional needs of their parents. Children of a narcissistic family do not receive love, but rather tyranny disguised as approval or disapproval. In a family with a narcissistic father and mother (s), the children will generally play the following roles, which will be assigned by the narcissist: the golden boy and the scapegoat.

The golden boy is the favorite daughter of the narcissist, who will be a reflection of him/herself. For the narcissistic parent, the excellent boy is flawless. He does everything always well, he never makes mistakes, and he is predestined to success. The narcissist pampers, protects, and defends the golden boy without really taking into account if he misbehaves. The golden boy learns, from childhood, to demand special treatment, to blame others for his mistakes, to manipulate and lie, knowing that he will not be punished for this behavior as long as he obeys and pleases the narcissist.

The scapegoat is the girl that the narcissist has a fondness for, the one that he / the narcissist turns into the "black sheep" of the family. The scapegoat is the one that tends to question the behavior of the narcissist more, to "answer" her, to challenge her authority. The narcissist has the idea that this girl does everything wrong, is rebellious, rude, and ungrateful. When the narcissist has open confrontations with this girl, she will try to turn the rest of the family members against her, as if she were "the enemy." The narcissistic father and mother will criticize, humiliate, and disapprove of the scapegoat, even if he has done nothing wrong. The scapegoat is used in the narcissist to pour out his / her shame and anger.

Hoovering

The term "hoovering" comes from the American brand of vacuum cleaners "Hoover," referring to what the narcissist tries to do with this manipulation technique, trying to "vacuum" his victims to have a relationship with him/her again. If you have had a relationship with a narcissist, it is more than likely that they will try to "hoover" with you so that you can become a narcissistic source of supply for him/her again. It can take anywhere from weeks to months or even years. Narcissists are stubborn and persistent people who know how to wait and who can have immense patience when it comes to getting what they want.

Here are some examples of hoovering. Behind them all, there is always the same: manipulation and lies to resume interrupted contact:

- A message worried about you: He wants to know how you are, how you feel, if you are depressed, sad, He pretends to worry about you to see if you fall again and return to him/her.
- He contacts you again as if nothing had happened: "How are you? How are you? It tells you things that have happened to him/her as if nothing had happened between you. Calls or writes to you for your birthday or Christmas.
- Manipulation using third parties, for example, children: "I know you hate me, but tell your nephew that I won't be able to go to his birthday but that I love him very much."
- You have cancer / have had an attack/plan to commit suicide. The narcissist checks how much you still care if you run to help him. It is like a child with a tantrum, check if shouting and kicking works with you or not.
- Messages that are supposed to be for someone else. They send you messages "by mistake," which "presumably" were addressed to another person (her new partner, for example) to provoke jealousy and see how you react.

- Soulmates: They contact you to tell you that they have realized that you are their soulmate, that you have to be together, that you will always be the love of their life, that you will never find someone who loves you like him/her.

Gaslighting

It is a pattern of emotional abuse used by the narcissist to manipulate the victim into making him doubt his perception, judgment, or memory. It usually makes the victim feel anxious, confused, and sad.

The term originates from the 1940 British movie "Gaslight," directed by Thorold Dickinson, based on the 1938 play "Gas Street" (known as "Angel Street" in the USA) written by Patrick Hamilton. In the film, a man manipulates his wife to convince her that she is crazy and thus be able to steal a fortune that she has hidden. He hides paintings, jewels, making her think that he is responsible for these losses but does not remember it. The term refers to the gas lights that the husband uses in the attic while searching for the hidden fortune. The wife sees the lights, but the husband insists that he is raving.

Some examples of gaslighting are:

- Pretend not to understand what the victim says or refuse to listen to her.
- Change the subject saying, "you don't want to talk about it" in situations where you have never talked about it before.
- Accusing the victim of having an overflowing imagination and of "always living in the clouds."
- He accuses the victim of being possessive, jealous, demanding, when he tries to turn the tortilla in a conversation so that they are not asked about something they have done, and that is not correct.
- Neglect the victim by telling him that his opinions are ridiculous and childish.
- Try to isolate the victim by telling them to believe more in what "other people" say (these people being the victim's family and friends usually) than in what he/she says. The narcissist seeks isolation so that the person is entirely dependent on him/her.

The Perversity of Gaslighting

Manipulators, sociopaths, liars, psychological vampires, it is also how "narcissistic abusers" are known, experts in entangling their victims with words to make them prey to their worst intentions.

Manipulators, sociopaths, liars, psychological vampires, it is also how "narcissistic abusers" are known, experts in entangling their victims with words to make them prey to their worst intentions.

Gaslighting or "narcissistic abuse" is more common than it seems and has harmful effects on the victims, the psychologist Isabel La Fuente Taborga warns ECOS, for whom it is imperative to know how to recognize the strategies that this class of manipulators uses.

It is a "subtle emotional abuse" that describes the professional when it comes to referring to the most common type of manipulation that exists between sociopaths and psychopaths. One of their main behaviors is that "they don't do things head-on."

In reality, gaslighting is sociopathy, later specified, because "it is within psychological pathologies, but of a social nature." Among the types of sociopaths is the narcissistic abuser.

"They Have No Scruples."

La Fuente explains that psychopathy sometimes has a biological component, but this is not the case. The narcissistic abuser is an abuser for reasons such as education, upbringing, etc., "it does not have to do with brain functions but with behavior patterns."

Most worrying of all, people with gaslighting characteristics are hazardous because, in the psychologist's opinion, "they have no scruples to act."

A "Toxic Person."

This wicked picture is also circumscribed in what is known as a "toxic person." "There are various types of toxic people; for example, negative people. But this type of toxicity is the most dangerous because they make deliberate actions from harming the other, "adds the specialist.

This abuser — as well as his victims — can be male or female. A boyfriend, a husband, a wife, a mother, a father, a brother, a friend, a coworker, in

38

the latter case, generally a boss or a female boss. In La Fuente's experience, the most common is that the narcissistic abuser is a partner or a boss.

The "Smokescreen."

Inner Integration's Meredith Marie Miller, in a YouTube video, addresses the potential victims of these manipulators directly, bluntly, to try to convince them that they should get away from them as soon as possible.

There, he narrates how the victim, when he claims the narcissist, sociopath, or psychopath for his harmful forms, usually receives, for example, the following reply: "I never did that, you are crazy, you imagine it." Or: "You are very sensitive; what's wrong, it was just a joke."

"It kind of trains the victim and he stops trusting his thoughts, his feelings, his perception of reality," falling into the trap of what is called a "smokescreen."

He adds that "the abuser is driving the victim crazy. You can even humiliate him. That is degrading more and more their self-esteem, their confidence. "

Then she gives one more example: "You can force the other person to have intimacy under the threat that they won't have anything again. And the woman thinks that she is not well and that she has to do what he asks her to please the man."

"Something Is Not Right."

The danger is the affected person, by accepting the perception of another, maybe the victim of a form of "brainwashing."

"You will never have the proof because the abuser will always lie to you, manipulate you. You have to trust yourself, and you cannot trust the other person. If you start to believe her, you deny your perception of reality. Trust your feelings: if you feel that something is not right, something is not right, "says Miller in her video.

Addressing the victims of gaslighting, he practically evicts the narcissistic abuser: "He never assumes his responsibility, it is always your fault. If you suspect that someone is manipulating your reality, do not try to confront him, leave that relationship. That will continue, and it will be worse. Flees! Don't try to convince him. He will never take responsibility for his deeds. Confide in yourself".

"Posttraumatic Stress."

Gaslighting is so subtle that society does not know how to recognize it. Psychologist Isabel La Fuente warns that "there are many victims of people like this, only that we are used to thinking of sociopaths or psychopaths as murderers, and we see these people only as 'selfish.' But the consequences are complicated. There is posttraumatic stress later on in the victims."

We asked if a narcissistic abuser can recover. "It is difficult," she replies. "First, they don't see people as people but as useful tokens for their goals. Second, they have no empathy, so they do not see that the other is being damaged in its entirety. And third, most do not have true affection for the other (they are narcissists); they only care that they look good." That they see the importance of being different."

MARRIAGE AND THE NARCISSIST

Narcissists and psychopaths often get married and stay married. That does not mean that it is a happy union. Indeed, your spouse cannot be satisfied, and the narcissist is never pleased, or at least not for more than a nanosecond! Narcissists marry and remain married because the "family" is a backdrop to their fabricated life. Stabilizes your image, after all, is what others do. Except the narcissist does it much better than anyone else. Just wait and see how unique and ideal your marriage and family are! The narcissist has many advantages to staying married. First, they are the BOSS of everyone and everything that happens in the home. They make all the decisions and do nothing of the work. They spend most of the money on themselves, and the things that make them look good are fantastic, beautiful, or convenient.

The spouse financially supports the family or contributes all of their income to the home that the narcissist controls. The spouse does the narcissist's dirty work. They play bad, make excuses, and cover their nasty husband. They defend their spouse's misbehavior towards others and remember all the narcissistic moments of glory and stellar achievement that date back to the beginning of time. They enforce the rules, obey the rules, flatter the narcissist, support their lies, and accept blame for everything. The spouse is also a good companion for parading at parties or events that involve the family. He/she will present himself/herself as the ideal and loving husband/wife and father, that satisfies all the whims in front of others so that no one becomes aware of the fact that he/she is married to the devil incarnate. Still, if the opportunity presents itself, the narcissist can be unfaithful.

The likelihood of this occurring will depend on the attractiveness and enchantment of the narcissist, the advantages that the "new source" can offer the narcissist. The narcissist may dismiss the spouse at this point, blame the spouse for not being a good spouse, or tell them to stop being a baby and "get over it." Narcissists strategically marry. They form alliances. It is not a bad idea when you think about it, because it is always advisable to marry your heart and mind. The difference is that narcissists make the rules and change them at will. What other benefits does marriage bring to a narcissist? -At a basic level, they marry an attractive couple that makes them look and feel good. Nothing new here. -They also tell themselves and the world that they are rational enough to maintain a long-term relationship.

Having a long-term wife speaks of stability and commitment. What happens behind closed doors is something else entirely. -The spouses

41

complete them by filling in the gaps as the always loyal secretary, campaign manager, and fan club. Narcissists can be away from home 18 hours a day, but they will always be the king (or queen) of your property. Until death separates them. -In some cases, they marry couples who are significantly younger for the same reason, and because younger women can expand their dynasty by having children.

How many dating sites abound with men wanting a second family at fifty, even at sixty? -The most important reason for a narcissist to remain in a marriage is money and prestige. It will take a long time to get out of wedlock. Divorce will damage your reputation and your self-esteem. It splinters into the image they have carefully constructed of a blameless and outstanding citizen. Not all married people are unfaithful because they are narcissistic. Sometimes it is a quick adventure. Sometimes a marriage simply ends. It is how it is. No one is wrong; it just happens. All married people who deliberately cheat someone out of wedlock are narcissists. They are liars. They do it for their gratification. Not all married narcissists seek sex. High-functioning narcissists are often brain narcissists. They can flirt and joke and send midnight text messages to a harem of admirers, but they aren't interested in sex. They just want admiration for the thrill of it.

Narcissism in Marriage

Narcissism in the couple is mediated by that person who at first dazzled us with his attentions and captivating character. Later, the authentic face and those tricks that articulate deception, manipulation, and emotional sabotage emerge.

When narcissism arises in the couple, anguish becomes evident, and fear appears because beyond what we can think, narcissistic men and women also fall in love. Now, its mechanism to love generates "a rope" that makes a knot around us: every day, it tightens more, and every moment, we lose more rights and wills and may even mislead our voice.

There is no shortage of people who claim to be an actual 'magnet for narcissists.' Why happens? Is there an explanation why we don't see this type of profile coming to protect us from it? Some theories indicate that, on average, it is the most sensitive and empathetic people who are captivated by this type of personality.

There is perhaps a kind of feedback, that in which one nurtures the needs of the other. However, it must be said that there is no conclusive data on this, because in reality, all of us, regardless of our way of being, age or status, can feel attracted by this profile. The reason for this is that narcissists tend to be very magnetic at first.

It is common for them to present features such as excellent friendliness, liveliness, a great sense of humor, wit, personal security, and that sparkling extroversion that never goes unnoticed. Now, under that dazzling patina is undoubtedly the real skin. That characterized by the impossibility of creating an emotionally positive bond with someone.

"An egotistical is one who insists on telling you about himself when you are dying to tell him about you."

Narcissism in The Couple: Keys to Act

The way narcissism appears in the couple responds to different realities. Thus, it is common that two particular facts can occur: the first, that narcissism starts from both members.

The second is that one of the two is clearly and exercising behavior that is both harmful and destructive to the relationship itself. There are, without a doubt, two situations that we must analyze.

Narcissism in The Couple: When We Both Act Selfishly

It is essential to differentiate narcissistic behavior from a narcissistic personality disorder. In the latter case, we would be talking about a clinical condition included in the Diagnostic and Statistical Manual of Mental Disorders (DSM-V).

Therefore, it may be the case that two people with this type of personality cohabit in a couple of relationships, or with this disorder. It is unusual, but it can happen. Also, another reality that sometimes occurs in the life cycle of a couple of relationships is the following:

- We leave aside the needs of the couple to prioritize ours.
- Not only that, but emotional sloppiness also appears. Also, they arise c portamentos, as the need for control and ups and downs in those moments that we want close to the couple and to the need time away.

What explanation does this type of relationship present? What happens when narcissism in the couple starts from both members? What happens is that this link is situated in an abyss in which, sooner or later, it will rush to an end. Some couples have stopped loving each other and yet are unable to make the step to a healthy resolution.

43

Laziness appears, and at the same time, the burden of dependency remains, not wanting to let go of what once "was ours."

My Partner Is A Narcissist. What Can I Do?

Narcissism in the couple is commonly manifested in one of the members. Thus, it is at the end of time when the other person is aware of the authentic personality of the loved one. It is that moment in which the previous fascination falls to open the eyes to the anatomy of the narcissist.

Keys to Reflect and Make Decisions

Livesley, Jang, Jackson, and Vernon (1993) point out in a study that in 64% of cases, the narcissistic personality has a genetic origin. Therefore, changes are not so easy.

Likewise, this profile usually falls within a spectrum. There will be those who show more abusive behavior, and those who only present a few characteristics.

These are some keys in which we must reflect.

- Never doubt yourself. When narcissism in the couple becomes evident, there are only two options, to react or get used to living in emotional abandonment. If we do the latter, we will end up doubting ourselves, our self-esteem, and even our own identity.
- Ruptures and reconciliations, is it worth it? Having a narcissistic partner means living on a wheel of distancing and settlement. It is possible that at some point, you have had the strength to leave that relationship. However, the narcissist is adept at being affectionate and "catching" us again. Evaluate what this means for your dignity.
- They need you to validate their self-esteem, but where is yours? Narcissists lack a central self. Thus, to stabilize and strengthen their self-image, they need someone to do it for them. They feed on the other person to reaffirm themselves. Reflect on whether this is worth it. Visualize for an instant how you see yourself in 5 or 10 years.

Conclusions

Without a doubt, we could point out that the best option is to proceed to a breakup. However, that decision is personal and would mean admitting that no one can change or position themselves on particular inclinations of their personality, ending its effects.

Thus, it must be assessed from each specific case: the danger of generalizing at this point is severe. Not all situations are the same, and not all narcissistic or narcissistic personality disorder people are alike.

However, and despite the existence of psychological approaches, such as conversion therapy, to try to generate changes in this type of patient, it is a complex process. To this, we must add the resistance of these people to go to therapy.

Therefore, narcissism in the couple is something that will demand a lot from us, first of all, to defend ourselves and make decisions. Let's do it prioritizing your well-being and integrity.

COMMON TRAITS NARCISSISTIC MEN ARE LOOKING FOR IN A WOMAN

Having a relationship with them can mean damaging your self-esteem and becoming their parasite.

We are not talking about those who have a severe personality disorder, but those who act with marked narcissistic traits. That is, those who are in love with themselves always. That is its primary and deadly characteristic. "To recognize them, you just have to notice that they are the ones who always speak from their grandeur and feel superior to the rest," says Perla Ben-Dov, director of the Graduate and Research School of the Faculty of Psychology at the University of Development. He points out that there are different levels of narcissism. The usual thing, she says, is to have the right level of self-esteem to feel safe, but the harmful something to feel excellent, unique, superior.

The worst thing is that these people, he adds, find it difficult to love because they are too practical with the rest since the only thing that would interest them is to achieve admiration and permanent self-gratification. "They work at poles, they idealize or disqualify you and turn you into rubbish." Furthermore, Ben-Dov declares that this narcissistic style is more frequent in men. They are usually very envious and easily see in others the aspects that they do not possess. And, as if that were not enough, they also have difficulty recognizing their mistakes. Pastry? "They have a hard time receiving criticism, and every time you show them something that doesn't work well, and they experience it as a wound to self-love or what is called a narcissistic wound, a break from self-love. It is that they are very insecure of themselves", affirms the teacher.

In this sense, the specialist explains that this way of showing oneself is only a facade because if one digs a little, a person appears with a greatly diminished image of himself. The dangers for one Domingo Izquierdo, professor of psychopathology at the UDP, points out that the risks of partnering with a person with these traits are the damages they cause due to the type of relationship they form, which they define as parasitic. "Those who partner with someone who is Narcissus come out with a lot of pain and are relationships that are difficult to shake off; they are very unsure of themselves and become too humble. So, we should be cautious when we are with someone who has narcissistic features, "he advises. Besides, he comments that the person with whom they are related, to avoid conflicts and maintain the relationship, immolate themselves, and become invisible with the successive negative consequences of canceling. That is goodbye, self-esteem, needs, satisfaction, and not to mention enjoyment. The

46

teacher also says that they can become violent and explode, at the slightest problem, with high attacks of fury. It is frequent, according to Perla Ben-Dov, that a daffodil meets a person who has depressive features, how to Identify Them Although it should not be forgotten that narcissism is a personality trait that varies from person to person. The harmful ones are those who act too self-referentially and don't care about the needs of their partner. According to university specialists, one aspect that tends to overlook the grandstanding of daffodils is that these gallants believe that they are physically more attractive and intelligent than almost everyone. Although many times they are, in a man, that is not everything. Another opinion that helps to identify them is that they are published in an article in the Journal of Psychology by two psychologists from the University of Washington in St. Louis, Nicolas Holtzman and Michael Strube. They claim that to distinguish them, you also have to look at the sound of their voice. To easily recognize them, we give the keys to analyze a good-natured, flirtatious but narcissist:

1. They redirect the conversation towards them.
2. They brag about their accomplishments even though they are not always real. Their families are "perfect."
3. They always speak in everything grandiloquent, alluding to fantasies, and myths about what they do.
4. When conversing, they use a high tone of voice and make exaggerated hand movements and show complete disinterest when others speak.
5. When they stop flattering, they fall into catastrophic reactions.
6. They choose couples who can be subservient to them, who place themselves at the service of their narcissistic gratification of the Narcissus.
7. They convince the other, who is totally and dependent on him.
8. They do not recognize the other's needs as necessary.
9. They are usually promiscuous, and it is a critical strategy that allows narcissists to maintain control. They are always looking for a better deal.
10. Narcissistic men tend to attract women who crave drama.

Common Traits Narcissistic Men Are Looking for In A Woman

They say that the opposite poles attract. Perhaps this explains why narcissistic people - who are characterized, among other things, by lack of empathy - tend to be invited to empathetic people, who represent the opposite pole to narcissism.

Although, at first glance, it seems like a good idea, as they could nurture and complement each other, it is not. These types of relationships, which are not uncommon, are usually doomed to failure.

What Is A Narcissist?

Psychologist Ruth Zazo Rodriguez, from Psicoadapta, explains that a narcissistic person is characterized by showing arrogant and arrogant she tends to exaggerate her achievements, knowledge, and abilities fantasize with significant successes, feels special and unique, and believes that only those who they are of her status they are worthy of relating to her.

"He is in great need of admiration and often, even if he doesn't show it, envies the successes of others. Likewise, he lacks empathy, that is, he does not identify with the feelings of others and does not care at all about other people, although he does get some benefit from them, "he adds.

This type of person needs to continually receive the admiration of others and exclusive and unique treatment, and they are obsessed with the opinion they may have of them. "If they are not recognized or criticized, they get angry or defensive, experiencing very intense, and may even lead to violence and aggression."

Narcissists hate - and try to avoid it by all means - to feel weak or show fragility, precisely because, in the depths of their being, this is how they think. They have low self-esteem, even if they do everything possible to hide it as much themselves as well as others.

All this causes them to establish complicated relationships, which can be described as toxic by having a fundamental inequality: narcissists seek to develop relationships with people who give them admiration, affection, and idealization, with whom they feel that their ego is continually elevated.

Empaths and Daffodils: A Relationship Bound to Failure

An empathetic person shows excellent management and control of the emotional world, with which they have a high capacity to understand and understand others. You can even border on the excess and that this virtue becomes a defect, assuming the suffering of the other as your own or not being able to find limits when it comes to helping you.

This is an attractive profile for a narcissist since he will always " try to understand and offer to the other what he understands will be good for him, satisfying his needs and offering his unconditional support," says Ruth Zazo.

The expert explains that, initially, narcissists manipulate the other by admiring their qualities or values, being charming and exciting. However, with time, they begin to devalue their positive aspects and react with anger, fury, or rage, everything that goes against their wishes.

When the empath tries to be accepted and loved by the narcissist, the latter, who only needs his love and does not care what the other may need, will seek to manipulate the empath and make him feel guilty for the existing problems in the relationship. For his part, the empathetic, who is compassionate, "will try to heal the narcissist by taking and experiencing his pain as his own; that is to say, it will try to supply in some way the misfortunes suffered in his life."

When the narcissist begins to mistreat or devalue the empath, the empath will tend to continue to insist and become more attached to the relationship if he realizes that his affective needs, desires, and illusions are also essential and make it known to him. The narcissist will brand him as selfish, and the relationship will become even more complicated: narcissists need continuous attention and assessment, as they are always there. Dissatisfied and need to feed their ego.

Finally, the psychologist emphasizes that these types of personalities communicate differently: "While the empath seeks solutions for the couple, the narcissist will try to blame him for everything, and thus manages to dominate and control the situation. The more affection the empath lavishes, the more control the narcissist will have."

It is not easy to recognize or accept that you are in a relationship of this type, although many signs indicate it. One of the first steps is to understand that everyone is responsible for their personal growth and that of no one else. Trying to do the job that belongs to the other is always a bad sign.

The limits are healthy in any type of relationship, and especially for empathetic people, who have more difficulty saying "no" and accepting that not everyone has to be part of their lives. Some people do because they help us grow, and others that should be let go.

COMMON TRAITS OF NARCISSISTIC PEOPLE

We all come across a narcissist at some point in our lives. However, not all narcissistic people are clinical cases with difficulties in living with a full degree of well-being: some are only partially so, in a way that is not always evident.

These are people who think they are better than anyone who underestimates others and who, when challenged, tend to act because they feel that their ego is being threatened. Studies affirm that at least 6.2% of the population is narcissistic and that the majority are men. Narcissists are often associated with different problems, from childhood behavior disorders, addiction to physical exercise (for example, anorexia), depressive disorders, or anxiety.

Narcissists Are Empty People

The narcissist puts on a mask because it is empty inside. What they appear to be is not really what is behind their facade. The narcissist makes friends quickly since he is usually open to others at first, even becoming sweet. But he has severe difficulties in maintaining relationships because it is difficult for him to care about another person. Narcissists' friends, sooner or later, tend to distance themselves from these characters because of their selfishness and are not trustworthy.

Narcissists eventually give themselves away, as their need to always be the first does not help build lasting friendships. And although they always brag about their achievements, they are frail people. They can be attractive and smart, and they can love being in public, but they become icy people in private when no one looks at them.

Now that doesn't mean they don't surround themselves with people. Narcissistic people need others to feel that they are being admired. They fear loneliness, and they fear to be alone with themselves because this can mean doing a severe analysis of conscience, which is the greatest nightmare for them. Narcissists fear to come into contact with their reality by having to accept that their true self is not what they are trying to make others believe.

50

Detect A Narcissistic Person

But how can we identify a narcissist? What clues do these people give us? Today we are going to discuss the key characteristics of a narcissistic person so that you can recognize that you are dealing with one of them.

1. Selfies Are Taken, And Photos Retouched Continuously

We have all taken a selfie on some occasions, and this does not have to be anything terrible. But narcissists spend all day taking selfies and posting them on social media. Social networks can be harmful to these individuals because they can be connected continuously, trying to show off and raise their ego. The opposite effect occurs, and they can suffer from FOMO Syndrome, feeling that the life of others is more interesting. Therefore, they enter a vicious circle that ends up negatively affecting their state of mind and their self-esteem.

Regarding the use of social networks, a study carried out in 2014 with a sample of 1,000 subjects, showed that narcissists differed from others for three reasons:

- They spend more time on social media than non-narcissistic people
- More selfies hang
- They edit more selfies until they get a "perfect" image

2. They Constantly Criticize Others

A narcissist will rarely speak of others, and if he does so, it will be to criticize or belittle the work of others. With this attitude, they may believe that they are dominant or better than others, but in reality, this does not leave them in the right place, since it is a symptom of insecurity.

3. They think that the world revolves around them

Narcissists are unconcerned with the feelings of others because they are too self-centered. If they talk to others, they can give the sensation of unique personal interest, theirs. So, if you ever meet a narcissist, he will always try to talk about himself and inflate the image of himself. Although they may be warm at first, their callous actions soon appear. It is because they only think of them and always seek to be the center of attention.

51

4. They Are Charming at First

Narcissists know how to win over others, and they have a very seductive personality. Not always, but often they are usually physically attractive. Their confident appearance attracts people, and they become a magnet that hooks those who know them. At first, their talkativeness makes it easier for them to access others, but their friendships are short-lived because they are not people who like privacy.

5. They Often Start Many Love Relationships

Narcissists often initiate many love relationships, although they are usually ephemeral. As I have mentioned in the previous point, they are people who are generally seductive, and the opposite intimacy is attracted to their magnetism. But relationships do not last long because they do not meet the requirements of a right loving partner. So, their bonds are broken soon.

6. They Are Uncompromising and Think They Know Everything

Seeing others as inferior, they always think they are right. Worst of all, they don't mind being criticized for not being empathetic and uncompromising. They are very little tolerant of others, and because they think only of themselves, they do not have to compromise and yield to other individuals.

7. They Need to Be the Best at Everything

These types of people are not very humble and have very high goals, almost always irrational. Also, they still want to go to the best doctor, the best hairdresser, the best restaurant, work in the best places, etc. So, they can brag about it and post it on social media for everyone to know.

8. They Usually Dress Impeccably

Narcissists continuously seek attention, and physical appearance is significant to them. That is why they always dress impeccably and are still in fashion. Such is their obsession with dressing well that it is their priority, even if they have to sacrifice their needs.

9. They Don't Accept Criticism

Narcissists do not accept criticism and are often very aggressive when they receive it. They always want to be the best at everything, and if they see that their ego is being threatened, they become defensive.

10. They Are Proud to Be Narcissistic and Admit It

In a study carried out at Indiana University in 2014, it was identified that to the simple question "Are you a narcissist?", They proudly answered, yes. This response, which may seem counterintuitive to most mortals, to a narcissist is unique. These results generated some skepticism in the scientific circuit, so Sander van der Linden decided to carry out another investigation to find out if it was true. To their surprise, the new study yielded findings that were the same as the original study.

Relating to Narcissistic People

Before judging narcissistic people negatively by the characteristics they present, it must be taken into account that, in part, they act this way because they have learned to adopt these kinds of customs and habits. That means that these people can change (and therefore there is no point in labeling them as if the fact of being narcissistic could not be modified) and on the other hand that in their eyes their behavior is reasonable, they find it spontaneous. Unlearning certain habits will allow them to relate more satisfactorily to others, but this requires time and effort.

HOW TO DEAL WITH NARCISSISTS IN RELATIONSHIP

When we start a relationship, it is because we want a deep bond with someone. After all, we need to give and receive love, affection, beauty, company in our lives. Well, narcissists do it for entirely different reasons. They feel an insatiable emptiness within them, and the only way to temporarily silence it is to fill it with the love and admiration of others.

According to Karpman's dramatic triangle, which applies to dysfunctional relationships, there are three roles: the Victim, the Persecutor, and the Savior. In the case of narcissists, there are two versions of the triangle: one, the real one, and the other, the narcissistic version. In his version, the narcissist sees himself as Victim, the person he is already abusing - that is, his "old" supply - appears as a Persecutor, and his new "supply" -that is, his new partner prospect-, is shown as Savior. But in reality, the narcissist is the Persecutor, his new "supply" is his accomplice, and his "old supply" is the Victim.

At the beginning of the relationship with a narcissist, when one is the "new supply" or supposed Savior, the narcissist is probably helped in harming the Victim. At that point, the alleged Savior is treated as if he were a hero or an angel, and the Victim is that unpleasant person who no longer appreciates the narcissist. The "new supply" is the answer to the narcissist's problems, just as it once was, the one who is now the Victim. And the cycle repeats itself. Here is a curious image to understand the dynamics:

Therefore, relationships with narcissists follow a very defined circuit, which consists of a three-stage pattern:

1. Over-Evaluation or Idealization

At this stage, the narcissist carefully chooses his target. In general, they want their victims because they have something that they are interested in owning, be it in the social, economic, or even physical sphere, to validate their ego. At this stage, everything is lovely. The narcissist seeks to show everything the other wants from a partner. They are overly loving, loving, and caring at this stage. They bombard their victim with love and flattery. They put them on a pedestal, and they adore him. The narcissist is full of dreams and hopes, which he shares with his partner very frequently.

At this point, the victim believes that the narcissist is their soul mate, and

54

they cannot find their luck of course, because the narcissist has dedicated himself to imitate everything that his victim has told him that he dreams of a person. This phase can last from a few weeks or months to just over a year. But then, that's when things change.

2. Devaluation

It is when the narcissist shows his real personality. You feel confident that you have unconditional love for the other, and you can "get comfortable." Little by little, the attention begins to decrease. The narcissist walks away. He becomes crabby, withdrawn, silent.

What has happened is that the narcissist gets bored very easily. And after the excitement of the first stage is over, he begins to wonder if he was correct in choosing his victim. He stops answering calls and messages, breaks his promises, and punishes his partner for disturbing him. And as the other person tries to get the relationship working again, he gets further and further away. The emptiness inside has returned, and if it has returned, it is that your partner was not so special.

He begins to project his emotional confusion on his partner. He begins to blame her for his shortcomings. However, a narcissist will never abandon a source of moving "supplies" for his ego until he has a safe alternative. So, he starts with his manipulation techniques: triangulation, devaluation, and gaslighting, which we will see in-depth later.

Life for the victim becomes unbearable: the narcissist changes his mind violently, accuses him of things he has not done, and maybe in a loving and agreeable moment, and then erupts in a fury. She doesn't know what to expect and is manipulated over and over again. Many times, he begins to lose his sense of reality and begins to have difficulty distinguishing the good from the bad, his limits from those of other people, etc.

At this point, the narcissist will either already be looking for another victim to start the cycle again, or the abused person will be bored and flee to lose himself from a troubled and challenging person.

3. Discard

It is a terrible name, but that is what happens. The narcissist, without remorse, ends the relationship because the other person has already stopped "serving" him. What your ex-partner arrives or feels to you matters little to him. This phase is provoked by the narcissist and can be slow and painful, or fast and aggressive, and will be colored by the manipulation that the narcissist does, inducing reactions, feelings and acts so that the relationship finally breaks down.

Very Important: The Rule Of "No Contact."

If you have survived a relationship with a narcissist, either by escaping or after being abandoned, it is imperative to comply with the "no contact" rule, to avoid further harm. A narcissist will seek his supply of emotional arousal wherever, so as long as one allows it, he will try to manipulate us. Therefore, it is essential to cut off all communication, liquidate any business one has, change telephone number and email, and get rid of everything that reminds us of the person. If the narcissist seeks us out, we must ignore him. This rule is fundamental because otherwise, you are exposed to being damaged again. Remember that this is a person who has a very harmful disorder.

Go Ahead

It is excruciating to recover from such a relationship. Dr. in Psychiatry Sam Vaknin recommends first accepting what has happened. That the link was not what we believed, and that we were gravely mistaken. After that, comes grief and forgiveness, and learning from this traumatic experience must be worked. It is essential to have the support of family and friends, and ideally, to have the help of a therapist to facilitate this painful process because you are damaged in your self-esteem, in your perception of reality, and in the ability to establish healthy relationships.

Am I A Victim of a Narcissist?

Some symptoms can reveal to us if we are victims of a narcissist.

1. We doubt ourselves. Do you notice that you suspect much more than before meeting him? When we are victims of a narcissist, we usually seek very frequently to verify that we have not been wrong, or that we have not misheard something, much more than before. It is because the narcissist tries to blame his victim for things he didn't even say or do, and in this way, he gets his emotional "supply."
2. Confusion. Because they do not know interpersonal boundaries, they also force this on others. We suddenly feel guilty about what others did, said, or felt. Even more so when they use a terrible technique called "gaslighting" on us, which we will mention a little

later (patience, dear readers). In this way, little by little, the victim becomes more and more dependent on the narcissist, to determine his sense of reality.

3. We think we are going crazy. A narcissist projects his disorders on us. That is, if he is a pathological liar, he will accuse us of lying, if he feels that he is going crazy, accuses us of going crazy, etc. Since he relies on the trust we have in him, abusing it, he will try to convince us of what he says, which can lead to a significant deterioration in our self-confidence.

4. Unexplained symptoms. We no longer feel "ourselves." Without knowing why, we are losing motivation. It is not known what happens, but we realize that it is something serious. It is a narcissistic abuse. There are a large number of symptoms that, separately, it would not be known what to attribute. But which are generally related to the signs of having suffered a trauma: places and words are avoided. There is a loss of interest and motivation, problems to eat or sleep, nightmares, irritability, hopelessness, psychosomatic illnesses, etc. Some victims develop Stockholm Syndrome and seek to protect and help those who cause it all.

5. Dissociation. Dissociation is an automatic response of our psyche to insurmountable stress, for example, the product of systematic aggression. We escape from where something unbearable is happening with us, and we feel that we are in one place, while our body is in another place. It can also occur from an emotional point of view, and there we feel alien to life and emotions. Or, there may be amnesia regarding what happened. This defense measure works temporarily, but it brings other symptoms, for example, anxiety, low self-esteem, somatization, depression, chronic pain, addictions, self-mutilation, ideation, and suicidal acts, among others. Unfortunately, many times the victim believes that these symptoms are the cause of the problem.

6. Post-Traumatic Stress Syndrome. Something highly characteristic of victims of a narcissist is suffering from symptoms of post-traumatic stress. In a nutshell, reliving the abuse, and the body and mind respond as if they are experiencing it again.

7. It, too, involves some other symptoms: numbness of the fingers and lips. Place, sounds, food, etc., that remind the abuser are avoided. There is memory loss, need to isolate after abuse. Inability to feel joy, confidence, and hope for the future, and fear of never being able to contact them again. Insomnia from fatigue and night terrors. Anxiety, disturbing thoughts, feeling of vulnerability, and loneliness. Obsessive ideas in which the narcissist is seen suffering accidents or being killed, which causes guilt. A tendency to always be defensive and overreact at the slightest stimulus.

And the worst thing is that many times victims realize that before meeting the narcissist, things were different. It also causes profound damage.

Daffodil Aggression Modes

Once we know the symptoms that can show us that we are being abused, we must understand that apart from systematic lies and trust abuse, there are three very sophisticated aggression "techniques" that a daffodil uses.

Devaluation: consists of making malicious, disqualifying or humiliating comments, in private or in a way that no one else hears. It can give you to understand that you are the worst of the worst, with a simple phrase: "you are very careless, that's why your son crashed." Or attack your self-esteem: "you gained weight, and you have more grey hair, you have to take care of yourself, I'm telling you for your good." It is never for your good, unfortunately.

Triangulation: consists of the use of a third party to destabilize us, for example, by comparing ourselves with others, by convincing ourselves that our friends or family think wrongly of us or are against us, etc. They may also speak ill of us to third parties. The most common forms of triangulation are: saying that a third party (a friend, colleague, etc.) has flirted with you. In this way, she causes jealousy and insecurity in her partner, who will try harder to satisfy the narcissist, so as not to be replaced. Furthermore, it creates an illusion of desirability and fosters rivalry, which also feeds the narcissist. That does not happen in a healthy relationship. Another way is to force the couple to think the same as him, even bullying for it. In this way, it overwhelms the integrity and dignity of the other person. For this, it uses third parties, to whom only one version of the facts has been told. Healthy couples do not need to incorporate a third party to resolve their differences. A third way is to offend people against each other, due to the narcissist. It does by speaking ill of the other behind his back, by getting other people to support him, in his role as victim blindly. It is achieved by isolating people, and becoming the valid interlocutor between them, so that all communication passes through him, with which he manages to manipulate all those involved. Finally, another modality appears when the narcissist wants to end a relationship: he tells others that his relationship is ending, putting himself as a victim again. Many times, one of your confidants becomes your next victim.

Gaslighting: This is a brutal "technique" of manipulation and erosion of the sense of identity. It consists of showing the other incomplete or false information so that they doubt their memory, their thoughts, and, ultimately, their sanity. It can consist of denying real things that have

58

happened, even creating and manipulating situations to disorient the other. The name comes from the play " Gas Light, "where a man tries to convince his wife that she is crazy, confusing her in that way. Some examples:

Hiding things from the other, or moving them from the place, to then say: "but if you put it there." Later, he accuses the other person of having a bad memory. "You always fail to recall where you put your keys. Why should I trust what you tell me now?"

You can change dates without warning and then tell the other that you misunderstood. Also, deny what he said or promised even minutes before, and even deny facts in front of people who cannot corroborate them. Or affirm false facts so that he doubts the other. Often this is compounded by manipulation of the worst kind, telling the other person, who believes more in what others say than in his word, pretending to feel betrayed and hurt.

Or, manipulate saying: "Didn't you see the face they made when you talked about X subject? I say this because I love you, please don't make a fool of yourself again."

According to Dr. in Psychology Robin Stern, if you are always apologizing to your partner, boss, or friend. If you sometimes wonder if you will not have stress or a nervous illness if you must justify some behaviors of your partner to your family. If you Despite having nothing to complain about in life, you feel a diffuse feeling of anguish and sadness if you find it challenging to make decisions, and if you live in fear of having a bad evaluation at work despite giving the best of yourself, Then it would be advisable to check if you are not the victim of a narcissist at home or practice.

How to Deal with A "Daffodil" (Or Lessen Its Influence)

The objective is to know in detail the narcissistic disorder, but also to look for a way to solve the problems that a relationship with a person in these conditions can bring us, and that is why I give you these recommendations.

In general, specialists roughly recommend zero contact. In other words, do not call him, do not answer messages, do not look for them, do not respond to any of his actions. Ideally, change your phone, email, and block you on social networks. Many times, it is inevitable to deal with a daffodil day after day, either because it is part of our family, or perhaps it is in our work environment as a boss or colleague. Here are two strategies to use:

minimal contact, and the grey stone method.

Minimum contact: as its name says, it consists of avoiding being in direct contact with the narcissist, whether in person, by phone, or by other means. For example, communicating by email, and handling it in writing - ideally copying others to have a backup of what is happening. It also involves avoiding contact alone. All this also serves to document any unusual situation, so that we can legally prove what is happening. In this way, it is not eliminated, but the damage that the narcissist produces in our life is minimized.

Graystone method: a "daffodil" needs to be supplied with emotions and creates dramatic situations, seeking encouragement in manipulation and deception, driving someone mad, satisfies their need for drama. This method consists of becoming a "grey stone," becoming the most annoying person we can work for them, without responding to provocations or insults. Trying that everything we say is minimal, neutral. Without telling him anything flashy at all regarding our lives. Nothing that contains any vivid emotion no worries that we have, or things that matter to us. Talk about everyday things, the weather. In this way, we will cease to be a "supply" for the needs of their voracious ego.

It is certainly not easy, because when confronted with the "grey stone," the narcissist will undoubtedly seek to make us react. It will provoke us. He will insult us, and he will say the worst of us. Here, the "greystone" must accept them, in a grey and neutral way. It is tough and requires a lot of self-discipline, but it will make the narcissist bored and start looking for other victims.

These problems are challenging to treat, and if we seek professional help, it is also necessary to be careful when choosing, because you must necessarily be a specialist in these sociopathic disorders. Otherwise, the "daffodil" can wrap it in its manipulation network, completely nullifying the help that we can receive. In this sense, it is also essential to have an entire support network, which is aware of these things, and which can, at least, help us to "breathe" and rest a bit from an already suffocating situation.

60

NARCISSIST VIEW OF MARRIAGE

The "narcissist" raises his feeling of self - esteem by being adored and admired by the "complementary narcissist," and it is so because a person has been sought who has no aspirations of his own and who must fit his own. He feels great because the other admires him with great exaltation; This can be observed, at least indirectly, in the sentences it issues:

"Now I do not feel well, and I am not comfortable in the situation I am in, because I see that I cannot bear the absence of it. I was fine with my wife and not now because she adored me. I have lost all that, and I am wrong, do you understand me?".

The "complementary narcissist" searches for someone to worship by exaggerating his brilliance, adjusting himself to him, anticipating his wishes, and giving up his aspirations. It is also possible to observe how, when entering the relationship, there is an improvement in the traits of his personality that he considers harmful; We see it in the following sentences that we collect from a session:

"I think I have always adored him because I considered him far superior to me. Sometimes I thought I was dreaming of having that person by my side and, above all, that he had noticed me. He was everything to me". "When I started dating A. all these things were taken from me, I mean all my complexes."

What happens, in these cases, is that the "narcissist" shows himself before the "complementary narcissist" assimilated to the "ideal," so that the latter feels dazzled by its exceptional brilliance and swallows his entire exhibition, dedicating himself to idealizing it. It means that it projects its "ideal" on it, to achieve an acceptable personal improvement. The "narcissist" assimilates with great pleasure the position in which he is placed, feeling great.

The end of the journey is both are assimilated to the "ideal" in a mutual identification; In context, the "complementary narcissist" feels happy to find what he was looking for so long. The "narcissist" perfectly fits the "ideal" that his partner places on him, feeling better than ever and causing inflation of self-esteem.

There we discover undoubtedly the inextricable union to which both aspire since both complete the "ideal" form, and that tends to merge. It is going to cause significant problems since when working from the "ideal" the following phenomena take place in both members:

61

a. an emptying of personal or human content, which are precisely the rejected ones
b. when working from this register, a mutual ignorance
c. the interdependence is of such magnitude that the individual development of each of them is impeded. These aspects block the mutual enrichment in your bilateral contacts and in which you can be with others.

This fusion, far from being the "wonder of love" as they understand it (or who surrounds them), expresses a significant weakness. The following speeches contemplate how those involved see the matter:

"All our friends were amazed at us because they saw us as the perfect couple because they observed in us two very close beings. I confess that I also think so". I will always think about it."

The Couple Crisis

When the mechanisms expressed are exaggerated, we enter into a couple of crises that frequently leads patients to consult and initiate psychotherapeutic treatment. Such crises show a high rate of recurrence, both with the same partner and with a different one.

This effect can begin when the "complementary narcissist" forces the "narcissist" to allow him to get out of there; This indicates that what was once a possibility is an obligation. Hence, it follows that the "ideal" becomes a prison because by being stuck in that place, there is no possible escape.

The "narcissist" then responds aggressively, humiliating, and offending his partner. The "complementary narcissist" supports it because he thinks he knows him and believes that, deep down, this is not how he shows himself, and he excuses him.

At the same time, the "narcissist" can allow himself to be determined more and more by the "ideal" since he cannot do without the admiration of which he is the object, finding himself imprisoned in that place. As determined there, he struggles to retain his identity, and that makes the partner feel disappointed. Aggression is unleashed because he thinks that he is forcing it and does not let him be free. It means that by fearing disappointment, that is, that the "narcissist" is not always on the pedestal on which he depends, he demands and assaults him in the way that he can, because he had found in him everything he expected from life.

Breakage or Maintenance

If the crisis continues for a long time, several things can happen:

a. They are still together but thoroughly disappointed, with great resentments towards each other and a great apparent coldness that covers these affections. They can even make their own lives independently, also if they are under the same roof. They are still united, but it is for not starting something new, continuing with the material advantages, or for the children. Let's see one of the cases studied by us:

39-year-old woman, married to a son and dedicated to a family business. Consultation for problems arising from a relationship she describes as "strange" because the two live together "without any kind of incentive."

He comes to the consultation demanding a solution for his situation: "I want to know if I continue or leave it because I see that we can neither leave it nor fix it." After a time of sessions, she realizes that she has idealized her husband for a long time and that, recently, she has seen what she is and does not accept it. From there comes the constant attack and denigration on her part.

b) The separation. If this happens, each of the members follows a different fate:

1. in the case of the "narcissistic," he usually quickly searches for a new relationship with characters identical to the previous one, giving a recurrence of the problem. It is not uncommon for him to denigrate his last partner, who becomes guilty of what happened. If abandoned, he experiences it as a catastrophe, since it supposes a "narcissistic wound," which can only be repaired with another relationship and, if he is not a partner, necessary paranoid attitudes towards the other intimacy develops.
2. The "complementary narcissist" after the breakup usually keeps within himself the idealized image of his partner, in such a way that he is not resigned to stop thinking about him (case P-2), even if he has another relationship. He usually continues to believe that it is essential for the "narcissist" and that no one can understand him/her.

Let's see a case:

23-year-old single woman and law student. About two years ago, their relationship was broken because the boyfriend had been unfaithful to her. Currently, she has a stable partner, but she remembers the previous one a lot, many times a day, her image comes to mind. Even dreams show her very vivid scenes where she is dating her old boyfriend again, and they are happy. She has even away so far as to phone him from a phone booth and hear his voice unanswered. She comes to the consultation because "it takes me a great job to shake my previous boyfriend from the head, and I think I will not be happy. I don't understand this problem of mine, because who I'm really in love with is the current one".

The previous lines have served to show us what the narcissistic aspects of the human couple are, something that, to a greater or lesser extent, can be shown in any relationship of this type. The desire that has moved us has been to publicize the processes and mechanisms inherent in couples since patients come to us for professional help are marked by one of the moments to which we have referred. Knowledge is necessary because it implies taking certain precautions and assuming certain risks that may arise in the treatment.

Without going back in the least, neither of them is configured, as quickly as possible, a set of rules and connections that pass through the "ideal self," in such a way that the "narcissist," embodying it, allows the other person to identify with him while reassuring himself that exalted position. Thus, both will point to an impossible "unity," since it is non-existent in reality and can break at any time. Indeed, as beautiful as this love story, it can never achieve total and absolute "unity," assimilable to the "androgyne" of the Platonic myth. Because sooner or later it will succumb to the suffocation of the participants.

It seems, therefore, that this system is not destined to last too long since the beauty of idealized contact is going to become sinister. It happens as soon as whoever is in the "ideal" position slides a millimeter out of their place and commits a slip shown as something unforgivable; right there, he finds the other, sword raised, to remind him where he has to be and where he is. So, we are faced with a major crisis in which great resentments can arise, since the aggression that appears at the moment in which the aforementioned "ideals" are not strictly fulfilled is updated.

Here there is a dramatic change since the position of each of them is modified, from becoming two beings identified with each other to being imaginary rivals, producing challenges and battles that remind us a lot of the "fight to the death of consciences" described by Hegel (14). It turns out this way because they try, each in their way, to be right and defend their position without giving a foot of ground to the other; only one can win the game, only one can win. They do not understand that, in this fight, neither is right nor none is wrong, hence the impossibility and not being able to articulate "theses" and "antithesis." Weak to the one who gets into the

64

middle of that Dantesque spectacle.

All this shows that when two people with a high degree of narcissism meet, a conjunction of two strangers is obtained, although they think they know each other, have brilliant communication, and be the envy of how many surround them.

If, as it seems, they work in the register of the "ideal," they are two unknown to themselves and the other; Only when they see "the wolf's ears" can they realize, if at all fleetingly, what they really are like and how far they can go.

It is not strange that these people, after enormous disappointments, end their days existing as two living dead, sharing food and shelter. Behind this theatre of human cruelty is discovered the great pain derived from the betrayal of the standard "ideal"; Milton's lost paradise.

The narcissism of the couple leads to an essential paradox: the more the two-in-one communion is sought, the higher the tendency towards "total union" and maximum agreement, the more the relationship is added in trivial appearances and an immense superficiality. Lacan would say that the two functions in the "imaginary register," which is the terrain of the delusions and illusions of the "I," and not because they belong to the imaginary, their influences cease to be convincing.

But there is no need to despair, because psychotherapy Psychoanalytic offers honorable outlets for these narcissistic labyrinths since it tries to help the patient to recognize. In the other and himself, everything that escapes the domain of "ideals" and that, because it is rejected, does not stop manifesting itself. At the same time, attempts are made to lower expectations, both within the couple and outside of it, opening subjectivity too much more real relationships. However, this beautiful company in which we embarked could not be said to be "sewing and singing." Because patients oppose a brutal force to the idea that to be harmonious a couple has to be based on the "unity" more absolute and mimetic in operation and faithfully comply with the maxim that Dickinson left written: "If we stay together, we are standing; if we divide, we fall. "

The Unbearable Coexistence with A Narcissist

"Honey, rest, today I do the shopping." That's a phrase Sarah never heard from her partner. Not before her pregnancy, but not during or even when the baby was born. Her partner's world revolved around a single person: herself.

65

A few months ago, Sarah ended the connection. Since then, she has been in psychological therapy. The therapist confirmed his suspicions: He lived with a narcissist for five years.

Little Empathy, Much Aggression

"Narcissists are considered by a lack of understanding," says Bärbel Wardetzki. She is a psychotherapist and the author of several books on the subject. People with this problem rarely listen, prefer to talk about themselves, and have very little tolerance when they are opposed to it in conflict situations, says the expert.

That's what Sarah first noticed: "He overreacted when we disagreed over small things and said things like 'drop it off, if not, we're done,' and that seemed very strange and inappropriate to me." If she did not verbalize her wants and needs with extreme clarity, he did not take her into account.

At first, Sarah was fascinated by her ex-partner's self-confidence, determination, and seeming bravery. Admiration is the elixir of narcissists, but if denied, "they can be too aggressive when someone does something they don't like," says Wardetzki. Instead of regarding and gaining the people around them, they despise them.

According to the expert, there is a big difference between being self-confident and being narcissistic: "People who say 'I like it' simply have good self-esteem. They also have doubts, but they can regulate their emotions and to console and support themselves. They know their abilities and their limits. "

The narcissistic person does not feel empathy for his partner.

There's Not Much Behind the Ego

Relationships with people with the narcissistic disorder are complicated. It is better to break them to avoid losing yourself in them.

Pathological narcissism, on the other hand, comes from extremely low self-esteem, according to the psychotherapist. Grave doubt must be "compensated by inventing an oversized self."

As is often the case, this behavior begins in childhood. Narcissists are "emotionally neglected children.

Some children cannot even draw a simple line on paper without their parents showering them with praise. Others are constantly humiliated.

The result, after all, is the same. Those who are always put on a pedestal and who are regularly despised do not feel taken into account. A child who grows up this way cannot develop a healthy self-image.

Sarah says her ex-partner's mother was an "ice-cold, emotionless" person and abandoned him at a young age. Then he was raised by his aunt: "His aunt was not a good person; she mistreated him a lot." Also, he never knew his father.

A Narcissist for Me?

Sarah labels herself as a "caring individual" who always wants to help and fix other people's things. Her partner was her project. Someone he wanted to help overcome a difficult childhood and show him what true love is: "He believed that if he could continue to hold on long enough, he would realize that I was the right person for him."

But it failed. Her refusal to meet her needs came to a head during the pregnancy: "She didn't understand when I wasn't feeling well and showed no interest whatsoever. I was under the impression that it was a hindrance and stressful to her."

As a future mother, she asked for more support. So, she got mad because he didn't react. Her ex-partner's usual response was, "You always yell at me, so don't be surprised if I don't treat you right." "Because I didn't give her the recognition, she thought she deserved, she also had romances (with other women) all the time," says Sarah. If she found out one of his lies, he denied everything and said that she was crazy.

Dealing with narcissists affects your self-esteem, "In a short time, they make you feel useless and regrettable, and you stop liking the person you thought you were. It is important to adopt a firm attitude and not feel intimidated".

Signs of Narcissistic People

Psychologist and psychotherapist Aline Vater refer to the classification system of the American Psychiatric Association, the so-called DSM-5, with nine criteria and of which at least five must be met to speak of narcissistic personality disorder.

Don't You Dare Criticize Me!

"The characteristic of a narcissistic personality disorder is not only the good opinion that a narcissist has of himself but the weakness of his arguments," says Vater. It may be the case of a worker convinced of his ideas, but who does not receive the desired applause from his colleagues, because they believe that his proposal is rather mediocre and, therefore, they do not react with enthusiasm.

His idea is debated, criticized, and ultimately not accepted. The person feels very hurt and rejected. The frustration is so great that he feels deep anger. However, she masks her bewilderment behind a facade of arrogance and arrogance. She does not understand why half of the colleagues were not able to see that her idea was "fabulous."

Loneliness and Without Empathy

In many cases, the narcissistic person not only has problems at work and with colleagues but also in his private life. "People with a pronounced narcissistic personality disorder often conflict with other people," explains Vater.

Also, these "show an extreme lack of empathy. They can know when the others are sad, but they really cannot put themselves in the other's place," explains the psychologist.

Vater advises in case someone might think they have such a disorder: "If someone has problems with other people over and over again, it is certainly good to get psychological advice from a professional familiar with narcissism." affirms the therapist.

Narcissism Rarely Comes Alone

Constant conflicts are not only extremely unpleasant for the narcissistic person's environment, but also themselves. The feeling of being alone, misunderstood, and not feeling loved is very depressing for those affected. "Narcissists often go (to a therapist) for treatment because of other symptoms," says Vater, for example, for depression or drug addiction. In psychology, these problems are called comorbidities, that is, additional disorders or diseases.

To reliably detect narcissistic personality, it is necessary to interview for several hours, which can often take several weeks. "Talking to someone who knows the person well is also helpful in making a diagnosis," adds Vater.

Recognize the Pattern

Doing therapy is advisable, but "by definition, personality disorders are patterns that have their roots in childhood and are stable throughout life," says the psychologist. It is not a question of curing, but of understanding why this model of behavior has been developed and "designing a kind of manual" that makes it possible for the patient to deal with this disorder.

Narcissists received either too much praise or much rejection from their parents in childhood. "In both cases, their needs were not met." It can result in the development of an oversized self. It is a person with a devastated soul.

Suppose that person, after time in therapy, in one of the conferences, is confronted with a situation in which he expects a lot from his colleagues. Her desire to be admired and valued has not waned. He continues to feel hurt and quickly embarrassed if a proposal from him is rejected.

However, this time, he no longer blames others for having his self-esteem shattered, but instead checks the pattern by which those feelings that he feels and torment him are governed. In this way, you could gradually change your behavior towards others: less anger, less exaggerated expectations, and more empathy. He would probably also be less alone.

DIVORCING A NARCISSIST

The separation and divorce are one of the most disturbing factors of psychosocial stress for welfare and often cause depression and anxiety pictures as part of the mourning the end of a relationship.

However, there is a situation that is even more traumatic for someone who decides to separate the divorce or separation of a couple with a narcissistic personality disorder. It is usually the beginning of hell because someone sick with narcissism is unable to forgive who considers treason and unjustified abandonment. The narcissistic disorder is defined by the inability to empathize with others, by utilitarianism in relationships and by a total lack of awareness of their defects and errors that could explain, in part, an emotional breakdown. The narcissist, in his vision of the world, never makes mistakes or needs help from anyone. The others are the imbeciles, the ones who fail, the ones who can't see the irreparable loss that means ending a relationship with him or her.

Having some personality traits is not the same as being a structural narcissist. Someone who thinks he is terrific or who spends a lot of time talking about himself and listens little is not necessarily this person who cannot feel real love. Who is unable to think of others and who organizes his life so that everyone serves him, helps him. And admire it. And once he has stopped needing them, he abandons them in cold blood, but he will never (and never is ever) forgive anyone who decides to leave him.

Legal proceedings involving divorce, alimony, or custody lawsuit are the perfect pretext for acting out narcissistic anger. Whoever dares to confront, criticize, or abandon a narcissist will never find peace and will live an eternal lawsuit. A narcissistic process of divorce will never accept that a stage is closed, as it is a wound to the ego. Her grudge is timeless, and her revenge plans too. They often use their children as weapons. They fill them with gifts, they organize a small amusement park on the weekends and then manipulate them and confront them with the ex-couple. They are stingy in handling money and never give it when it is needed, but when it suits their interests.

Narcissists are wrong partners and parents. Their prognosis is reserved because they never come to ask for help. If they do, it is only to convince the therapist or to the legal system or whoever is necessary, that they are right and are victims of the circumstances. They lack introspection and frequently describe an inner world of coldness and indifference. Nothing moves them except when something affects them personally.

Some clues can be useful to avoid lovingly relating to a narcissist: lack of interest and curiosity about the life and activities of the couple, about their family and friends; Difficulty speaking about what you feel and being authentic; resentment towards many people, although the offense occurred many years ago; inability to forgive, recognize mistakes, and apologize.

Couples of narcissists manage to separate when they realize the tremendous emotional cost of continuing the relationship when they see their children damaged when they know that nothing they do will be enough, and they will always be criticized.

It does not matter that you have been married (or in a domestic partnership) for five days or 50 years.

It is hard to imagine that the person you are divorcing or separating from today is the same person you once promised your eternal and unconditional love.

As the saying goes, the same traits that caused you to fall in love with a person are what made you fall out of love at the end of the relationship.

Legal, financial, and emotional decoupling becomes even more complicated when you're entangled with a narcissist.

Divorcing from someone with a narcissistic personality disorder or narcissistic characteristics can be a difficult, long, lengthy, and arduous process if you allow yourself to be sucked into their vortex.

1. Determine If Your Ex Is A Narcissist

Your ex may be arrogant, heartless, mean, or egotistical, but that doesn't necessarily make her a narcissist.

Narcissists are notable for lacking empathy and not accepting any responsibility, even a little.

People lack empathy do not feel sorry for the kitten they ran over, for the family mourning the loss of their pet, or even for the child who has seen the accident.

Sometimes they invent their feelings to look good in front of those they want to manipulate.

71

They blame the family for allowing their kitten to wander the neighborhood alone. They'll blame the fucking kitty for not straying out of the way. Or they could even sue the cat's family for the inconvenience of having to clean its wheels of blood.

Now imagine asking such a person at the center of his universe for divorce.

Are they going to have ideas to worry about this brought about, or behaviors from them led to this decision?

Probably not.

Will they work with you to parent the children and make the children feel safe with the changes and uncertainty in their lives?

Probably not.

If they cheated on you, they would blame you for not believing them. Even if they attacked you physically or emotionally, it is you who forced them to do so.

They will portray themselves as the prey; They will try to make you pay.

Pay for the things that they have done.

Once you control and accept the fact that you are a narcissist, your guard must be awake and must allow that they will be challenging to deal with in a divorce.

They don't give a damn if it's a kid at play or meat knives. You can kill them with gentleness, and they will keep looking for you and provoking you.

2. Save Rational Feelings for The Right Viewers

Bringing rational thoughts into any conversation with a narcissist is like carrying a water pistol to a knife fight.

Rational thoughts are for the narcissist like vegetables for a young child, they will feed as much as you want, but they will just spit it out.

It's like the child who wants ice cream and throws a tantrum to get it, and the narcissist doesn't want to listen to you, he just wants to win.

They want an explanation to show the world that they were right!

His tantrums come in the form of detours, designed to keep you off-balance, distracted, and defensive.

While you're spending energy explaining that you don't even drink a beer on weekends and that your accusation says nothing about your ability to be a parent, it's too late.

You've already bitten the hook and are discussing his favorite topic (your inability to be a good father) versus his (his ability to be a good mother).

Instead of arguing with your ex, speak calmly and rationally to your attorney and allow him to speak for you.

Which brings us to the next point

3. Hire a Narcissist Divorce Lawyer

If you have a Tesla electric car, you won't take it to a combustion engine mechanic, will you?

The same logic applies to legal representation. Not all divorce attorneys are on the same level.

Some are excellent negotiators. Others are loud, aggressive sharks.

But you need someone who is well versed in the tactics narcissists use in court to create a strategy that will keep their divorce process and especially custody in the legal process.

4. Know the Way Ahead

If you have children, as a man in a macho country like Spain you will have to convince a variety of people, each with their agendas and prejudices, that you are not a danger to your children.

Your audiences include therapists, psychoanalysts, and judges. At each step, the narcissist will try to demonstrate that you are unbalanced, incompetent, and a threat to your children.

Do you remember the old movie "Gaslight?

If you react emotionally to accusations during procedures, you are giving a reason to the image of yourself that your ex-partner has made.

In expecting the unexpected and the worst behavior of your ex, you cannot lose your balance or be surprised.

5. Document. Save. File. Share

It is relatively easy to edit a text message, email, or voicemail that you have left before sending it to your attorney as evidence against you.

The only way to counter your claims is by providing the original message that was sent, and this includes screenshots from your phone, "messages sent" from your email outbox, and audio recordings of everything you say to them.

The best way to keep track of this is to minimize communication with your ex and avoid all chances of causing it.

If you see evidence of bad judgment, aggressive behavior or abuse on social media, Capture it before filing for divorce because your ex can delete offensive posts, or their accounts, in seconds.

6. Have A Plan, Stick to It

You plan to reasonably divide your assets and responsibilities so that you and your children can move on with your lives.

For your kids, this plan perhaps includes time with you (because in most cases the mother keeps guard and custody), even if your ex is a first-class psychopath. For you, it includes having as little contact as possible with your ex.

But the narcissist sees things differently. For them, it is to win or lose; everything for them, none for you. Any assignment you are given is considered a personal defeat, so you will save any expense to avoid reaching your goals.

Even if they finance € 50k in legal fees to get what they want and you have to sell your car for € 25k, they will feel justified in their actions because they can blame the unfair judge and not own the final decision. The judge's decision could fuel his complex martyr for years to come, which is a victory for the narcissist.

7. Lock Yourself in A Circle of Wagons

In the Wild West, a caravan could better defend all members against attack by surrounding tanks and fighting from all sides. By divorcing a narcissist, you can expect them to hit you from all angles and blind you when you

74

least expect it.

By surrounding yourself with close family, friends, and counselors, you won't have to fight your ex alone.

8. Forgive Yourself

Going back to where we started, it's hard to imagine why you ever married a narcissist. But that's it. You cannot change the past. So, Forgive yourself! Narcissists, by nature, want to win at all prices

During their courtship, you were the prize, so they will likely take advantage of the charm, romance, S, and affirmation to claim your identity and prevent others from accompanying you.

Her confident attitude, charm, ability to "always close the sale" might be part of what attracted you to her in the first place.

It is after the sale is made, the deal is made, the validation of winning your love has been given, that the narcissist changes and often focuses on other prizes and goals (from job offers and bets to sports cars and lovers).

This cold and calculated change will eventually lead him to file for divorce.

Learn from that lesson and become aware of why you fell into a narcissist's trap

Nothing happens; this time, you didn't see it coming. But from now on, you know what narcissistic behaviors and should keep that in mind next time, as long as you are ready to find a new and more worthy partner.

Particular Case: Divorce from A Narcissist

Even the separation from such a manipulative character as a pronounced narcissist is painful. Divorce naturally presents the person concerned with even more significant challenges. Persistent harassment, in some cases to stalking, is just one of many ways such a person tries to "keep you busy." His view of the world and himself, separation/divorce means one thing above all: an "attack" on his person, on his ego. In his arrogance, he sees this ego as being superior and superior, even error-free and flawless, so you can wait a long time for your share in the failure of a relationship or marriage to be seen and recognized.

But how does a narcissist deal with separation? He is often not sad or sad.

Instead, an overwhelming resentment flares up in him - paired with lust for revenge. When he realizes that he can no longer recapture his old partner, the kindness that may have been shown at the beginning of the contact quickly turns into harassment. The repertoire is almost infinite: letters, threats, excessive demands, emotional manipulation, and much more. In the event of a divorce from a narcissist, it can, therefore, unfortunately, be expected that the narcissist will fight with "hard bandages." Last but not least, this can affect the areas of finance and custody of children together. Here it is extremely advisable to get help from outside (e.g., initiate friends, if necessary, seek legal advice or a victim protection office).

Conclusion and Outlook: How Can I Finally Get Rid of a Narcissist?

After separation or divorce from a narcissist, you need to show yourself as unimpressed as possible by his manipulative, sometimes aggressive behavior and, above all, to remain steadfast. Fight doubts about the separation (sowing precisely that is his strategy), stay consistent, and never go into his games. It is best to break off contact consistently. If continued contact is necessary, for example, because of children together, each interaction should take place sober and targeted. Do not try to appeal to his "reason" or appeasement. Rational arguments are unlikely to change anything about the situation and its behavior. Even if you miss your partner, you should keep in mind: Your decision is definite and remains the right one for you. A separation or divorce is your (well-considered) decision, and you do not have to ask for his / her permission.

TIPS FOR DIVORCING A NARCISSIST

First of all: Everyone has narcissistic parts in them. Some more, some less, like the Viennese psychiatrist and neuroscientist Dr. Raphael Bonelli, explains. Conversely, just because a person is not beautiful, he is far from being a narcissist. Nowadays, this term is used much too lightly in relationship matters as a homicide argument. There is a clear definition. Basically, the narcissistic personality disorder, which will be discussed in the following, can be characterized by three essential characteristics: A real narcissist idealizes himself, devalues others, and is always next to himself. "Only he is beautiful, only what he says is true, and only what is good for him is good," says the expert.

No Partnership at Eye Level

In a relationship, the narcissist is dominant. A partnership on an equal footing is not desirable. After all, you want to think about it, feel more powerful and more prominent. It does not prevent the narcissist. More men than women are affected by this disease from not looking for the most beautiful, here and there the smartest of all women. With it, he can decorate himself, increase his value even more. However, if the woman dares to part with him, the narcissist shoots from all tubes. "For him, it is an insult to majesty. It is improper and completely unacceptable that the woman wants to part with him," said Bonelli. The narcissist is deeply offended. "That's why separations, where a narcissist is involved, are often so bloody."

The narcissist experiences the separation brought about by the woman as a personal defeat; he cannot bear this. And don't understand either. How can she leave him when he's the best? According to the motto, "you will see, you will come back," the separation is simply not acceptable. The man makes every effort to bring the ex-partner back. "Sometimes even just to drop it. Because: A narcissist will not be left," the psychiatrist illustrates the possible reactions of the person concerned. Things get even more complicated when children are involved. "Sometimes, he misses the children he doesn't care about as an instrument of power." Sometimes he tries to get the woman to stop seeing her.

The Narcissist as A Manipulator

"A real narcissist is unscrupulous. He has no moral values and no inhibition to lie, steal, and cheat. Everything is allowed as long as it

77

benefits him. Because he is the highest, and the end justifies the means," asks Bonelli represents the patient's point of view. It is not uncommon for a so-called gaslight effect to occur in a relationship with a narcissist. "The narcissist manipulates the partner deliberately using incorrect information." Usually, to create a free space - mostly sexual, but sometimes also of a financial nature. "The victim is increasingly unsettled until he finally no longer trusts his perception. He feels very uncomfortable in the partnership, but don't assign the feeling to an apparent reason.

It can take years, even decades, for the victim to see through this evil game, the consequences of which can range from mental illnesses such as depression or delusional states to changes in the entire personality. Once the separation is inevitable, the person who dared to leave the narcissist is completely devalued. The insight that he is the one who would have to change to continue the relationship does not exist. And that's not all: "It is not uncommon for the narcissist to go through an extreme war of roses, trying to destroy the other." On a personal, social, or even financial level.

It Is How the Separation Works

So how can you pause this vicious cycle? The expert advocates precise wording. For example, you say: I want us to remain friends. Or: I don't want you to suffer." Such formulations do not help here. Especially not if the partner is a narcissist. One should not be squeamish, and the decision to separate should be expressed clearly. To emphasize what was said, it could help to break a taboo that the person affected by the narcissistic personality disorder has set, or at least to threaten it.

Sometimes you can involve a person in the separation interview whom the person concerned does not particularly like. If, despite all efforts, the message does not get through to the other party, it is essential to use harder guns. He had to be made to understand that he was severe and, if necessary, was ready to take more drastic measures. "It's best to say or do something that hurts him." If you want to pull through the separation, consideration in the sense of "It must not hurt" is out of place. If you catch a sore spot of the narcissist, he finally manages to break away from his partner in his injury. "Better to be a little too rough than not clear enough." Because with the latter, you would only drag the process out unnecessarily.

What to Do with Kids in Case of Narcissistic Marriage and Case of Divorce

Many disturbed people, especially relational manipulators, move freely in society, often occupying essential positions. They have a "health mask," which makes them invisible and difficult to identify. They are individuals moved by predatory aggression, without empathy, remorse, and guilt. They have constant tendencies aimed at the exploitation and victimization of others, which they achieve through the use of lies, deception, and manipulation.

The psychopath, in particular, unlike the rest of humankind, does not worry or feel displeasure or feel any guilt when he hurts someone. To achieve the goals he has set, he uses various tools of mental manipulation. He can pretend tenderness, solidarity, loyalty, and he can also cry, but always to the "benefit" of his atypical needs. Its sentimental points are "chameleonic." It also captures the needs of the prey, is very insightful, aims, and then "collects" the gains and thus acts with each victim.

They are mechanisms with human features. They can't do otherwise. Making objects others for them is essential and automatic. Pouring violence and destruction onto their human objects is an automatism of their nature. Birds fly, fish swim, humans are creative and act not only to satisfy the need to survive physically but also need to survive emotionally through the relationship with others. Psychopaths, on the other hand, capture, plunder, exploit, and destroy their objects. Nothing personal, I'm like that.

These dangerous subjects with an often harmless appearance, there are many partners who, both in constant relationship and after separation. To make life very difficult for the ex-partner and the children.

The Technique of The Graystone

The technique of the grey stone and the counter-manipulation techniques are reserved for those who cannot carry out severing contacts with them (no CONTACT) or for those who in the early stages of detachment undergo surprise visits by the abusing subject. It is useful in cases where there are children or common work interests.

Counter-manipulation is not a technique for seducing or attracting a perverse subject again nor for implementing a vendetta against him, but only for not letting himself be overwhelmed and deprogrammed in the interactions that may prove inevitable.

79

In the cases, in fact, of inevitable contact, the victim must transform himself into a stone. Firm, immobile, without emotional reactions of any kind, he must look at the subject in the face without any expressiveness, he must have a high or low tone of voice and a constant timbre. Short phrases, do not collect any provocation (love bombing or insults), must not appear comely or unkempt. In short, it must not reveal its true self that once attracted the pathological narcissist or the psychopath. One must (or rather one must pretend) to be grey, colorless and immobile. The perverse narcissist and the psychopath seek energy and vitality to feed themselves, and they do not find those who are immobile and off. After a while, they will go away. This technique, in some cases, can save. In nature, many animals pretend to be dead to protect themselves. Predators are not so intelligent and are overconfident. It is a weapon to our advantage. Of course, implementing the technique is not simple and requires two requisites: not being preyed to anger and having decided to quit.

The Gray Stone method is based on knowledge of the narcissistic and psychopathic personality. These do not experience emotions and, therefore, do not enjoy an abundant inner life. On their own, they are fatally bored. It is why they need to create situations with a high dramatic content to obtain constant stimuli, using deception and manipulation. They love to respond to their provocations and lies. They need to feel that they manage to destabilize the other. The idea of this strategy is to turn into an extraordinarily bored and grey person.

Do not respond to insults and provocations, never tell anything about you; use only minimal and neutral words and phrases.

Try to divert the psychopath's attention away from you by shifting it to trivial household problems such as school hours or plumber problems.

If some problems worry you, if you have family or work troubles, do not let the manipulator participate, who, sooner or later, will use this information to his advantage.

Also, as far as possible, unless the situation is dire, do not show the problems of the children (for example, do not report that they have nightmares or insecurities with the group of friends: they will use this information to manipulate them, probably against you).

The grey stone method is a kind of "zero reaction. "When we communicate, we use words and also non-verbal communication, which is represented by gestures, tone of voice, body posture, gaze, and it represents 90% of communication between two individuals. The manipulator uses words and non-verbal communication to his advantage, in a positive way to seduce and attract and in a negative way to intimidate, enslave, blame. For example, he will use "adverse listening," that is, he will not look at you during the conversation or look at other people or do other things, raise his tone of voice, or beat his fists, will have his gaze fixed on you.

Counter-Handling Communication

Communicative counter-manipulation is a technique that must be acquired and takes effect after months. In the beginning, you will feel your heart pounding, and you will have a stomachache. However, you will have to continue insisting. On the other hand, the psychopath, when you adopt another communication scheme, will be surprised and angry. Noticing that you are getting out of control, for this reason, it may become more pressing and offensive or more accommodating and seemingly sensitive to enslave you again. Of course, you must not give in or believe in its change.

It is carried out with short, simple sentences and an emotionless tone. Some examples could be these: psychopath.: "Think only of yourself" - victim "this is your opinion" psychopath. "You had never done such a thing before" victim "doesn't feel persecuted if I do what I think is right" psychopath. "You always want to be right" victim "sometimes it happens to me" (Isabelle Nazare Aga-The art of not being manipulated)

Some requirements are:

- Short sentences
- Be on the vague
- Use the sentences made, morals, general principles.
- Use the impersonal form
- Smile if the context allows it
- Be polite
- Do not enter into discussions if they bring quarrels or humiliations
- You no longer justify yourself

In short, make yourself seem indifferent. Phrases like " it's your opinion," "you can believe it," "if you think so," "it is possible," "it depends" "you say this to me?" "The future will tell us," "I have a clear conscience," are correct. Also, know how to refuse, knowing how to say no, is one of the principles of personal self-affirmation. The psychopath exists to affirm power and control over others. He can be extremely persistent when he wants to get something; in this case, be like broken disks, repeat the same phrases, as indicated above, without letting out nervousness and tension.

Finally, in case you are divorced, and the interactions concern the management of children, know that you will not have to leave margins wider than those established by the Court.

Try to divert the subject's attention away from you by shifting it to small household problems such as school hours or issues with the plumber.

If some problems worry you, if you have family or work troubles, do not let the manipulator participate, who, sooner or later, will use this information to his advantage.

It often happens that relational manipulators, psychopaths, and narcissists consider the child as an extension and a property of his, demand maximum availability from you. If, on the one hand, it may have defamed you with friends and relatives or even in front of children, however, considering you an object of property, it will feel entitled to call you or enter your home without notice and limits.

If you leave space for him, you will always be in tension and nervousness, and you will not be able to untie himself from his fatal presence definitively. Communicate with the psychopath only in writing with short messages and on issues strictly related to the contingent need. Do not answer after a specific time; it would be good to have a mobile number only for this purpose that you will keep off at times set by you and do not provide any information about your life and write it all down. Try to communicate with them in the presence of third parties and always print both and your messages, emails. Also, do not let it violate the agreements and contact a lawyer and judge in all cases where they do.

Lastly, to stop him in cases of greater intrusiveness, in addition to the report, prepare a dossier that concerns him and that, if it was inevitable, can be sent to those in duty (superiors or family members), to put him with. his back to the wall. The latter remedy must be used only if the aggressiveness is not very strong, in which case, the total interruption of contacts and the recourse to the competent authorities is the only way forward.

Finally, if you want to end the relationship and fear that it could turn the facts into a case for the separation or custody of minors or harm you in another field, prepare a strategy in time and make use of the records. They are especially useful in cases of persecutory acts, physical, verbal, or psychological violence because they can be used in both criminal and civil proceedings.

It is lawful to record a conversation between those present provided that it does not take place within the walls of the private home of the unsuspecting registered subject. If the registration takes place in the home of the registered item, unaware of this, or another secret place belonging to the same (for example, the partner's house), the registration constitutes a crime.

But be careful: the member of a conversation is always enabled to record it, as the crime "triggers" when a third party registers the conversation. It is because the recipient's capture of the interlocutor's words and gestures cannot be considered undue, as it constitutes merely legal documentation of what has already been learned. In other words, the registration among those present is illegitimate, in the registered residence, only if the booking is made by a third party.

On the contrary, it is lawful to register the home of the registrant or in place belonging to the same, for example, inside his car or even in a public street or within an open business. In such cases, there are no crimes concerning the violation of privacy. According to the Cassation, in fact, "those who dialogue accept the risk that the conversation is recorded."

The registration can be delivered immediately to the Judicial Authority, to the Public Prosecutor with an act of complaint, if the same is intended to demonstrate the existence of the crime represented by the same claim. It can produce, to the Public Prosecutor, by the suspect or offended person by respective defendants the Investigation, at any time. In the event of a civil trial, it is filed in the file.

The systems outlined here are useful but must not replace the zero contact, which must be implemented if the situation permits, as the no connection is the only real tool that allows removal from social predators and those who use manipulation and psychological violence.

HOW TO START RESPONDING AND MANAGE CONFLICTS

The best advice in case you are trapped in a relationship with a manipulator/trice (histrionic, border, narcissist, etc.) is always the NO CONTACT, but what happens if we cannot or do not want to detach ourselves from these people? It is essential to learn some narcissistic counter-manipulation techniques.

For example, if our mother or our son is manipulating us? What do we do?

Narcissistic manipulation You must learn to:

Communicating with the manipulators more healthily and effectively: this is the first step to start again, indeed, to start living - learning to trust yourself, but also and above all (much rarer if the abuse scheme narcissistic starts from childhood) of the outside world.

Adopt behavioral strategies aimed at preserving yourself and avoiding conflict.

The goal of counter-manipulation is not to harm the manipulators, to take revenge, or in turn to manipulate because we remember that affective manipulators are primarily people who suffer and seek confrontation and conflict to channel all their negative energies.

Our goal is to ensure that they do not use us as a channel and accept that they cannot love us as we want - even if we want it so much, also if it would be right for the role they play in our life yet if we have explained it to them many times.

Counter-manipulation, therefore, is not a means of communicating by reacting. Still, it is a way of not communicating at all, not to enter that vortex of predefined thoughts and actions (schemes) that we know well, and that makes us suffer or simply empty us.

We must learn to have the answers ready, without offending, without being aggressive, but placing ourselves in a detached way, without adding to the message, the emotional connotation that could imply underlying meanings or further irritate the manipulator/manipulator causing the conflict.

The first rule, therefore, consists in:

- This action involves a painful strain on spontaneity. Still, it teaches you how to control yourself (in various situations) and requires that you learn to operate a sort of emotional avoidance.
- Avoidance is not repression (involuntary inhibition) but rather "voluntary and elaborate oppression." it allows you not to lose contact with your truth, but learning not to share it with those who use it against you and therefore defend yourself against constant suffering and lack of energy (emptying).
- It is essential to give up spontaneity with this type of person, even though they appear to be emotional, true, impulsive, etc. Etc.; this truth is granted only to them and not to you. Your truth is only information that the manipulator will use to defend himself, attack you, or make you feel guilty later.
- Unfortunately, manipulators do not have the maturity to understand, learn from experiences or emotionally process their skills; they do not have the empathy to know that that sentence, that criticism bothers you or hurts you, but they have only learned that if I do a, I get b. Up to now, every time they provoked, humiliated you, etc., they got a conflict and, in the end, a heated confrontation, through which you learned who they are not and would like to be.
- Manipulators do not know how to get in touch with their shadows, and for this reason, they must project them onto the outside world, renouncing the benefit of being able to grow (take responsibility for the relationship) and learn from the intimate knowledge of themselves.
- They are not interested in the truth and your effort to underline that you are not so that it is not true, etc., only leads you to lose energy and to be mistaken as crazy. For this, you give up the desire to restore what is right and do what is right for you and the situation.
- Especially if the manipulator you are dealing with is a wife or husband who can harm your children or have the power to harm them, be intelligent. Do not react.

There are some different styles of counter-manipulation based on the context and the type of relationship you have with the manipulator-manipulator:

- Neutrality (emotionless and non-judgmental communication)
- Humour or irony (better the first because the second, if not used well based on the context, can be a provocation).

85

- Self-mockery
- Collusion (give a reason and try to see it as he/she even if it is not so).

EXAMPLE with a narcissistic mother:

You are too little rigid with your children, bah! These do as they wanted when you were little you didn't fly with me (between the lines I am a mother better than you, and you can't do it, without me you can't stay).

- Neutrality (emotionless and non-judgmental communication): "True, how times change "
- Humour or irony: "By catching flies, we were paralyzed, haha haha," or "But you were at home when there were flies"?
- Self-derision: "my mother, what a mother's disaster, then I start playing with them so much. I am so small near you"!
- Collusion (give a reason and try to see her as he/she even if it is not so): "Yes true, you are right."

The Inner Mantra

Find a "mantra," a guiding phrase, a sort of inner warning that neutralizes you and reposition you in the emotional condition necessary to prevent anger from making you take the behavioral step.

Or imagine an arrow that heading towards you breaks on an imaginary glass that protects you.

Discovering that a loved one has a personality disorder helps us to detach ourselves from the idea that something is missing in us: "IT IS NOT MY Fault" and allows us to start healing from the post-traumatic stress disorder that often characterizes the narcissistic abuse, with invalidating and self-sabotaging tendencies.

We are not unworthy of love, and it is instead the manipulator/manipulator who feels inadequate in providing it.

It is a long path that requires a process of regeneration aimed at the RECONSTRUCTION OF A SELF-ESTIMATE torn by years of psychological and emotional abuse practiced by those who instead - should protect us and love us a husband, a wife, a parent

It is almost IN NATURAL to believe that those who love us can harm us. Still, sometimes it happens, because all the evil that we are unable to face in our interior, coming into contact with ourselves, we run the risk of projecting it outside.

In this sense, for dramatic and childish personalities, the other acts as a channel/scapegoat/container; it is the filter through which to purify oneself or someone to attach oneself to obtain supplies as a newborn baby does with its mother.

In this sense Winnicott spoke of a "sufficiently good mother": a newborn uses the mother as a container and the "sufficiently good" mother processes the emotionally disrupted contents of the child and returns them so that he can face them because he is still "emotionally disregarded given his age. "

A manipulator is an angry child trapped in the body of an adult who needs to be looked after and sucked in energy without being exposed.

Dealing with A Narcissist in The Court

The narcissist wants to win and will use any sneaky means to do it. Remember that these people are pathological liars and can stage Oscar-winning performances in courtrooms.

Pathological narcissists are the most poisonous and dangerous opponents that can be faced in any court.

The types of cases in which you may be involved are the following:

- Criminal proceedings in which you have fallen victim to a crime committed by a pathological narcissist;
- Divorce proceedings, in which goods/money are at stake;
- Child custody cases;
- Return procedure for goods/money due.

If it is a divorce case, the narcissist will appear confident and calm. At the same time, the subjugated former partner will have already been severely trampled by this ruthless individual in the months and years preceding the trial and will often appear stressed and lacking self-confidence and the law.

If you are in this situation, not having conversations and avoiding eye contact with the narcissist inside or outside the courtroom will be essential for you. Better to find a place on the sidelines where to sit outside the courthouse while waiting or at intervals, so that the narcissist and his lawyers and followers cannot intimidate you or make you nervous.

87

Many people who face a narcissist in court fear that he will be able to manipulate there too and that the lies told are believed. It is essential to ensure that the legal representative of your choice is aware of what Narcissist Personality Disorder is. A lawyer who knows nothing is likely to be manipulated by the narcissist and can advise you to negotiate when it is not in your best interest to do so.

If the narcissist pushed you to the limit in the past, now it's up to your lawyers to play hard.

Narcissists are likely to react when their lies are exposed, and their bad behaviors brought to light. Eventually, you are revealing information that they had no intention of letting the world know so that their anger can become uncontrollable. Often their lawyers do everything to keep them "good," calm, and content (a rather tricky, if not impossible task).

They probably have hidden or diverted goods: they are very skilled in concealing their earnings.

Is it possible to empower a narcissist in court? Of course, but one must be well prepared. It is essential to be armed with irrefutable, undeniable, and corroborated evidence.

Avoid giving the narcissist credible alternative scenarios to the facts. An experienced lawyer knows how to put a narcissist in trouble with the right questions, to remove the wind from the sails subtly, but effectively.

Example:

- I am led to believe that you are entirely qualified in your profession. Excuse me, what is your highest academic qualification? So, it doesn't have a formal qualification, I understand. "
- Contradicting or diminishing the narcissist's inflated vision of himself and his fragile self-esteem will shatter.
- A trained lawyer knows how to play with words so that a narcissist understands that he has no control over everything and everyone.
- When we are in the confines of the courtrooms, we must stay as far away from the narcissist as possible and never look in his direction. The fact that never being looked at causes a narcissistic wound: they hate being ignored!
- As we know, the narcissist believes he is above the law and not subject to the limitations of ordinary citizens. As for them, they are superior to anyone in the courtroom, including the

88

judge and lawyers. Nobody can have the audacity to make them responsible for their actions! Anyone who testifies against them will be labeled a liar and corrupt.

- Never show any reaction to their words or behavior. They knew how to step on your Achilles heels first, and they will try again. Make sure these attempts are accepted with indifference.
- It can be challenging to communicate to magistrates and lawyers how unacceptable the behavior of a pathological narcissist has been.
- The goal of a good lawyer will be to snatch any information from the court and lead them to discredit themselves when their explosive fury makes its appearance.
- Always tell the truth. Never be tempted to embellish the truth or paint a fake picture.
- And remember never to drop to the narcissist level.

BREAKING FREE

There is a bit of Gockel in most of us. We live in the age of narcissism, and it is often said lightly. And indeed: each of us has narcissistic features. "We need it to keep our self-esteem stable," says psychotherapist Dr. Bärbel Wardetzki. We strengthen our ego with praise, recognition, and love. It becomes difficult when there is no self-esteem at all, and someone constantly needs a "narcissistic supply" to feel worth it at all.

Then caution is advised. The author of the book "Eitle Liebe. How narcissistic relationships can fail or succeed. "(Kösel) prefers to speak of a" person with narcissistic structures " instead of a " narcissist." "And that ranges from very strong to very weak," says the psychotherapist. Such people can be downright dangerous if you want to have a romantic relationship with them. We reveal how you recognize a "person with narcissistic structures" (in the future, we will briefly call him "narcissist") and how you can best deal with him.

1. Don't Be Blinded

Whoever gets into a relationship with a narcissist usually believes at first to have found the dream prince or dream woman: he carries one on his hands, lets red roses rain, and always stresses how happy he is to have found one. Christine Merzeder calls this strategy, "Love Bombing." She was with a narcissistic partner for twelve years - and then a psychological and physical wreck. With her recently published book, "How creeping poison. Surviving and curing narcissistic abuse in relationships "(Scorpio) wants to draw attention to the victims.

Usually, an uncomfortable gut feeling tells you that you are wriggling on the hook of an egomaniac: Because it feels strange how he lifts you onto the pedestal ("You are the most beautiful woman in the world), unbelievable that he shares all our hobbies, overreaching when he orders for you in the restaurant.

2. Take Warning Signals Seriously

On cloud seven, it's easy to ignore the chaos below. For example, that Mr. Right has left a hell of a lot of burnt earth elsewhere: gone bankrupt, divorced x, divorced with the ex, hopelessly no contact with the child is always blaming others for their problems," says psychotherapist Wardetzki. You should also get attention if you do too well compared to previous partners: "They only used me - but everything is different with you." Another typical pattern: relationship hopping: The glow of the last partnership is probably still warm when he lights up a new love fire.

3. Expect That He Always Wants to Be the Center of Attention

The reason why narcissists often get involved in a new relationship so quickly or lead several at the same time: "Narcissists are like junkies," says Mercedes, "they cannot be without narcissistic intake." Desires and needs are only gradually noticeable. "You have no feeling of belonging, " says Bärbel Wardetzki. They are not looking for a partner at eye level, but a mirror that keeps their magnificence in mind. There is no such thing as "Our Song," only the "I, I, I" record is playing. Also typical: "You don't get a word in conversation with him. He doesn't ask, "How are you?" And forgets essential data about the partner, "says Bärbel Wardetzki.

4. Don't Talk Bad Behavior Nicely

Is the honeymoon phase once over, narcissists extend their claws: "They enhance themselves by manipulating, emotionally exploiting and devaluing their counterpart," says Mercedes. There are violent scenes for the smallest "wrongdoings" in the company. He runs over your mouth, criticizes appearance, outfit, or general education. Mercedes calls such verbal attacks "micro-violence." It is essential to put a stop to it as quickly as possible: "Resist against the hurtful behavior of the other," says Bärbel Wardetzki. "Set limits." But expect that Mr. or Mrs. Ego will not find it funny if you give up contradictions: "Narcissists cannot deal with criticism at all," says Bärbel Wardetzki.

5. Strengthen Your Self-confidence

The attacks with which the narcissist bombarded his partner are particularly treacherous because they often hit the Achilles' heels: "You are so fat" when you are struggling with a few kilos too much, "You are so incredibly stupid" if you suffered in school as a child. It describes the strategy as "scanning" a person. You can only oppose this if you are at peace with yourself and mentally stable. "Stand by yourself and who you are," advises Wardetzki, a psychotherapist. If you have strong self-confidence, you will not be blown away by the pejorative remarks of the other person, but can assess them for what they are: desperate effort for attention. Psychotherapist Wardetzki advises to set clear boundaries and to express your wishes and needs. "Dealing with narcissists requires sensitivity," she says - and healthy nerves.

6. Don't Let Yourself Be Unsettled

While one can still overlook small taunts and survive power struggles, there are even more treacherous methods by which people with extremely narcissistic structures torture their victims in relationships. In her book, Mercedes describes the strategy of "gaslighting." The name goes back to the 1940s film "Gaslight," in which a man tries to drive his young wife crazy. Through lies and manipulations, the victim should be so unsettled that he no longer trusts his perception. Punctured tires, undetectable sums of money, strange nausea after meals - the arsenal is diverse. Christine Merzeder looked after more than 1000 victims in a self-help forum for victims of narcissistic abuse. "Some have even attempted suicide because of such manipulation," she says.

7 Keep in Touch with Friends and Family

Not only does extreme narcissists play with their partner's self-image - it is also often the case that ego-bloodsuckers try to portray the partner as untrustworthy, silly or even malicious, or to seal off the relationship with friends, acquaintances or who Family is described as corrupt dealings, as Christine Merzeder experienced. Her ex-husband, she says, tried to convince her that her brother had made derogatory comments about her. "He wanted to drive a wedge between us," she says. However, she was not put off by this and kept in touch with friends and family - very important in order not to perceive the relationship as the only elixir of life and to have allies in the event of a separation.

8. It Is Not Your Fault

Psychologists like Bärbel Wardetzki believe that narcissistic relationships often find complementary partners, that there is often a "grandiose" narcissist and a "depressed" one- inferior "team-up. The weaker part draws from admiring the other. Christine Merzeder is of a different opinion: "Each of us can fall for a narcissist, even mentally stable people." Under no circumstances should one be blamed for this. Psychotherapist Wardetzki also says this: "Finding the blame for a messed-up partnership with a narcissist on your own would be completely wrong. It doesn't work. Narcissists are often not able to relate. "People who cannot find their way out of the labyrinth of" vain love "on their own advise them to seek

92

professional help. Christine Mercedes, for example, found support with the Australian Melanie Tonia Evans with the Narcissistic Abuse Recovery Program (NARP).

9. Don't Believe in Promises That Everything Will Change

Mercedes is even convinced: "Narcissists cannot change." One of the most famous narcissist researchers, psychoanalyst Otto Kernberg, once said that the often-voiced assumption that narcissists were resistant to therapy. "However, before the midlife crisis, Mr. Ego is unlikely to see Dr. Love will. "He's just looking for his next victim," says Mercedes.

10. Prepare the Separation Well

The sun king or the sun queen has spanned the bow too often? Anyone who decides to separate from him/her should prepare well, advises Mercedes. If you turn off his ego oxygen, he becomes uncomfortable. You have to expect aggression, stalking, and smear campaigns, she says. Bärbel Wardetzki explains: "A narcissist must always be right, a separation that does not originate from him will, therefore, hurt him insane." You have to be able to substantiate allegations against him, for example, in a divorce process or custody dispute, says Merzeder: "Narcissists It often succeeds in taking mediators or judges for themselves, so that the victim then stands as the culprit. "Nevertheless, she does not want to miss the experience with her narcissist:" That made me strong, "she says today.

RECOGNIZE WORST TACTICS OF NARCISSISTS

"Toxic" people such as vindictive narcissists, psychopaths, and other types of people with antisocial traits adopt maladaptive behaviors in their relationships that end up exploiting, diminishing, or injuring their partner, family, and friends. They use many misleading tactics that distort the reality of their victims and deflect their responsibilities.

Here are the tactics that people with more or less severe personality disorders use.

Gaslighting

By "Gaslighting," we mean a manipulation tactic that makes use of these formulas or their variations, for example: "It didn't happen," "You imagined it," and "You're crazy" is a sort of negation. Gaslighting is perhaps one of the most unfair manipulation tactics because it attempts to distort and erode your perception of reality; it dramatically affects self-confidence, which may even push an individual to choose not to report abuse and mistreatment.

When a narcissist, a sociopath, implements this technique towards you, you may unconsciously accept it as a way of reconciling the disharmony between your versions of the facts. Two different beliefs challenge each other: is the other person right, or can I trust what I remember happened? A manipulative person will try to convince you that the former is an inescapable reality, while the latter is a sign of your dysfunction.

To resist these attempts at manipulation is essential to rely on your version of reality - sometimes writing things as they happen as they happened, telling the story to a friend, or bringing the experience back to a psychotherapist can help counter the Gaslighting effect. Having the support of external people can distance you from the distorted reality described by the evil person and help you gain confidence in yourself.

Projection

A clear sign of meanness is the inability of the other person to realize their shortcomings and the attitude of using any power in their possession to avoid being held responsible for it. This behavior is like a projection. Projection is a defense mechanism used to divert responsibility for negative behavior or trait by attributing it to someone else. It acts as a

94

digression leading to avoiding one's duties.

Although everyone makes use of the projection in some way, according to Dr. Martinez-Lewi, an expert on Narcissistic Personality, the predictions of a narcissist are often psychologically offensive. Rather than admitting their flaws, imperfections, and mistakes, malevolent narcissists and sociopaths prefer to unload their traits on unwitting victims in a way that is painful and overly cruel. Instead of admitting the possibility of improvement, they prefer that their victim take responsibility for their behavior and be ashamed. This is how the narcissist projects any sense of shame he feels towards others.

For example, a pathological liar might accuse his partner of lying; a wife in need of affection could call her husband "sticky" to make him seem dependent on her; a rude employee could call his boss inefficient to try to escape from reality regarding their poor productivity instead.

The narcissist accustomed to offending and behaving in a petty way loves to play to transfer the blame to others. The aim of the game is simple: he wins, you lose, and you or the world, in general, takes responsibility for all that is wrong with them. In this way, you babysit their fragile ego while you sink into a sea of doubts about yourself.

The advice in these cases? Do not "project" your value system onto a narcissist as this has the possible consequence of further exploitation. Extreme narcissists usually have no interest in introspection or change. It is essential to end relationships and end interactions with toxic people as soon as possible to focus on your reality and validate your identity. Avoid living in someone else's dysfunctional shadow.

Meaningless Conversations Aimed at Confusing You

If you think you can have a satisfying conversation with a "toxic" individual, be prepared instead to deal with meaningless dialogues, which have the intent to destabilize you.

Malevolent and sociopathic narcissists often use tricks such as talking frankly, circular reasoning, ad-hominem arguments, projection, and gaslighting to confuse and mislead you in-case you disagree with them or challenge them in any way. They do it to discredit you, confuse you, and frustrate you, distracting you from the actual problem and making you feel guilty for the fact that you are a human being with thoughts and emotions that may be different from his. In their eyes, the problem is your existence.

Just spend ten minutes arguing with a hostile and ill-disposed narcissist to forget only the reason why the discussion started. Maybe you just questioned their absurd claim that the sky was red, and now your entire childhood, family, friends, career, or lifestyle are under attack. This is because your contradicting them touched their false belief that you are omniscient and omnipotent, resulting in a wound to their ego.

Toxic people are adept at taking long and exhausting monologues. They thrive on drama and live for it. Whenever you try to provide a point of view that contrasts with their ridiculous claims, you just feed them. Don't feed the narcissist - instead, give yourself a confirmation that the problem is their offensive behavior, it's not you. Stop interacting the moment you notice that the situation is getting worse and use your energies to take care of yourself.

Trivial Statements, Generalizations, And "Mind Reading"

Evil narcissists are often intelligent people, but many of them are intellectually lazy. Rather than spending their time carefully considering a different perspective, they generalize everything you say, responding with general statements that do not take into account the nuances of your position or consider the multiple aspects you have mentioned. On the other hand, why strive to reason? Better to brand yourself with a label that dismisses your position in one fell swoop!

For example, if you point out to a narcissist that their behavior is unacceptable, they will often respond with general statements about your excessive sensitivity with phrases like "you're never happy" or "you're always too sensitive" rather than discussing the actual problems. Of course, you may sometimes be particularly sensitive, but it is also possible that most of the time, your attacker is insensitive and cruel.

Hold on to your truth and resist these generalizations keeping in mind that they are nothing more than an illogical way of thinking in black and white. Toxic people who make use of generic statements do not represent the whole spectrum of experience - they serve only their limited knowledge and disproportionate self-conception.

In the eyes of a malignant narcissist or a sociopath, your different opinions, legitimate emotions, and life experiences are nothing but defects in character and a sign of your irrationality.

Narcissists are ready to turn what you're saying so that your opinions seem absurd or offensive. Let's say you point out to your friend with whom you

96

have a toxic relationship that you don't like the tone he is talking to you about. In response, he or she might attribute things to you that you never said, saying, "Oh, so would you be perfect instead?" or "So I'm a bad person, huh?" even if you have done nothing but express your feeling. This causes them to invalidate your right to express thoughts or emotions about their inappropriate behavior and instill guilt in you when you try to set limits.

Then there is another common form of cognitive diversion and distortion compared to the alleged "mind-reading." Toxic people often assume they know what you are thinking and feeling. They frequently jump to conclusions based on what bothers them rather than stopping to reflect seriously on the situation. They react based on their illusions and their logical errors and do not apologize for the pain they consequently cause. Known for attributing to other words they have not said, they depict you as the person with the intention or the bizarre point of view, although this does not belong to you. They accuse you of considering them despicable - even before they have given you time to express yourself about their behavior - as a form of preventive defense.

Even just saying, "I never said that" and leaving in case the person continues to accuse you of doing or saying something you haven't done can help you define clear limits in this kind of interaction. As long as the toxic person can blame others by diverting attention from their behavior, they will have been successful in convincing you that you should be ashamed of trying to question them.

Look for The Hair in The Egg and Diminish the Results Obtained

The difference between positive criticism and negative criticism lies in the presence of personal attacks or impossible standards. These so-called "critics" often don't want you to improve, and they just want to look for the hair in the egg, humiliate yourself and make you the scapegoat as often as possible. Offensive and sociopathic narcissists try to downsize your achievements to feel justified in being dissatisfied continuously with you. This happens when, despite having already provided all the possible evidence to validate your position or having done everything possible to satisfy their requests, they expect further sacrifices from you or ask for more evidence to support what you say.

Do you have a successful career? The narcissist will then wonder why you're not a millionaire yet. Have you already done everything necessary to make them feel satisfied? However, you should have maintained a higher degree of "independence." The yardstick moves continuously, and the new requests are designed to make you pray for approval and recognition by the narcissist on your knees.

By raising their expectations higher and higher from time to time or changing them completely, manipulative and toxic people are capable of instilling in you a generalized sense of incapacity and inadequacy. By emphasizing an irrelevant fact or one thing that you may have done wrong and analyzing it extensively, narcissists divert attention from your strengths and lead you to develop an obsession with any possible defect or weakness. They guide you to think about what their next expectation will be that you will have to meet - to the point where you will do everything to meet their every single need - only to realize then that the horrible way they treat you doesn't change anyway.

Don't get sucked into this spiral, if someone continues to dig up, again and again, an irrelevant question to the point where they don't even consider all the efforts you've made, they don't do it to understand the situation better. They do it to make you believe that you have to try something for others continually. Instead, you have to prove something only to yourself. You must be aware of being enough and prevent others from regularly making you feel incapable and not up to par.

Change the Subject to Escape from Responsibilities

This tactic could be summarized with the phrase "What about me?". The intention is to distract you from the actual speech to shift your attention to an entirely different matter. Narcissists don't want you to be able to call them back to their responsibilities, so they turn the talk around so that their point of view is the center of attention. Are you complaining about how they neglect their children? They will come up with a mistake you made seven years ago. This kind of diversion has no time or content limit, and often begins with a phrase like "Well, what about that time."

On a broader level, this kind of diversion is used to derail discussions that endanger the status quo. A gay rights speech, for example, could quickly be sidetracked by someone who focuses on another issue of social justice to distract people from the main talk.

Don't get sidetracked - if someone tries to do it with you, you can try the "broken disk technique" and continue listing the facts without giving in to distractions. Redirect their attempt to redirect you by saying, "It's not what I'm talking about. Let's focus on this issue. " If they don't care, give it up and use your energy for something more constructive - like not arguing with someone who shows deep immaturity.

Threats and Blackmail

Pathological narcissists feel attacked when their perception of being entitled to everything, their sense of superiority and their self-esteem are somehow questioned, and instead to deal with disagreements by making compromises. They prefer to deny you the right to have a point—out of sight, trying to instill fear in you about the consequences of disagreeing with them and not meeting their demands. For them, the answer to any challenge is an ultimatum, and the formula "you have to do this or I will do this other" becomes a daily catchphrase.

If someone's reaction to your setting limits or having an opinion different from theirs is to threaten you until you give up, be it a small veiled threat or a clear admission of what they intend to do, it is a signal alarm that indicates that the other is profoundly convinced that everything is due to him and has no intention of reaching a compromise.

Insults

Narcissists tend to precautionarily magnify anything they perceive as a threat to their superiority. In their world, they are the only ones who can always be right, and anyone who dares to say otherwise creates a narcissistic wound that often results in anger.

In the worst cases, these people choose to express their narcissistic anger through insults when they can't find a better way to manipulate your opinion or manage your emotions. Insults are their most natural way to knock yourself down, humiliate yourself and offend your intelligence, your appearance, and your behavior while invalidating your right to be an individual with your point of view.

Insults can also be used to criticize what you believe in, your opinions, or your positions. A well-argued and the documented view becomes instead "stupid" or "idiocy" in the eyes of a malicious narcissist or a sociopath who feels threatened and cannot answer with a respectful and equally convincing idea. Rather than focusing on your positions, they target you as a person and try to diminish your credibility and intelligence in every possible way. It is vital to stop any interaction that consists of insults and communicate that you do not intend to tolerate it. Do not internalize offenses: remember that if they resort to insults, it is because they are unable to attack you with smarter methods.

99

Damaging Conditioning

Toxic people condition you to associate your assets, talents or happy memories with abuse, frustration, and offense. They do this by diminishing the qualities or traits they once idealized and, at the same time, sabotaging your goals, ruining holidays, and holidays. They may even separate you from your friends and family or make you economically dependent on them. Like Pavlov's dogs, you are primarily conditioned with time to be afraid of doing those things that once made your life satisfying.

Narcissists and sociopaths and other toxic people do this because they want to shift attention to themselves and how you can satisfy them. If there is anything external of them that can threaten their control over your life, they want to destroy it as soon as possible. They need to be the center of care at all times. In the idealization stage, you were the center of the narcissist's world - but now the narcissist wants to become the center of yours.

Narcissists are also pathologically envious and want nothing to intrude between them and their influence on you. On the other hand, if you understand that you can get approval, respect, and love from other people, what prevents you from leaving them? In the eyes of the toxic person, a little conditioning is the best way to keep yourself on the thorns away from happiness and your dreams.

Defamation and Stalking

When toxic personalities cannot control the way you see yourself, they begin to control the way others see you; they act like victims, letting you be labeled the toxic individual. A defamatory campaign is the first step to sabotaging your reputation and tarnishing your name so that you don't have friendly people to lean on in case you decide to detach and cut bridges with them. They may come after you and harass you or the people you know as a way to "unmask" the truth about you; these acts aimed at exposing you serve to hide their abusive behaviors, projecting them onto you.

Some libelous campaigns may also act to pits two groups of people against each other. A victim in an abusive connection with a narcissist usually does not know what the other says about her during the link, but often discovers the falsehoods after being abandoned.

100

Toxic people will gossip behind you (and in front of you), slander you with yours and their loved ones, tell stories that paint you as the attacker and them as the victim, and accuse you of the same behaviors that you fear you could report about them. At the same time, they will abuse you methodically, deliberately, but secretly so that you can use your reactions to prove that they are the real victims of your abuse.

The best way to deal with a defamatory campaign is to calibrate your reactions carefully and to rely on facts. This is especially important in the event of a highly confrontational divorce with a narcissist who could use your responses to their provocations counter to you. Document any form of annoyance, cyberbullying, or stalking and communicate with the narcissist through a lawyer whenever possible. If you believe that the other is exaggerating with stalking and abuse, you may decide to take legal action; Finding a lawyer who is knowledgeable about Narcissistic Personality Disorder is crucial in this case. Your character and integrity will do the rest when the narcissist's mask begins to collapse.

Love-bombing And Devaluation

Toxic people make you go through an idealization phase until you are immersed and absorbed enough to start a friendship or a relationship with them. Only then do they begin to devalue you, insulting precisely those things they previously admired so much. Alternatively, the individual toxic places you on a pedestal, devaluing, and attacking someone else who endangers their sense of superiority. Narcissistic abusers do it all the time - they devalue their exes with their new partner until the new partner begins to receive the same mistreatment as the ex-partner of the narcissist. In the end, what will happen is that you will receive the same kind of abuse. One day you will be the ex-partner who will want to denigrate with their new livelihood. It's just that you still don't know.

Be aware that the way a person treats or talks about someone else can potentially translate into the way he will treat you in the future.

Preventive Defense

When someone points out that they are "good guys" (or girls), that "you have to trust them" right away or emphasize their credibility without any provocation of any kind, be wary of them.

Toxic and abusive people exaggerate in exalting their ability to be kind and compassionate. Often, they tell you that you should trust them regardless, without first building a solid foundation of enough trust. They may "exhibit" a high level of empathy at the beginning of your relationship to tease you, to take off this false mask only later. In the phase of the devaluation of the cycle of abuse, when the wrong cover slowly begins to fall, they discover themselves as actually cold, insensitive, and disrespectful.

Sincerely kind people rarely need to demonstrate their positive qualities continually - they exude their warmth far more than they talk about it, and they know that actions are worth much more than just words. They know that respect and trust need reciprocity, not words.

To counteract preemptive defense, consider why a person should decide to enhance their functional qualities. Is it because they believe you don't trust them or because they know you shouldn't? Trust actions more than empty words and notice how actions show what someone is, not who he says he is.

Triangulation

By "triangulation" is meant the act of inserting an opinion, perspective, or the possible threat of a third person into the interactive dynamic. Often used to validate the abuse of the toxic personality, while invalidating the victim's reactions to that abuse, triangulation can also be used to invent love triangles that make you feel insecure.

Evil narcissists love triangulating their partner with strangers, work colleagues, ex, friends, or even family members to evoke jealousy and insecurity in you. They also use the opinion of others to validate their point of view.

This diversionary tactic serves to draw your attention away from their abusive behavior and bring it towards an image of them as a desirable and requested person. It also leads you to doubt yourself - if Marta agrees with Tommaso, does that mean I'm wrong? The truth is that narcissists love to "report" falsehoods that others would have said about you, while in reality, they are the ones who are slandering you.

To resist triangulation strategies, understand that whoever the person the narcissist is triangulating you with is also being triangulated by your relationship with the narcissist. Anyone is made fun of by this person. Return the triangulation against the narcissist by finding the support of a third party who is not under the influence of the narcissist - and also by finding your esteem for yourself.

Test Your Limits and Then, "Suck Yourself In."

Narcissists, sociopaths, and other toxic personalities continually try to test your limits to understand which ones they can overstep. The more violations they manage to commit without consequences, the more they will take things to extremes. It is the reason why victims of emotional and physical abuse are often increasingly misused every time they return to their abusers.

The abusers tend to "suck" the victims towards them with sweet promises, false remorse, and empty words about their intention to change only to abuse their victim in an even worse way. In the abuser's sick mind, this testing the limits is a punishment for reacting to the abuse and also for returning. When a narcissist tries to press the "emotional reset" button, the further delimits your limits rather than making them retreat.

Particularly manipulative people do not act thanks to empathy or compassion, but only to the consequences of their actions.

Aggressive Little Arrows Passed Off as Jokes

Plainclothes narcissists enjoy making malicious jokes against you. Usually, they pass them off as "jokes" so that they can afford to say terrible things while keeping a clean and peaceful air. Yet every time you take it for an insensitive and crude statement, you are accused of having no sense of humor. It is a tactic often used in verbal abuse.

Still, the scornful grimace and the sadistic shimmer in their eyes unmasks them - like a predator playing with food, a toxic person enjoys your suffering and being able to get away with it. Besides, it's just a joke, right? Mistaken, it's just another gaslighting technique that leads you to believe that their abuse is a joke - a way to divert attention from their cruelty and focus the spotlight on your supposed sensitivity. It is crucial that you assert yourself in these cases and that you point out that you are not going to tolerate this kind of behavior.

Pointing out to manipulative people that you noticed their tactics to knock you down could lead to further gaslighting by the abuser, but keep your stance contrary to their behavior and immediately end the interaction if necessary.

Condescending Sarcasm and Paternalistic Tone

Diminishing and denigrating someone is the strong point of a toxic person, and their tone of voice is only one of the tools in their possession. Sarcasm can be a fun way of communicating when both parties agree, but narcissists use it always as a method of manipulating and denigrating you. If you try to react in any way, it is because "you are too sensitive."

By being consistently treated as an infant and targeted when you dare to express yourself, you will begin to be especially careful about expressing your thoughts and opinions in order not to be reprimanded. This self-censorship allows the abuser to silence you with less and less effort because, unfortunately, you will begin to do it independently.

Whenever you are greeted with a sarcastic or paternalistic tone, point it out thoughtfully and assertively. You do not deserve to be spoken to as if you are children - nor should you ever silence yourself to meet the expectations of someone else's superiority complex.

Make You Ashamed

"You should be ashamed" is one of the favorite phrases of a toxic person. It can also be used by someone non-toxic, of course, but in the world of narcissists and sociopaths, shaming you is an effective method that targets any behavior or belief that could endanger the toxic person's power over you. It can also be used to destroy or diminish the victim's self-esteem: if the victim dares to be proud of something, making her feel ashamed for that particular trait, quality or goal can serve to diminish their self-worth and remove any pride they can handle.

Evil, sociopathic, and psychopathic narcissists enjoy using your wounds against you. So, they will also shame you for any abuse or injustice you have suffered in your life as a way to traumatize yourself again. Did you survive child abuse? A malicious narcissist or a sociopath will say that you must have done something to deserve it or will boast of their happy childhood to make you feel lacking in something and unworthy. What better way to hurt yourself than to turn the knife over in an old wound? These people try to reopen the wounds, not to help you heal them.

If you suspect you're commenced with a toxic being, avoid revealing any vulnerabilities or past trauma. As long as they don't show you their real character, there is no reason to disclose information that could potentially be used against you.

Control

The most important thing is that people who love to manipulate you want to keep control in any way they can. They isolate you, continue control over your money and social networks, and manage every corner of your life in detail. Still, the most powerful mechanism available to them to control you is to play with your emotions.

It is why abusive and sociopathic narcissists artfully create conflict situations out of nothing, to make you feel wrong. It is why they continuously engage in clashes on irrelevant issues and get angry about small things. That's why they move away emotionally, only to idealize you again as soon as they start to lose control. That's why sometimes they behave honestly and sincerely and sometimes not so that you never manage to achieve a sense of psychological security concerning who your partner is.

The more influence they have over your feelings, the less likely it is that you will be able to trust your reality and the truth about the abuse you are undergoing. Knowing the manipulative techniques and the way they work to erode your perception of you can provide you with the tools about what is happening to you and, at the very least, lead you to develop a plan to take back your life, away from toxic people.

HOW TO ESCAPE FROM A NARCISSIST

We have seen that the only way to break the chain of psychological/physical abuse perpetrated by a perverse narcissist is to escape the "no contact." When it is impossible to disappear, it is necessary to limit the contact to the bare minimum. Most people are slow to notice how they abused, and when they realize they try every type of strategy before closing the bridges thinking they can bring the relationship to an average normal level. Here are some of the most common mistakes we make when trying to save the unsolvable:

1. Forgive and Excuse the Perverse Narcissist

Some of us have brought up for forgiveness. Undoubtedly forgiveness is a significant and commendable step towards those who regret what they have done and are willing to start over on new, more transparent, and clean bases. We must take it into account. However, that forgiveness is what perverted characters want: they interpret it as a concession to continue to mistreat us, as a weakness of those who have forgiven. Devoid of spirituality and depth, the perverse narcissists do not conceive forgiveness as an elevated spiritual concept but see it as a symptom of the stupidity of the mistreated. We should not, therefore, expect him to rejoice with our forgiveness, that he will see it as an opportunity to "make himself better." In the mind of the perverted narcissist, every forgiveness is a let through to increase the charge of abuse and continue to test ourselves. Remember: even when we turn the other cheek, a narcissist (lover of low blows) can ruin our lives.

2. Ignore It If You Are Still on The Same Roof

In this case (especially in the process of separation), many spouses in conflict have the terrible idea of continuing to live together. Although avoiding, without any kind of verbal, gestural, or emotional exchange, the situation will still be agitated. This strategy can only work when we forced to go to the same places because of children or work, but it destined to fail when we are still in the same house. Ignoring a narcissist can trigger his irritation and aggression. If we stop reacting to his provocations, it is almost certain that he will use his children to take revenge on us or be pitied by them. The abusers need someone to follow their dirty game and get very nervous when their destabilizing strategy doesn't work correctly.

106

3. Deny the Existence of Mistreatment or Diminish Its Importance

Many self-help books on the market advise supporting the narcissist when he/she is "nice" with us, taking "what they have good" and forgetting or ignoring their unpredictable and wrong side. This method can only work when we train our dog not to bark at visits, but it is completely useless and even dangerous when we are at the mercy of perverse narcissistic men and women. The denial of psychological or verbal abuse excites any abuser and is the preferred advice of people who want to wash their hands when we confide in them. If the mistreatment attenuated and minimized, it ends up disappearing without leaving any trace. Also, since there is no abuser and one abused.

4. Try to Help or Change It: Let's Heal Together

Any attempt or effort to improve the emotional and psychological condition of a psychopathic partner is doomed to failure: changes are not of interest to him. It does not matter our sweetness, the enthusiasm of the advice we shoot, the passion and the renunciations that we are willing to do for him/her, the couple's therapy sessions that punctually deserted or the courses that teach us to master our emotions for a better deal with it. We have to get used to the idea that we are dealing with a mental structure programmed not to change. Expecting him to recognize his mistakes and making an effort to make him understand where he is wrong is an exhausting and useless exercise since all the abusers consider themselves perfect and infallible; moreover, what we consider an offense to our dignity, that is, the severe mistreatment episodes on his part will directly trace back to something we did. The more time you pass by the perverted, the harder it will be for you to distance yourself. Why not better use this precious time and effort in your personal growth? The more time you pass by the perverted, the harder it will be for you to distance yourself. Why not better use this precious time and effort in your personal growth? The more time you pass by the perverted, the harder it will be for you to distance yourself. Why not better use this precious time and effort in your personal growth?

5. Respond Aggressively to Those Who Want It at Any Cost

If on the one hand, it is understandable to lose patience when the psychopath says he does not know where he spent all your savings, if you

107

have discovered the receipts with gifts made to lovers or stops in the hotel with other women, remember never to lose the calm when they deny everything peremptorily with the most varied excuses. Their denials and tales meant to make you lose control (and save your face), so they can tell anyone that you are the mentally ill and abused.

The best way to deal with such an attack if there is one! Is going to unload you emotionally elsewhere, away from their eyes. Even without benefiting our situation in any way, going for a walk can temporarily ease the tension, recharging us to face more calmly the implacability of the psychopath in defending the thousand unsustainable versions of the same fact. If you are not afraid to tear off their mask and say them in the face or front of all their infinite lies, get ready to face the so-called "narcissistic anger." In these moments, all their seductive and friendly gifts will disappear by magic to give rise to the deformed mask of the monsters. You will seem to have catapulted into Dante's hell in the arms of some auxiliary of Lucifer. The only positive side of witnessing their outbursts when unmasked with no appeal is no longer having doubts about their disturbing nature. Those who do not know narcissistic anger remain longer in the fog of seduction convinced of the existence of a "good side." No doubt, exposing them involves a series of risks, it is giving the green light to a relentless and long defamation campaign with peaks of verbal violence, suicide threats, stalking.

6. Never Establish Doubtful Alliances

The temptation to seek the support of other people as usual. The illusion is to exert some pressure on the psychopath with the imagination that is intimidated for fear of being scolded "by the people." Attention: if these alliances work with people from your circles, know that they are easily maneuverable. By offering his favors, his availability, and his services and by covering "friends" with kindness, he is likely to seduce them on his side before you even decide to speak. Beyond the hoax, the damage: you will end up with new enemies who will accuse you of wanting to shout revenge against a "perfect person." Remember that you had the misfortune of sharing your intimacy and your dreams with the masters of the scam, with people capable of using any weapon to attract you in their distorted logic using preventive lies. And so, when you finally decide to tell someone about their abuses and misdeeds, the probability of seeking the solidarity of a person previously informed by them is very high (typical examples: "my wife is going through a difficult time, she is under stress, she has become paranoid, believe that cows fly, think if you see her a little lost and confused, don't forget to tell her that I love her so much "in my fiancee's family there are many schizophrenics, imagine what the unfortunate thing

108

forced to endure That's why she's always mad at me. ") think if you see her a little lost and confused don't forget to tell her that I love her so much "in my fiancee's family there are many schizophrenics, imagine what the unfortunate thing forced to endure! That's why she's always mad at me. ") think if you see her a little lost and confused, don't forget to tell her that I love her so much "in my fiancee's family, there are many schizophrenics, imagine what the unfortunate thing forced to endure! That's why she's always mad at me. ")

This does not mean that the harmed should choose silence but that it is preferable to confide in a more mature than average person. We keep in mind that those who challenge the status quo they come across the unbelief, hostility, and doubt of others. Talking to someone, we trust, however, causes the breaking of the humid veil. It is the very first step in getting out of the vicious cycle of abuse. We must, however, choose carefully with whom to let off steam to avoid even more excellent isolation. We take it for granted that it is in the psychopath's DNA to manipulate others precisely as he did with us. So far, nothing new on the front: they are usually the same ones who lent themselves to act as puppets in the perverse game of deceiving you and overwhelming you; the same who covered their betrayals and justified their lies for fear of losing "a friend" to whom they owed some small favor.

The help offered by others must be real, not just in words. We must seek the support of people we have always known, even before the entry of the perverse narcissist into our life. People who recognize our change for the worse and who can help us take the first legal, economic, logistical, or emotional steps to abandon it to its fate can only help.

7. Remember Not to Lose Hope and Not to Use Drugs

When victims of abuse lose clarity (because they are conditioned by "gaslighting"), it is almost customary to resort to the violence of drugs to combat depressive symptoms (insomnia, hormonal changes, panic attacks, gastritis, etc.); others develop eating disorders (excess or lack), obsessive (gambling, internet addiction, plastic surgery), others indulge themselves (chronic depression).

Psychic maltreatment weakens the will to pursue the goals of our life. The impossibility of finding a relief valve to such suffering makes the most iron desire to live fragile.

Psychically abused people, however, do not know that mistreatment is the deteriorating agent of the optimal use of intelligence and memory; they do not see that it destroys the emotional potential and with it the self-love,

109

the will, the pride for having reached an important goal, etc. It is the psychological abuse that prevents us from thinking, from forcing us to doubt the objectives for which we have fought, it is the deteriorating agent that leads us to commit grave errors that, in other moments/circumstances of our life, would not even be conceivable.

Once the conditioning phase is over, aware that our conduct wrong and dysfunctional - constituted the most terrible injustice committed against ourselves, the struggle to recover us takes over.

Let us remember that the most excellent satisfaction of a psychopathic manipulator is the destruction of the victims without appearing directly responsible.

That's why at the first symptoms of abuse or manipulation, it is essential to have the courage to run away without hesitating.

HOW TO HEAL ISOLATION, FEAR, AND LONELINESS

The most crucial step to take to recover emotionally after having a relationship with a narcissist is to put yourself at the center of your world, becoming aware that there can be no other people but himself who can take care, respect, and guarantee protection and emotional stability. Treating ourselves as we would like others to do with us is the only way to keep people who intoxicate their lives away with blackmail, manipulation, and guilt. After breaking the relationship with a narcissist, it is essential not to hang up and go back to check if the person has changed to alleviate the sense of emptiness and his lack. The pathological narcissistic most cases, it never turns. When the desire to return to a relationship with a narcissist is present, a process of splitting and removal is triggered, according to which negative memories separated from those definite few. Everything that made them feel bad is removed, remembering only the feeling of intoxication and pleasure that his words procured when he told how much he loved and cared about the relationship. These words, however, never translated into actions, much less formed the basis for starting a project of everyday life. Going back on one's steps on the back of nostalgia and lack can be avoided only by remembering the pain and the verbal and physical aggressions received; in this way, you will avoid confusing addiction and obsession with the lack of a healthy relationship.

How do you experience the period after the end of a relationship with a narcissist?

The period following the end of a relationship with a narcissist is very complex and painful to go through, and it can compare to post-traumatic stress disorder. The Posttraumatic Stress manifests itself as a consequence of an extreme traumatic factor, in which the person experienced or witnessed an event that implied death, or threat of death, a threat to one's own or others' physical and psychological integrity. The answer characterized by intense fear, feelings of helplessness and fear, the traumatic event is relived frequently with unpleasant memories that manifest themselves in the form of images, thoughts, nightmares, feeling as if the traumatic event was recurring, an uneasiness psychological concerning events that resemble some aspect of the traumatic event, difficulty falling asleep or maintaining sleep, irritability or bursts of anger or crying, difficulty concentrating, hyper-vigilance and exaggerated alarm responses. The onset of the Post Traumatic Stress Disorder can also occur months after the traumatic event and its duration can vary from one month to chronicity. The symptoms of those who experience the trauma from narcissism similar to the DPS are:

111

- Intense agitation, fear, nervousness, anxiety, anger, sense of loss, fear
- Loss of appetite
- Depression, little or no interest in achieving one's life goals, loss of enthusiasm and in severe cases lack will to live
- Difficulty in social relationships, a significant decrease in sociability, and fear of encounters with potential partners
- Self-destructive performances such as alcohol and drug abuse, intimate promiscuity, obsessive thoughts, to alleviate the pain of loss
- Isolation, decrease or elimination of friendships and family relationships
- Emotional instability
- Significant decrease in coping strategies (defense): difficulty making decisions in daily life, feeling overwhelmed by feelings of despair, perception of being paralyzed and blocked
- Physical ailments such as sudden mood swings, weakened immune system, hormonal failure, migraine
- Sleep disturbances: lethargy or insomnia
- Obsessive thoughts: continually thinking about the relationship with the narcissist, what he does, who he is with, miss him, think about me, etc.
- Loss of self-confidence
- Irritability and feeling of losing your head
- Strong dependence on the narcissist despite knowing that this person is not healthy for himself but at the same time inability to do without it
- Perception of not being able to survive without the narcissist

How can I deal with the traumatic phase after I have ended my relationship with a narcissist?

When the relationship with a narcissist is interrupted, the reaction of dependence and separation anxiety becomes more acute, which becomes all the stronger, the more time that has passed since the last time you saw him. Probably after having tried several times to separate from a narcissist, although not succeeding in the intent, because the sense of loneliness and obsessive thoughts have pushed him/her again, you get to imagine that what you feel is true love, because you can't help it. Still, in reality, it's just addiction. Authentic love is a healthy, secure, non-obsessive, and mutual feeling where one is not devalued and blackmailed, and above all, where actions follow words.

What are the thoughts that make it difficult to separate from a narcissist?

112

- No person can replace you and help you get rid of a narcissist, and it's a battle you have to wage on your own
- It is only a waste of time to expect the narcissist to change or modify or recognize his / her behavior; the narcissist does not change
- It is only in your power to get out of the emotional tunnel you are in and go back up
- Do not believe that you can face this situation
- Imagine no alternative to the relationship with the narcissist
- The pain of loss is too severe, so it is better to take what the narcissist gives in the relationship (nothing, since the narcissist deludes)
- Failed to accept the idea that your loved one is a narcissist with no possibility of change

Review these dysfunctional thoughts allows you to compare what we think with what we feel, making contact with our emotions and the reality that we are living. The liberation process passes through taking responsibility for one's actions and accepting that no one has the power to make happy but that we are the only ones able to identify and satisfy our needs and subsequently to share part of our life with a healthy person and not with someone who wants to replace us but who only wants to bend to his will. The partner of a narcissist not seen as he is but is a pawn, a functional tool to fill the gaps that the narcissist lives. The way to liberation is to start from yourself.

The Toxic Relationship

It is easy to fall in love with a narcissist. The men who belong to this psychology category are often bright, beautiful, capable of "selling well."

And then, to make matters worse, they are masters in the art of courtship and know how to make a woman feel unique and special.

The beginnings of history with the pathological narcissist are almost always romantic and passionate: the daffodils are full of surprises, initiatives, and attention.

But as soon as the relationship is consolidated (and you are beginning to believe that you have found the perfect man), suddenly and without motivation, he cools down.

It clears the meetings, becomes surly and in a bad mood, begins to criticize you, and puts forward doubts about his feelings, while at the beginning he declared himself in love and convinced that you were the right one.

The narcissus will justify himself by saying that he understood that he did not want a story (when he said the exact opposite in the early days), that he was not ready to commit himself, that he wanted to be alone.

Many women, at this point, already feel too involved to withdraw and accept a broken relationship in which he alternates moments of tenderness and passion with moments of coldness, bad moods, escapes, and silences.

If He Comes Back, It Is Not Out of Love

Sometimes it happens that falling in love with the beginnings does not turn into love.

The narcissists, though even in love, seldom leave their partner but prefer to drag (even for many years) a disengaged "relationship" characterized by continuous escapes and returns.

The mistake that many women make is to welcome back the narcissus, hoping every time it is different and convincing themselves that if he comes back, it is because, in the end, "he cares."

Sad to say, these hopes punctually rejected.

Even in the best case that he had felt the absence of his partner and wanted to try again seriously, it is a man with a personality structure that makes him unable to be in a relationship.

As soon as the enthusiasm of finding himself disappears, doubts begin the boredom, the sense of suffocation that leads him to further estrangement.

Often, however, the reasons for his return are much more prosaic and are dictated by loneliness, the lack of other alternatives, and the need for confirmation after different sentimental experiences have not gone in the desired way.

In long-standing relationships, the partner is often perceived as a "secure base" and experienced as a symbolic substitute for the mother figure that gives stability, welcomes, and consoles. For this reason, it is indispensable but, at the same time, not very exciting and little desired sexually, always available, and for this reason, felt as dull, evident, and suffocating.

In cases of severe narcissism, the partner's return is motivated by practical and selfish reasons. The narcissist tends to use people and to consider

114

them as objects that satisfy his needs. This type of narcissus will remain in a relationship as long as it can gain some advantage: sex, the image returns, and often economic and material benefits. A man with these personality traits never throws away a woman's phone number. It could always be useful!

Years Pass and Love Does Not Grow

Women trapped in a relationship with a narcissus console themselves thinking that if he keeps coming back, it means that he is tied up and that he has a vital feeling even if he doesn't want to admit it.

Unfortunately, the years spent together count for little (or nothing) for the narcissus, which, having an internal image of others as unfavorable and rejecting, carefully avoids any attachment.

For this reason, his sentiment towards his partner does not grow with time but remains superficial.

However, despite the lack of involvement, he will continue to return until she changes the rules of the game, setting limits, and demanding a commitment.

In my clinical experience, I was able to see how this inability to internalize positive experiences also reflected in the memory of the narcissus.

A narcissist patient of mine had been seven years with a man who loved her very much but could not remember a single day spent with him, and above all, she could not recall the emotions she felt while being in her company.

When he was gone, tired of his coldness, he had looked at his gifts, the books with the dedication, the photos were taken together, and wondered when she was surprised because all this could not remember.

Narcissus Strategies to Induce Addiction in The Partner

In the relationship, the narcissus uses the stick and the carrot: it alternates the escapes to the moments of sweetness, the most pungent criticisms to the declarations of love and compliments.

These ambivalent behaviors confuse the partner who receives a double message: you are important to me/you don't count for me, I crave you / I don't want you anymore.

The double message inherent in the relationship paralyzes the partner who no longer knows what to believe and makes her dependent. The narcissist uses some strategies to maintain control of the link and induce in the partner a state of dependence and impotence.

1) Silence and Escape

The narcissus runs away to get air from what he considers too stifling a relationship but also to punish his partner. Responding to messages with hours of delay or not replying at all is a well-calculated strategy to have power over the partner and to make them understand who dictates the rules in the relationship.

2) The Criticisms

The criticisms are the expression of a genuine disappointment (the narcissus is angry at his woman because he has disappointed his unrealistic expectations). Still, they are also a way to make her insecure and not to give her any power.

She doesn't have to know how attractive and desirable he considers her; otherwise, she would take advantage of it.

For this reason, fierce criticisms of sexuality (how many daffodils accuse their woman of not knowing how to make love well except then jumping on her at the first opportunity!) Or on the physical aspect of the partner are frequent.

These criticisms mean the exact opposite: he feels that he feels defenseless in the face of his woman's attractions and wants to convince her and himself not to feel anything.

3) Promises and Declarations of Love

If the partner leaves, the narcissus takes her back, playing the card of sentiment.

He says he is in love, explicitly speaks of the desire to have a family and children or suggests that he could fall in love in a day not too far away.

Sometimes he can be sincere (although it must be remembered: the

116

narcissist is capable of experiencing emotions but not feelings. His "I love you" means "I love you right now" and is more motivated by the passion of the situation than by an authentic conviction) at other times play consciously with the feelings of the partner.

She knows that by telling her what she needs to understand, she will forgive: just say the right words, and she will abandon all reservations and welcome him with open arms.

4) Demonstration of Weakness

If the sweet promises and little words do not work, the narcissus will play its last card: the card of weakness. He will try to pity his partner by showing himself weak and lost, and he will talk to her about his problems, he will show himself fragile and in need of a guide. He will behave like a small child with his mother, making her understand that he needs her.

To Conclude

Unfortunately, if you make the mistake of trying again, you must know that nothing will change.

Indeed, his position in the couple will further deteriorate: he knows that in the end, she always forgives him. This awareness leads him to devalue his partner further and will stimulate further disrespect.

If you have repeatedly fallen into this pathological dynamic and you cannot get out of it with your strength, you need to get help.

FEAR OF BEING SINGLE

Fear of staying single. Do you have one too? Are you also afraid of being alone, that is, without a boyfriend or a husband or partner for a while and maybe for a lifetime?

Did you know that this is a widespread fear, that of being or of being without a partner?

Do you know that it is a fear that men have more than women?

Well, yes, even men are terrified of being without a partner, perhaps for the rest of their lives.

Fear of remaining single: where does it come from?

Let's proceed step by step: the fear of being alone, in general, that is, without anyone standing by us, not necessarily a partner, is a very healthy, natural, as well as very human fear.

We are social beings who can survive and live well only if placed in a context, in a community, in a network of relationships.

None of us can live well alone, isolated, and without a community around us. Whether we like it or not, we depend on others.

Be careful, however, that these statements do not seem like justifications for dysfunctional behavior. We depend on each other in a reciprocal and balanced sense, that is, to the same extent that others rely on us, and we all depend on others, in a more or less stable way, according to the moments and circumstances.

We humans are, in fact, a community.

Although many pretend, they don't understand it and don't remember it. And this is very serious.

We are biologically and psychologically "built" to be and to live with others.

That is why it is "inhuman" to mistreat others, to be rude to relatives and strangers, not to respect what is familiar.

And that's why all of us, knowingly or unknowingly, are terrified of solitude and isolation. Because loneliness means death, Neither more nor less.

Fear of Staying Single. How Many Faces Does It Have?

Then some are afraid of being alone, that is, without a partner or companion. They have this fear because having someone who loves us and whom we love is reassuring, beautiful, pleasant. If it is the right person, a partner gives us support, affection, warmth, intimate pleasure. It's not cheap.

Many women and many men for fear of not having a partner, accept, as we know, unacceptable situations or experience anguish that makes them live badly. The anguish that even, for a very well explained paradox, makes them most wrong choices, especially as regards relationships.

Because if you are anxious about how your life as a couple goes or about not being a couple, q anxiety causes you to enter a negative vicious circle and you move further and further away from a good life as a couple.

Then some people cannot, cannot, do not tolerate, to pass any phase of their life as a single person. But what do I say period? They can't stay a month, a week, and maybe not a day without a partner.

I call them the "serial boyfriends," those who collect relationships as a couple as collectible stickers of footballers. They started being a couple when they were very young, and they cannot conceive of themselves outside a couple.

They don't want to experiment single even out of curiosity, just to have a different experience and to see themselves from a new point of view. As soon as they "burst," they rush to find someone to hang out, what a life, guys.

We also know that the fear of loneliness grips many people with apparent success, those who have money and power, or maybe just a very positive image that makes others believe, those who do not intuit the truth of the void, that they are reliable and sturdy.

But that, to calm the fear of loneliness, they must accumulate flirtations, lovers, or only an infinite series of broken hearts.

Fear of loneliness has many faces, often unsuspected.

This is to say what? That there is a fear of loneliness, understood as a fear of isolation and exclusion from the human community, which is atavistic, often more reliable than we think and which belongs to all of us.

Then there is the pure solitude and being single typical of "serial boyfriends" or "serial seducers," those who perceive all their inner emptiness and try to fill it with the most diverse partners. Without ever succeeding, because it is the drug that creates the disease in this case.

Then there is the "normal" fear of staying single, perhaps all of life, a concern that is very common, but not for everyone. It is also compelling.

It is often so powerful, so intense because many of those who try it are very sensitive to external influences.

And according to external influences (that is, according to the famous "judgment of others") who does not have a partner or a companion is forced to live worse than the others, to have no support, is a loser and unhappy and perhaps even unfortunate person.

These are all bales, but we often tend to believe lies and bales and take what is not suitable for good. Above all, look a little, if you are a bit fragile and particularly sensitive to the judgment of others.

Believing lies does not make you live well. I advise you to get smart and expose the lies, even those of the "judgment of others."

I advise you above all to get your idea of the world - as realistic as possible and above all as useful as possible for you - and to find valid strategies, yours, and that is good for you, to be calm, happy, and get what you want.

You are not caring about the opinions and judgments of others. Because those, yes, give you a distorted idea of the world and make you make choices that don't work for you.

They also increase your fears, including the fear of being single, and make you a less free person. Also, to find and choose the right person for you.

Fear of Staying Single: 5 Steps to Overcome It and Find Love

Let's go back to us, then, let's go back to you if you're afraid of being single. How do you overcome it, and above all, how do you recover all the serenity you need to find love?

The first step to being less afraid and feeling better about yourself is to accept what you think and what you think. Are you afraid of being single? Don't be ashamed of it. Accept it, and it's human, it's healthy, it's understandable. Act with understanding and benevolence towards

120

yourself.

The second step is not to complain. Life is lovely, and at the same time, it is dotted with difficulties, more or less significant, which require patience, intelligence, and even proactivity, that is, the ability to take situations in hand actively and proactively. Complaining is useless, and it makes you ugly and unpleasant, also if you are beautiful and charming.

The third step is to consider that the fear of being single is only a fear, which has no objective basis. Maybe you were left, you suffered for love, and you surrounded by men who are half socks. This may be more than true, but it is equally valid that, out there, there are men who want to give and receive love and share their life with another person, it is about finding them and intercepting them. Then to approach them and to stay close to them, with warmth and affection, on an equal footing.

The fourth step is to convince that the fear of loneliness, in the round, and the fear of single, is often fear of others. It is also useful to convince ourselves that we are all human, and we all share the same concerns from most to least. The others want to get closer to you, but they don't do it out of a thousand fears, perhaps out of respect. Exactly how it happens to you. Take the first step. Be smart and smart, protect yourself, and, at the same time, approach others with a pleasant disposition and without expectations.

Make a gentle gesture, smile, be available to listen, without selling yourself off and without talking too much about yourself, out of place and out of time. Always take the reins of a relationship in your hands, whether it's a peer, a younger or older person, a man, or even a man you like. Use all the charisma you are capable of, with gentleness and elegance. Limit negative feelings towards others, such as envy, resentment, and anger. Ignore those you don't like, but don't waste energy with negative emotions.

The fifth step is to stop using smartphones, computers, and various gizmos for relationships with others. Don't use social networks. If you want to show your friends photos of your holidays, choose the ten most, not the most, images and invite them to an aperitif to show them. Do not let off steam on your "bad luck" on Facebook, stop chatting, especially with men and especially if it does not strictly service communications.

Be human, surround yourself with rational people, create authentic relationships. This way, you find yourself, love, and you will no longer be alone or single anymore.

If you want to find out how and where to find interesting men and how to give birth to and nourish desire in a man, watch the preview videos of the path How to make a man fall in love and keep it.

DATING AFTER A NARCISSIST

Getting over relationships with psychopaths, sociopaths, or narcissists takes longer than usual. Survivors feel frustrated that they didn't get through the end of the relationship quickly, as in previous relationships. As if that were not enough, they find themselves forced to answer questions from friends and to confront therapists who are not always prepared about psychological abuse. Frustration increased when they asked to forget everything and go on as if nothing had happened. Whether they have lived in a long-lasting marriage or whether it is a summer passion, the process of overcoming a relationship with a psychopathic subject is more complicated than the others. As a time frame, we are talking about a period that varies between 12 and 24 months to seduce emotions, Conditioning that was a mere exercise for these dark characters, very skilled in manipulating multiple people at the same time. Why does it take so long to get through it all?

Falling in Love

All right, it was a fabricated 'love' in which your personality was imitated, like in a mirror, to manipulate your dreams better. You fell out of love because this was the goal of the psychopath, that's why you can't talk about a healthy breakup. You have been dealing with a person who, through the conditioning of your mind, has introduced an explosive cocktail of despair and unexpected desire into your life. Psychopaths know how to reward prey at the beginning of the relationship by reinforcing their positive image. These are gifts that they offer for free during the entire idealization phase. By placing you on a pedestal, they prepare you for the identity erosion they intend to do in retrospect when they no longer need you. By leaving behind one of the most painful experiences of your life, you guaranteed a permanent place in your mind. Through their lies, triangulations, the clouds of smoke they launch to confuse you and, many times, even though veiled threats, psychopaths make sure to stay in your thoughts day and night. When abandonment finally arrives - many times, it is the prey induced by the psychopath to decide to end the relationship because of his erratic behavior - he finds himself with the brain submerged by dissociated thoughts. On the one hand, the preys remember the phase of love bombing and the good they felt for the psychopath, on the other they go back to thinking about his lies, the denial of reality, infidelity, humiliation, the psychological conditioning that prevented her from extracting the truth from the fog. To this phenomenon, we attribute the

122

name of cognitive dissonance, and it takes time to overcome it.

One must be patient because it is reasonable to alternate conflicting memories when any relationship ends. Very dangerous, however, are the memories of the idealization phase because when they come to the gala, they induce the prey to break the zero count to return to merge into the toxic spiral once again.

The Chemical Reaction

Psychopaths and narcissists develop a strong intimate, and emotional bond in their prey. Many preys attribute to them a certain charm, an excessive intimate experience, and a very particular way of training the brains of others to bring each individual of their circles to depend on them for the validation of small and insignificant daily decisions. By demonstrating their adoration for you in the first stage, the psychopaths get the effect of letting you drop your guard, which leads you to entrust your value to them exclusively as people: your happiness depends on the loving bombardment that has occurred imposed at the beginning. To the initial euphoria provoked in your brain by the release of more dopamine deepest darkness takes over (the stimuli that produce physiological motivation and reward such as good food, water, or artificial as narcotic or electrical substances, but also listening to music, stimulate the release of dopamine in the brain) in the moment of abandonment. At that point, like a drug, you go to need more and more the approval of the psychopath who, however, totally loses interest in you because continually looking for further stimuli that challenge his ability to conquer.

Triangulation

Any infidelity in a relationship with an average person leaves traces and feelings of great insecurity. Very well, with a psychopath, we not only suffer multiple infidelities and betrayal but, in addition to the usual pain produced by any cheating, the humiliation of feeling used as objects also takes over. And not only that, since they leave traces of their misdeeds and then clearly deny it the action of a puzzling relational perversity! - end up damaging your psyche. What is behind this cruel way of doing? The basic idea of the psychopath is to make you fight to be better than the other women/men belonging to his Court: by inducing you to play to make private investigators keep you up and running as you have probably never been in other relationships, much healthier. Psychopaths can fabricate negative emotions and implant them in your intimate to use them as a weapon against you when they see fit. To justify their most execrable actions, they usually fish out these prefabricated emotions especially in the phase that precedes the definitive abandonment to convince the world that they are leaving you because of your character instability: your insecurities and your jealousy become, of point-blank, the real cause of his abandonment/disinterest in you.

You Have Known Evil, And It Had the Face of An Angel

The rules applicable to most people are not valid for psychopaths. Let us remember once again: they are beings who do not feel guilt, love, or remorse of conscience. During the whole relationship, you tried to understand, forgive, and become better. However, your ex has used all these feelings and all your actions against you. You made the mistake of projecting your consciousness as empathetic humans onto them when you could not explain certain bizarre behaviors. Still, at a particular moment, your brain realized that it was dealing with a disturbed personality that was clearly outlined, such as puzzle pieces that came together by themselves.

Disgusted, frightened by the darkness and wickedness of individual characters, you have tried to explain to friends, family, and colleagues every detail of your experience without apparently nobody being able to understand the extent of the damage you had suffered.

They thought it was any relationship that ended badly and that you were exaggerating because all too sensitive.

Your Psyche Is Injured

Most of the survivors say that immediately after abandonment, they felt an inner void that went beyond depression. It is as if their soul has disappeared (which is why many authors speak of 'energetic vampirism'). They say they felt a sort of general insensitivity and that nothing of what they loved before had been able to lift their morale. They were certainly going through the toughest moment of the entire healing phase!

However, it is in moments of profound prostration that we learn to definitively cultivate respect for ourselves, to plant new personal boundaries, and to seek our deepest identity. When you overcome this terrible moment, you will find yourself much more connected with your needs and those of others. You will be wiser, you will discover what inner peace is, and you will have more experience in your emotional baggage to

124

share with those who need it. By working hard on you, no toxic person will be able to manipulate you anymore. As soon as you have gained self-confidence, you will learn to appreciate and value the healthy, honest, and kind people around you.

THE ART OF SAVING

All relationships have their ups and downs, but a relationship with a narcissist can be particularly tumultuous. Your body naturally activates "attack or flight" style defenses, releasing stress hormones, such as adrenaline, cortisol, and epinephrine, to cope with the extreme emotional trauma of this type of emotional abuse.

It is a primitive response intended to protect us from danger, but, in the case of an abusive relationship, it is possible to become dependent on these feelings and their biochemical associates. When we end an abusive relationship, how we deal with this mess - or not - determines whether we are willing to solve specific problems or if we tend to make them even more complicated.

Feeding Dependence with Obsessive Search

Immediately after the break, after a short recovery break, it is likely that you will begin to engage in activities that create stress that can stimulate the release of the hormones you have become dependent on. These activities can arise from conscious decisions, or they can be actions you cannot even understand the meaning of what you are doing.

One way to recreate the stress response is compulsive research on the topic of narcissism. Reading about others' narcissistic abuse and emotional wounds can make you experience secondary trauma, which releases stress hormones and lightens withdrawal symptoms. This type of behavior is not unusual when processing something sensitive like a breakup. In reality, education is a natural and necessary phase of the healing process. Still, it can become a severe problem when it begins to invade other aspects of your life, preventing you from progressing to higher stages of healing. For example, if the toxic relationship has ended for years and you are still researching narcissism and attending forums on narcissistic abuse, it means that your recovery phase has come to a halt. It is a severe indicator in this regard.

Identifying A Serious Problem

If you experience poignant sensations due to the breakdown of a relationship, and begin to perform obsessive searches, take a deep breath and pause. Here are the five indicators that warn you of a problem that should not underestimate.

First: Obsessions

Obsessions are persistent thoughts, ideas, or mental images that don't go away, no matter how hard you try to crush them. They are not rational thoughts and can be debilitating.

One of the obsessions that you can develop after the breakup is to ask yourself how the relationship would have gone if your way had been different, in the sense of being able to change the mind of your ex. Another example is mulling over the things your ex's said, asking if more could do to save the relationship.

While mild versions of these thoughts are somewhat typical after a breakup, when those thoughts prevent you from concentrating on the routine chores of your daily life, you need to be very careful. If you are thinking about your ex-partner so much that you cannot concentrate on work, losing deadlines, or ignoring your responsibilities, you can aggravate your conditions. Failing to handle these thoughts could be the sign that you have taken the path of obsession.

Second: The Compulsions

A compulsion is a repetitive behavior performed to reduce stress and anxiety. Addictions often go hand in hand with obsessions because they transformed into the only way you know to deal with the problem.

If you have obsessive thoughts about your ex and are trying to explain his behavior, starting to research it signals your attempt to understand why he did what he did. So, what you are looking for is an explanation that will help you know how to stop obsessive thoughts.

Other examples of compulsive behaviors include checking out the social media of the former or the social media of new partners, participating in an excessive number of forums on narcissistic abuse, or jumping from one recovery program to another without ever respecting the strategies recommended.

126

Ironically, compulsions do not eliminate obsessive thoughts, and they are only temporary relief. Furthermore, the continuous compulsive habits deepen the neuronal pathways associated with the impulses, which leads you to engage even more in negative behaviors without even thinking about what you are doing.

If you are stuck in this cycle and neglect your daily responsibilities because of all this, consider seeking professional help to cope with your situation. For example, if you are a parent and spend all your time researching narcissism and chatting on forums instead of spending quality time with your children, it is time to make some changes in your life.

Third: Mental Contamination

If the interactions with your ex involve criticism, humiliation, or betrayal, you are likely to be dealing with mental contamination. It is an internal feeling of "impurity" caused by negative social interactions.

It is not difficult to understand how a relationship with a narcissist can lead to mental contamination. During your relationship, you dealt with the typical narcissistic behavior of distributing permanent judgments and criticisms. Narcissistic abuse victims almost always fight spiritual corruption as they work to overcome the rupture.

As long as this persists feeling back to rely on any compulsive behavior that we have developed as a mechanism coping (strategies that relate to the mode of adaptation with which you face stressful situations, not), so we continued to do obsessive research to try to find an explanation.

Fourth: The Ruminations

Continuing to mentally repeat the main topics discussed with your ex, again and again, means ruminating endlessly. The speculations do not just ask us what we could have done differently in a situation, but rather allow specific thoughts to remain in mind for too long, taking them even further.

If you are dedicating yourself to compulsive research on narcissism, your ruminations will take you back in a desperate attempt to find an answer. You can read articles on the psychology of narcissism or join online forums of people in similar situations, of course. But know that your goal is always to learn all you can about why your ex has behaved in one way or another and what you could do to improve the relationship.

The speculations can misunderstand. You can convince yourself that you are only trying to solve a problem; however, the problem you are trying to solve does not have a real solution. So, the behavior continues until it begins to impact your daily life, feeding on your compulsive research on narcissism. For example, if we start doing compulsive research on narcissism at work instead of fulfilling our duties, we risk losing our job, which has a devastating impact on our livelihoods.

Fifth: The Intrusive Thoughts

We can all suffer from intrusive thoughts from time to time. Still, they can become particularly unsettling when they concern about the emotional and mental anguish of ending a relationship with a narcissist. Intrusive thoughts are unwelcome, often creepy, and distressing ideas that pop overhead. They disturb us a lot, and we can't stop it from happening. Examples of intrusive thoughts: imagine yours or your ex with new partners and be convinced that they have changed; imagine having a loathsome feature that forced your ex to abandon you; be sure you are too old to find new love; feel the overwhelming responsibility of informing your ex's new partners of who they are.

There is a subtle distinction between intrusive thoughts and obsessions: obsessive thoughts are situations that we cannot stop thinking about, while intrusive thoughts are involuntary and can involve hurting yourself or doing it to someone else. If not adequately addressed, intrusive thoughts can turn into obsessions that will lead you, once again, to the same cycle of compulsive research on narcissism.

Making the Decision to Heal

To start healing and getting your life back in hand, you need to identify these habits and take steps to stop them. Due to the added emotional aspects of a relationship with a narcissist and the subsequent breakup, it is not easy to do. We must work hard to establish new habits and interrupt the return cycle to the obsessive search to make sense of things.

It is certainly possible to overcome these behaviors by seeking the help you need to form new habits and change the way your brain reacts to defend you.

SELF-LOVE, SELF-CARE AND SELF-ESTEEM RECOVERY PLAN

How to rebuild my self-esteem after the relationship with a narcissist? They do so by being aware of the aftermath left behind by a bond based on suffering and constant boycott. Thus, something that should know in the first place is that this reconstruction and healing craft is not an easy process.

Some have spent years with a narcissist. Living next to this personality profile implies, for example, that at a given moment, the person opens his eyes, identifying various ideas that he had ignored. The first is that living with these people hurts. Second, there is usually a very long period in which you are fully aware that the best thing is to end that relationship. However, the heart cannot; a dependency is a strong glue fueled by fear.

Many people fear to end this bond because they do not know how the narcissist will react. Furthermore, it is common to fall into the rebound effect; that is, to break the relationship and after a while, start it again. It is a round trip, where despite promises that individual attitudes and behaviors will not repeat, they are given back and with the same impunity.

Leaving a narcissist is an act of need, courage, and health. However, after the breakup, an important stage begins, the reconstruction of long-abused self-esteem.

Keys to Rebuilding My Self-esteem After the Relationship with A Narcissist

Broken bones heal. Wounds, burns, and chafing heal with proper care in a few weeks. Injuries to the tissue of self-esteem, self-concept, values, and even identity, do not improve with betadine or with antibiotics or over time.

To rebuild my self-esteem after the relationship with a narcissist, I need concrete actions. It is not enough to let time pass, because otherwise, the emptiness will still be there and we will be, basically, figures who walk the world broken. No one can find happiness again without the muscle of self-esteem recovered, because that psychological competence threads absolutely everything.

Let us, therefore, see what keys can help us to rebuild it.

129

Away Blame, It's Time to Rewrite Yourself

When we leave the relationship with a narcissist, many biases, words, and ideas remain in our minds to deactivate. Something that carries out this type of profile with its effective partners is reprogramming and cancellation. They make their victims believe that they are inferior, that are not worth what they want, and that their needs are secondary. Therefore, we must turn off specific images of our mind:

- You are not to blame for anything that happened. Whoever damages are the only culprit. However, it is useless to focus on hatred and vengeance either. You have to turn the page, and more importantly, you must take control of your life.
- Make a list of those phrases and images that still embedded in your mind (contempt, humiliation, situations where you were always in the background, etc.).
- Assume that those memories cannot erase, but the idea is that each day they lose their power over you. We should not tear out pages from the book of our life, just turn them and rewrite new chapters after learning from what we have experienced.

Empower Yourself: I Am, I Am Worth, I Decide

When the relationship with a narcissist ends, there is usually a whole host of insecurities. What do I do now? How do I take control of my life, or How do I leave all the bad memories behind? The key is to empower yourself, and you have to live in the present and not in the past.

- There is nothing better than starting new projects. Often, by feeling competent in new tasks, new jobs, and situations, self-esteem regains its power. We give way to a new version of ourselves.
- Therefore, do not hesitate to meet new people, to make your days have new incentives to put you to the test: other jobs, courses, hobbies

Practice to Rebuild Your Self-esteem Focuses on Courage, Not Feeling Insecure

Psychiatrist Alexander Lowen, author of the book Narcissism: The Disease of Our Time, points out that this personality profile is characterized by acting coldly; They are seductive, manipulative, and strive for power and control. It is easy to fall into their networks because they are capable of captivating, and once they succeed, a process of constant violation begins where they strengthen their self-concept.

Whoever manages to get out of these relationships often ends up having a social phobia. He is afraid to relate; he is afraid to go out into the world once again because the person feels insecure because he is scared of being hurt again. Hence, to rebuild my self-esteem after the relationship with a narcissist, what I need most is courage.

We can start with small objectives: sign up for yoga, make a makeover, etc. Later, we can give way to other decisions, such as a trip, new friends. The idea is not only to recover self-esteem; it is to strengthen it and live according to our values, where freedom, well-being, and happiness permeate every moment of our existence.

SET BOUNDARIES WITH NARCISSISTS

Learning to be assertive requires self-knowledge and practice. Many times, due to toxic embarrassment and low self-esteem, some people, codependents especially, find this problematic because:

- They don't know what they essential or touch.
- When they know this, they do not value their needs, feelings, and desires and put the needs and feelings of others ahead of them. They feel anxiety or guilt when they ask for what they want or what they need.
- They believe they have no rights.
- They are afraid that this person will get angry with them and judge them (for example, that they will call them selfish).
- They are ashamed of feeling vulnerable, showing feelings, or saying what they want or need.
- They are afraid of losing someone's love, friendship, or approval.
- They don't want to be a burden.

Rather than being assertive, codependents communicate dysfunctionally. As they have learned from interacting with their parents, they were often passive, complaining, being aggressive or critical, or blaming. If you complain, attack, blame or criticize someone, that person will act defensively or behave the same way you are. Assertiveness comes with practice.

Why Limits Sometimes Don't Work

You have repeatedly communicated your limits assertively, and it is not working. It may be because:

- Your tone is not firm or blame or critical.
- There are no consequences for violating your limit.
- You back down when they challenge you with reason, with anger, with threats, calling you things, with the treatment of silence or with answers like:
  1) Who do you think you are telling me what to do?
  2) You are a selfish
  3) Stop controlling me
- You threaten to do things that are too scary or unrealistic to do, like "If you do that again, I'm leaving."

- You don't appreciate enough the importance of your needs and values.
- You don't exercise the consequences consistently every time that person violates your limit.
- You back out because you sympathize with the other person's pain and put their feelings and needs above yours.
- You insist that the other person change. The consequences are not to punish someone or for someone else to change, but they require you to be the one to change their behavior.
- You don't have a support system that reinforces your new behavior.
- Your words and your actions are contradictory. Actions speak louder. Actions that ultimately reward someone for violating your limit prove that you are not severe. These are some examples:
  1) Tell your neighbor not to go without calling first, and then let him enter your apartment when he shows up without warning.
  2) Tell your ex-partner not to contact you and then write or see him.
  3) Tell someone not to call you after 9 pm and still pick up the phone after that time.

Things You Can Do to Earn Assertiveness

Reflect On:

1. What specific actions have you joined in or allowed to violate your values or compromise your needs and wants?
2. How does that affect you and your relationships?
3. Are you willing to take risks and strive to keep your limits? You might lose people in this process (friends, partner)
4. What rights do you think you have?
5. What are the consequences you can live in? Try to keep what you say and never make threats that you cannot continue. Remember that all the effort will not have served if you do not maintain the limit and the consequences of violating it.
6. How are you going to handle the other person's reaction?

Remember that being assertive and setting limits is a process that takes time and practice. At first, you will surely feel fear and guilt for setting a deadline. Do not shun them, hold that fear, and that guilt, you will see how, with each limit you put, they will be less and less present until they disappear entirely. Not setting limits and accepting everything others do to you is not loving yourself.

HOW TO FIND A NEW REAL LOVE

Of course, it is not an easy question to answer, and I think there is no absolute answer. We can each have different meanings, and both can be valid.

Love is found in mind and not in the heart, as it colloquially said. We also know that we feel " butterflies in the stomach " due to neurotransmitters in the abdominal area. These are all scientific explanations of love, but I think the concept of love goes beyond simple segregation of substances in the brain.

You may have the belief that love is part of evolution for survival, or you may also believe that it is something that God gave us, by divine means. Whatever your belief, I think the importance of lovelies effect it has on our lives, in that which is capable of creating, by merely existing within us.

True love unites humanity, and it is capable of making a person achieve things that he could never do with any other feeling.

Love makes us fight battles and chase dreams. Real love is capable of making you give up your own life if necessary.

That's right, and I think true love is the most potent feeling we can have. Neither fear, nor sadness, hatred or anger, or any other emotion, are capable of creating and moving the world as love does.

Although many people governed by fear, I think many act out of love. They get up to work daily with enthusiasm, and they have goals to fulfill, wishes to go further and experiences yet to be discovered. Love is a pillar that gives meaning to our life.

The Levels of Love

Not all loves are equally intense. I believe that there is only one type of true love, the others are just "wishes," "wants," or simple "I like," which are confused with real passion.

People like to say "love" to any weak, fragile, and brittle feeling. But I think it shouldn't be a word that describes common and lightly taken feelings.

Loving your job is not the same as loving your body. Love for your children

134

can be more reliable than your self-love. We do not like in the same proportion.

It could say that there are love levels. Some are fragile as a crystal, and others as resistant as a diamond. So, I think the stronger a "love" is, the closer to true love.

- From hate to love there is no distance
- Love and hate are part of the same.

Let's take an example. Suppose you have a neighbor who always has his music too loud at night. It causes you trouble sleeping and generates in you an emotion of anger or hatred at a certain level, that is, a feeling that you may think has nothing to do with love. But now we will see that you are wrong.

One day when you get home from work, you realize that your house has ransacked. Criminals have entered to steal. It causes you a feeling of hatred towards those people who have taken your belongings that you have bought with effort and years of work.

So here comes the critical question: Would you hate your neighbor, who does not let you sleep, in the same way as you hate the people who just robbed you?

No? Do you hate the thief more? Well, that means that you love your neighbor more than that thief who took your belongings. Please analyze it for a moment

This story is not over yet. Then you leave your house after realizing that you have robbed, and you see that neighbor who won't let you sleep. You go up to him and ask him if he saw someone come into your house. He shakes his head but invites you to check the recording of his outdoor security cameras to see if the thieves caught.

- It turns out that the recording of their security cameras helps the police to start the police investigation to catch the criminals.
- Even though you hated it before, now you feel grateful to your neighbor.
- What can we learn from this?

Well, with that act, you raised your level of love for him and reduced hatred. Therefore, we can say that love and hate are not opposites; they are

135

part of the same thing; they are within the same measurement scale.

If you hate someone, you also love them to some degree. It is like the relationship between cold and heat. Coolness is relative to the way you interpret it. If something is cold, it will also have a heat level, and there will always be a more chilled level.

Hate is not the opposite to love; they are the same thing. What is contrary to love is fear

The highest level of love is what I call true love or real love, and in a moment, we will see how to identify it.

Where to Find True Love?

In my opinion, real love is hard to feel and much harder for someone to think for you. It is not something you can find since it cannot search because you have no physical form. True love is something that simply arises without waiting for it.

You can find it in your partner, when you wake up every morning, in your job, in your profession, in your parents, but above all, it is more common to find it in your children.

Why am I saying this? I think there are not so many cases of pure love in the world, as the love of parents for their children. Now we will see why.

Truthfully, I have long analyzed the concept of love, and believe me, and I have not found any that is so similar to real love, as the one felt by a mother or a father for a child. A passion is so unconditional that it surpasses most other respects.

Most couple loves do not love, and they are just "wanting." Most passions towards a trade/profession are not loved; they are only "likes." The same is true of love for the environment or animals. Almost nobody or practically nobody is capable of giving his life for that thing or person he loves. But this is an act that if you can find in mothers and fathers, towards their children.

Of course, I am not saying that all parents have a true love for their children. I hope it was! What I am saying is that I have not known a love that resembles real love, like the love that can exist from a mother to a child.

You may already know from experience that it is difficult for true love to

136

emerge towards a couple you met 3 or 6 months ago. I doubt very much that you dare to give your life for that person, or that you continue loving him after 20 years when they only lasted 1 or 2 years of relationship.

True love transcends time, and as you know, it is common to find a love like this from a mother or father towards a child. Even if 20 or 30 years go by without seeing that loved person, you will continue enjoying him, thus for eternity.

True Love Is Not Reciprocal

Note that I say that true love generally comes from parents to their children and not the other way around. Many children indeed have a true passion for their parents, but many others do not.

More mothers have true love than children who love their fathers. Just as there are parents who do not deserve their parental title, there are also children who do not deserve to be called children.

True love does not have to be reciprocal to exist. It is the unconditional love that does not expect anything in return. The nature of real love is not to receive, and its quality is to give, help, and contribute.

So, don't expect to find true love. Searching for it would be like expecting someone to have a passion for you. What do you want that for?

I think it is better, and more comfortable, for you to feel inside yourself a real love for someone, to wait for someone to feel that love for you.

How to Know If It's True Love?

The only thing and the most important thing that each of the inhabitants of the planet has is life. Therefore, I believe that true love is one where one person can give his life to save another.

It means being willing to give up the most precious thing you have; your life, to preserve the life of those loved ones.

So, do you want to know if you love someone? Simple, answer these two questions:

- Am I willing to lay down my life for that person?
- Can this love I feel transcend time?

137

The first question is more comfortable to answer. If you are willing to give your (literal) heart, as long as that person you say, love continues to live. Then you have a passion that surpasses your existence.

I believe that giving your life for someone is the noblest act of love that can exist.

When you feel capable of giving your life for someone, then you will know that true love for that someone resides in you. Any other feeling underneath this act is a simple will, even though people commonly call it love.

Regarding the second question, I would tell you that it is a bit misleading, since I know if you ask those people "in love," it will most likely say yes. But I think the only way to answer this question is precisely by letting time pass.

A clarifying example

It sounds quite typical and melancholic, right? Especially in adolescents and young people who feel that the world is ending with their first "love."

Well, if you came right now and told me that, I would say something like this:

"It is not valid, and you do not love him. If you like him, you don't want him to come back with you. He left because he wanted to go, thinking about his well-being, his interests, and his happiness. If you want me to come back to you, then you are thinking of yourself, not that person.

You don't want him/her to be happy. What you want is for her to be by your side, so that you are well and you are so glad. You are looking for your well-being and personal satisfaction.

Please realize that you don't love him, you just want him you want him for yourself, to be with you. If we see it well, it would be like an object you want to have to feel that your life is complete. That's not true love, and true love is so great that it surpasses even your own life, your desires, and your needs.

It is not a common thing that you suddenly find after a night of drinks or a trip to the cinema. True love transcends time.

Also, realize that you both don't love each other, that person left thinking about him, and you want him to come back thinking about you. The difference is that you are obsessed with owning it, and that person is no

138

longer comfortable with you.

Although it sounds harsh, your story is not a different magical love story, it is one more story, where you have the confusion between wanting and loving.

Please allow time to heal you and life to flow. I guarantee that it will be so."

The Difference Between Wanting and Loving

Can true love be found in a partner? I think so, but it is extraordinary. As we have seen, most people confuse love with wanting, wanting, or possessing.

I think that most people, what they are looking for in a partner is a better half, not a true love.

While love is something sublime and powerful towards someone, the better half is simply someone who comes to complement or fill a part of your life.

The more time they spend together, the closer their relationship becomes. And when they separate, they feel that they are missing a part of their life, which is entirely normal. When separating, routines and habits change, what generates an imbalance is their way of living.

Wanting is close to possessing, when you want something or someone, you want it here with you.

If you want true love, then I would tell you not to look for it, love will arise when you least expect it.

There is no spell or formula for love. It is not something you can choose, or you can force, it is something that will happen naturally.

Do not try to find a partner or the love of your life, instead focus on becoming the person you want to be. Follow your instinct and seek to be that person of value that you would like to meet. In this way, you will attract only those people of great importance to you, because they will be a reflection of who you are inside.

Part 2

Co-Parenting

CO-PARENTING WITH A NARCISSISTIC

A narcotic simply cannot be suitable for children, as most exes need to search for supplies. Conversations on topics as emotional as your children are the best place for drug traffickers to generate reactions that feed their black hole.

Every little thing was difficult, and if I called the difficulty, they called me back for wanting everything my way. For example, when my son was little and spent the day with him, I sometimes forgot to ask him if he had napped or not, and for how long. This information was helpful so you could plan how the night would go. Therefore, I texted her to ask and not receive an answer for three days. It is the man who is glued to his social media account and, thus, to his phone.

Now that example seems like a small thing. Right? Don't worry so much about it. Let it go. Right?

Yes, but then imagine that every interaction you have is peppered with this shit. It always arrives 5-10 minutes late does not return clothing or toys. He never answers questions. She tries to communicate about doctor visits or childcare events, and he leaves while he talks. He tells his son that he will take them to a place where he did not intend to take them; they are too young to understand when it does not happen. He demands more time with the child, but every time he offers an extra night, he is 'busy.'

None of that is BIG. No one is hit or yelled. But these little things are designed to irritate you, to make you crack. So, when you finally explode and punish him for letting your son get sunburned, it can drive you crazy. You're overreacting. We could be friends if you were just less angry, he says with a sad face. It only makes you madder because he wouldn't know the

141

friendship if he got naked and danced on a piano and now, he's trying to lecture you. * insert a bitter laugh

Well, you can't be a parent with this person. Anything you ask for will be denied. Whatever you show, emotion will be used against you. The more you try to maintain life in each house similarly, the more it will do differently.

The only option, if you want to maintain your sanity (which is why you left, after all), is parallel parenting. In your house, you do. Who knows at home? You don't ask for anything, and you don't care, you certainly don't ask. As far as he is concerned, you are a big fan of his fatherhood. It will screw it up endlessly and will also make you feel much better.

You talk positively about him in front of the kids, or you don't. Mostly not at all. You model the correct way to deal with a narcotic for your children. You don't talk to him face to face about children—your email. Be brief: there is no emotion, only facts. You request information only if necessary and provide the deadlines by which it is due. If the deadline passes, you act without it.

You are not a doormat, nor are you a source to him. You are a rock, and he is a hot wind. Yes, in 1000 years, it could exhaust you, but luckily it won't be alive that long.

Your children must see this. You build them, make sure they know themselves. Make sure they can fend for themselves; make sure they know they decide who they are, no one else. He cannot help himself, and when they are no longer small and begin to question him, he will reveal himself. They will see what you see; they will learn it themselves. It is a painful lesson, but you cannot tell them that they will never believe you. Could someone has informed you when you were on that pedestal?

THE JOURNEY THROUGH SEPARATION

Making Decision of Divorce

The separation and divorce are one of the most disturbing factors of psychosocial stress for welfare and often cause depression and anxiety pictures as part of the mourning the end of a relationship.

However, there is a situation that is even more traumatic for someone who decides to separate, the divorce or separation of a couple with a narcissistic personality disorder. It is usually the beginning of hell because someone sick with narcissism is unable to forgive who considers treason and unjustified abandonment. The narcissistic disorder is defined by the inability to empathic towards others, for utilitarianism in relationships, and for a total lack of awareness of their defects and errors that could explain, in part, an emotional breakdown. The narcissist, in his world view, is never wrong, nor does he need help from anyone. The others are the imbeciles, the ones who fail, the ones who can't see the irreparable loss that means ending a relationship with him or her.

Having some personality traits is not the same as being a structural narcissist. Someone who thinks he is terrific or who spends a lot of time talking about himself listens little is not necessarily this person who cannot feel real love. Someone who is unable to think of others and who organizes his life so that everyone serves him helps him. And admire it. And once he has stopped needing them, he abandons them in cold blood, but he will never (and never is ever) forgive anyone who decides to leave him.

Legal proceedings involving divorce, alimony, or custody lawsuit are the perfect pretext for acting out narcissistic anger. Whoever dares to confront, criticize, or abandon a narcissist will never find peace and live an eternal lawsuit. A narcissistic process of divorce will never accept that a stage is closed, as it is a wound to the ego. Her grudge is timeless, and her revenge plans too. They often use their children as weapons. They fill them with gifts, they organize a small amusement park on the weekends and then manipulate them and confront them with the ex-couple. They are stingy in handling money and never give it when it is needed, but when it suits their interests.

Narcissists are wrong partners and parents. Their prognosis is reserved because they never come to ask for help and if they do, it is only to convince the therapist or the legal system or whoever is necessary, that they are right and are victims of the circumstances. They lack introspection and

143

frequently describe an inner world of coldness and indifference. Nothing moves them except when something affects them personally.

Some clues can be useful to avoid lovingly relating to a narcissist: lack of interest and curiosity about the life and activities of the couple, about their family and friends; the difficulty to speak about what you feel and to be authentic; resentment towards many people, although the offense occurred many years ago; inability to forgive, recognize mistakes, and apologize.

Couples of narcissists manage to separate when they realize the tremendous emotional cost of continuing the relationship when they see their children damaged when they know that nothing they do will be enough, and they will always be criticized.

" When you are clinging to another stage of your life, detained in time, you cannot move forward, " says psychologist Sebastián Girona, a specialist in couples therapy. The past is an excellent place to visit from time to time, but it is the wrong place to stay and live. "

Girona analyzes two positions regarding the possibility of an ex-partner feeding on hatred. On the one hand, narcissism. On the other, truncated projects. "Many times, separations that cannot be accepted involve a profound, painful narcissistic wound, difficult to digest. In other cases, not being able to cut implies staying attached to what could have been," he says.

"Sometimes, people who cannot finish separating themselves interpret any sign of the other for the side that suits them best. Then there is a distortion of the reading of reality -the psychologist warns-. Grudge prevails because, in this deep narcissistic wound, they take it personally when, in reality, many factors cause a couple to end."

Reasons and Consequences of Faithfulness Conflicts in Families of Divorce

Divorce is a process that ends the marital union is legislated almost everywhere in the world. The last Latin American country to legislate it was Chile, in 2004. In the United States, the divorce and annulment rate are 3.2 per 1,000 inhabitants. In Chile, the divorce rate corresponded to 0.1 per 1000 inhabitants in 2009, reaching 2.7 in 2014. An investigation by the Organization for Economic Cooperation and Development (OECD) showed that in general, there had been an increase in divorce rates accompanied by a decrease in marriage rates in the countries belonging to this organization.

144

In this article, we will talk about the divorce and separation of the couple, since when there are children, the common coexistence between parents and children ends. Divorce can occur in a wide range of situations. The parents decide to divorce having tried until that moment to keep the children away from the marital conflict, the one in which the children intensely involved and exposed to the conflict that precedes the separation to the one which continues after it.

Children raised in a home where parental harmony exists have better physical and mental health. On the contrary, familial discord affects them profoundly and produces numerous consequences in different spheres of their life.

As Cohen & Carol mention, the pediatrician, as well as the family doctor, are somewhat equivalent to the old "family doctor." He is aware not only of the physical problems that affect children during their development but also of the stressors that may be present. In the case of noticing that there is parental discord in the family, one of their tasks could be to ask about it, talk to parents about how it affects the child, and refer them to couples or family therapy, depending on the case and the disposition of the family.

The pediatrician can also perform anticipatory guidance with parents facing a separation or divorce. He can maintain a relationship with both parents and insist that, beyond the legal situation, what interests and worries him is the quality of the relationship that both keep with their children.

It analyzes some of the consequences that divorce or separation can bring to children, to provide recommendations to pediatricians to help guide parents to understand some reactions and how to protect the well-being of children.

Consequences on Children After Divorce or Separation from Parents

Divorce produces alteration of the child's well-being if it is contentious and if it is associated with worsening of the economic situation, behavioral and emotional malfunction of the parents, ineffective upbringing, loss of contact with one of the parents, the persistence of conflicts between the spouses and absence of agreements in education. Alterations in parenting that occur in contentious divorces can be stressors capable of generating poor adaptation in neuropsychological responses, making deterioration in children's physical and mental health.

In general, most of the difficulties of adaptation in children after separation or divorce is resolved within 2-3 years and 3-5 years after the second marriage, if any. The possible traumatic effect of divorce decreases as time passes, and especially if parents reach parenting agreements. In some cases, however, it has been observed that emotional problems can increase with age and may not be expressed until late adolescence or adulthood.

The relationship between gender and the effects of conflictive divorce is a widely discussed factor. The investigations have been inconsistent or have not been able to establish the relationship between gender and parents' divorce.

A review found that boys were more negatively affected than girls. These children had a more celebrated history of psychiatric consultations during childhood and adolescence and had more symptoms of separation anxiety, 16 more fears for collars, and more behavioral problems. Conversely, other studies have observed that girls are more negatively affected than boys and may be explained by the role of emotional restraint that they must sometimes offer to one of the parents.

This inconsistency could suggest that both men and women are affected, but in different ways. 10

It has been observed that parental divorce increases the risk of alcohol consumption in adolescents, which may be related, among several factors, to less parental control or a worse family socioeconomic situation.

Many children experience feelings of loss when a parent leaves the family home, but some feel relief. This relief will be explicit if a hostile and violent environment is interrupted when the couple separates. It should be noted that divorce is a process and not just an event, at least to understand the effects on children.

Children are more likely to present psychological problems when there is a conflictive relationship between the parents before, during, or after the divorce. Generally, inter-parental conflict is more significant in the immediate period of the separation and is expected to decrease with time. However, up to 44% of divorced families remain in conflict for prolonged periods that go beyond three years, and even they may end up understanding all of life. This conflict affects the quality of life of children, generates anxiety disorders and alterations in academic performance.

Long-term Consequences on The Emotional Level of Parental Discord and Divorce

The divorce of the parents can change the look of the children around love and relationships, perceiving that they are unstable and susceptible to disappointments. Furthermore, a high level of parental conflict can be transmitted as a negative model for managing contacts, developing more ordinary coping conflict skills. Greater exposure to parental conflict in childhood is associated, in adolescence and adulthood, with couples who end their relationship faster, have unsatisfactory relationships, and greater violence within the couple.

The parental conflict has a more significant impact on risky behavior in children than parental divorce. It has been observed that adolescent daughters have a less positive vision of love relationships, are less likely to engage in it, and if they do, they are less stable. Wallerstein and Corbin found that a poor father-daughter relationship was associated with a social adjustment of daughters (up to ten years post-separation) and that during adolescence, these girls were more likely to have early and promising sexual activity. It has also been observed that when mothers can support the rise of romantic interests, daughters can develop adequate sentimental skills.

Primary Care and Residence

It is called "primary residence," that gift of the child lives longer. In Chile, this is usually the maternal home. However, to facilitate the transition between a type of two-parent family to one parent, both parents can participate with the same rights and duties in the upbringing and education of their children, which is what is intended through the concept of "co-custody," 35 or shared custody.

This system is one in which the father and mother share the authority and responsibility for decision-making regarding their children, and both see themselves as equally significant in their lives. It is considered a favourable system to avoid the negative consequences that divorce may have. It has been shown that a higher level of support and control by the non-resident father, after a divorce, has positive implications on the well-being of children 37 and positively influences the self-esteem of these children.

It has also been observed that adolescents who have joint custody after a divorce present a significantly lower risk of alcohol abuse than those who do not, 39 and there are fewer psychological complaints from adolescents who have joint physical custody compared with those residing with a single parent.

Despite this, it is most often the case that "sole custody" is given, one in which one parent exercises "full" responsibility for the child. Even so, over time, there can be changes, for example, in adolescents, that when they feel "controlled by" the parent with whom they live, they express wishes to go live with the other, with whom they have fantasies that they will be free and happy. In fact, most teens in this situation, shortly after moving to a new house, decide to return to their primary residence.

Another type of agreement, although even more infrequent due to the difficulty, is that the children live in a home and it is the parents who take turns living in that house, which will require greater fluidity in the quality of communication between them and at the same time, unambiguous rules.

In general, both the studies of children of divorced children and our own experience in this field suggest that children's social adaptation depends on whether or not interparental conflict persists.

Regarding the presence of the non-custodial father in the children's lives, an 8-year follow-up showed that young people exposed to high levels of inter-parental conflict present worse psychosocial adaptation, even when that father continues to be actively involved in their lives. In the same study, it was observed that children who did not have personal contact with the non-custodial parent did not have worse results than those who maintained close Contact but with a high level of conflict, suggesting that a constant parent-child relationship does not necessarily by itself, it mitigates the consequences of a conflictive inter-parental relationship 24. Some studies suggest that if the child maintains close and satisfactory Contact with the non-custodial parent, even in the presence of conflict between the couple, the effects of the divorce may not be harmful. Another study shows that the migration of a parent to a remote location could even protect children from inter-parental conflicts and persistent disruptions if the parental conflict is intense.

Role of The Pediatrician in Divorce or Separation Cases

Paediatricians must be prepared to deal with multiple crises in the lives of the families they serve, including separation and divorce are often issues parents consult with them.

In general, the paediatrician can tell parents that the low level of inter-parental conflict is considered a protective factor, and it has been shown that a good relationship with parents can be a defence against the undesirable consequences of a divorce. It must be emphasized that the effects of divorce occur not due to the separation itself. Still, due to the inadequate way of the parents to face it, therefore, the adverse effects can be prevented, and paediatricians are considered to play a role fundamental to educate in this regard.

Young children are not able to understand environmental circumstances, but they do perceive changes in their environment, caregivers, and routines. They need stability in the daily routine and sufficient Contact with a primary caregiver to develop a secure attachment. The secure early attachment will be the basis for the development of future relationships, and high-intensity conflicts are linked to the development of insecure and disorganized attachment styles. In situations of external stress, infants may show signs of irritability, withdrawal or apathy, change in sleep patterns or appetite.

The recommendation, in this case, would be that the non-custodial parent visits him in his home, while the child spends the night with the custodial parent. Avoid changes in your routine. Agree on fundamental milestones such as feeding, sleep, and game times.

Regression is a common reaction in preschoolers. You can protect children in this process by delivering more one on one attention and reporting adequately to their level of development will be familiar routines and how to continue the relationship with their parents.

Erik Erikson 42 points out that between three and four years of age, the sense of moral, right, and evil begins to develop in children, which carries with it the concept of guilt. This guilt, added to the self-centeredness of that age, makes them often accuse themselves of their parents' problems and divorce.

The recommendations at this stage are to repeat that they are not to blame for the separation, that this is a matter for the adults, and that it is the parents who will best resolve how the family will continue.

Also, at this age, it is necessary to emphasize the continuity of routines. The child can start to sleep with the non-custodial parent, as long as this is well prepared by both parents. Maybe spring for a few hours, until you complete a long time.

Children from 6 to 8 years old can interpret the separation from their parents as the collapse of all the environment that surrounds and protects them. It is also common for children to express feelings of guilt and disloyalty, with both parents, being happy to stay with their non-custodial father, and at the same time guilty for leaving the parent with whom they live, a situation that can be reversed at the moment to return to the primary home.

Schoolchildren can blame themselves for relationship problems and eventual separation, with fantasies of reunion and harmony between their parents being frequent. They can present mood swings, especially more enormous sadness and anger.

In the event of a divorce, parents can help their children at this age, fostering trust and confirming the stability of this new and different family organization. They need reminders that the divorce is final and that they are not to blame. At all ages, but especially in this age, clear limits should be maintained, and consequences should be exposed in case of violation of the rules, which ideally should be expressed in a concordant way by both parents. It is also essential to provide space for children to express their feelings openly.

Adolescents may better understand the complicated and abstract situations involved in parental discord and divorce, but they may also have difficulty accepting it. They may assume excessive responsibilities and be concerned about matters that are incumbent on adults, sometimes in situations in which the parents themselves seem to be experiencing "second adolescence," with the ensuing confusion in the rules that govern family discipline. These teens may feel limitless, which can lead to insecurity or lead to unhealthy behaviors. Some studies have shown that adolescents living in families of divorced marriages are at higher risk of externalizing problems (alcohol use, violation of rules) and internalizing problems (depression, anxiety.

At this stage, parents should help their children delimiting how far they can share their problems and should keep intimate those situations for which a teenager is not yet fully prepared, such as legal, sexual, confidential, or financial matters.

In all phases, pre, peri, and post-separation, it is necessary to give adequate information to the children. In this regard, the following general considerations can be made 44:

- It must be clearly stated that the married couple will separate, giving the reasons that are most understandable for their age; explain to them that they did not cause or motivate the separation; Tell them that they could not have influenced or prevented the separation, clarify that this is a situation of marriage and that it has nothing to do with them (in the cause)

150

and that they will not be able to do anything for an eventual reconciliation.

- Emphasize that both are still parents despite the end of the marriage; tell them that they do not have to choose between one of the two parents; Let them know that their parents understand that they have doubts that they will always be willing to listen and respond to them.
- Let them know that it is normal for them to have rage, grief or confusion and that this cannot only speak to them within the family but also outside of it and clearly show them that the parents loved each other when they were pregnant and that they are the product of that love act.

The following suggestions regarding access to children depend on each case:

- It is recommended that the meetings of the father or mother with the children with whom he does not live do not take place in artificial environments and dedicated only to fun; the activities to which they give rise must be linked to everyday life: taking them to or from school, doing homework together, etc.
- Depending on the type of relationship, the convenience of children under three years of age, sleeping outside their home can be explored. If they do, the parent who lives with the child must be easily located, in case the child wishes to return to the primary home or contact her custodial parent.
- In all other ages, the outings must be predictable, stable in their frequency, reporting the exact time at which they will be picked up and dropped off, and that the father or mother strictly complies with it to instill confidence in agreements stop such.
- Between the ages of ten and fourteen and adolescence, it is sometimes expected that the child wishes to distance contacts with the non-custodial parent. In these cases, stays away from home should be according to your wishes, since the relationship with your friends is what interests you the most.
- Either because they are men or women or because of their different ages or interests, it is convenient to consider some encounters with some sons and daughters, and not all at once, without this resulting in an imbalance that shows some degree.

The preceding are not rigid rules, and if separate agreements have been reached than those described here and have been satisfactory for parents

151

and children, it would be preferable not to modify them.

In response to increases in divorce rates, many countries have adopted a compulsory educational program at the time a divorce is requested. These programs are generally brief and informative, focusing on how to help children cope with the situation during and immediately after the divorce process. A research group in Australia 45 has implemented a mediation program that includes children and has been found to affect reducing conflict levels and better managing them. New designs are also proposed to be applied in court to carry out a collaborative divorce instead of a cross-border approach.

The situation of separation and divorce in the family produces intense and extensive changes in various dimensions. The decision of how the family will live after a divorce is an issue that requires in-depth discussion and a deep commitment to continuing exercising co-parenting.

We have tried to provide some guidelines to paediatricians to help parents involved in the conflict to privilege the well-being of their children so that children can go through this experience without adverse effects, and on the contrary, learn what it is. It is possible to achieve solutions to problems that are difficult to handle.

Ways to Heal, Avoid or Manage Triggers, Rage, And Meltdown

These are varied and can appear from the beginning or in later stages of the divorce. We find parents blinded by rage because they do not tolerate the decision to separate that the spouse has taken, even if the couple's difficulties are manifest. Rabies can also arise due to economic factors, non-acceptance of the decline in quality of life, or non-compliance with the payment of the food quota. Satisfied alienating parents are jealous of a new relationship from their ex, afraid of being replaced as a father or a mother. Also, the birth of a new child makes them fear that their own will be displaced.

The alienating parent tends to overprotect their children. He sees the world as dangerous, and the other parent represents a possible source of danger, as he cannot control it on visits. The most frequently cited reason is the fact that the other parent is not able to take care of the children and that the children do not feel well when they return from the visit. The message to the children is that the other parent is no longer a family member and that it is a hassle to see him. In this context, the slightest change in visit plans is a pretext for cancelling them.

When this type of behavior is carried out by the woman, he usually alleges alcoholism, drug use, and bad company from the father. Another argument used is the age of the children, who are left with third parties during visits, non-compliance with the quota, or its reduced amount. Sometimes we can meet a resentful woman, desirous of revenge in the face of her husband's betrayal and contempt, who does not hesitate to sacrifice her children to harm the other. Wallerstein (1989) called this behavior "Medea Syndrome."

When the obstruction is carried out by the man, in general, he alleges alleged mental disturbance of the woman, which puts her children at risk, arguing treatments that she would have had, whether psychological or pharmacological. He also alleges alleged sexual misconduct by women, which he usually confirms with a new relationship. The presence of this man in the home increases harassment since he sees it as harmful to sons or daughters. You can also allege alleged negligence in the care of these, physical or psychological abuse. Many times we are in the presence of a man wounded in her machismo, authoritarian, and violent, who has not been able to retain the woman by her side.

These women, on many occasions, have escaped prolonged violence, and are accused of abandoning their children, who stay with the father and refuse to see her if she does not return home, which poses a risk to her integrity. When children stay with the mother, in severe cases, their mission is to control and observe her, disqualifying her. They do not respect or obey her, encouraged by the father.

The objective of these behaviors is to exclude the other parent from the lives of the children. The alienating parent is mistakenly put in the role of protector, often causing irreparable damage to the father / mother-child bond.

The abuse most often invoked is emotional. One parent accuses the other, for example, of sending the children to sleep too late. In reality, differences in moral judgment or opinion between parents are classified by one as abusive behavior by the other.

The most severe form of abuse that is invoked is physical abuse or sexual abuse, usually summoned by the mother. It is a delicate subject since it has been challenging to obtain a space for consideration and protection for the victims of such crimes. Still, I am referring to another circumstance, when it is a false complaint, to distance the father from the life of your children permanently, or members of your environment, for example, grandparents, new spouse, etc. It occurs in destructive divorce contexts, especially if the children are small and more manageable. Many times, the mother's doubts are transformed into certainties by legal or mental health

153

professionals.

Consequences of The Estrangement of Their Sons or Daughters in The Remote Parent

The consequences suffered by parents away from the lives of their children are multiple and depend on the type of SAP. Feelings of anguish, uprooting, loneliness, frustration over not having a family appeared in the research sample subjects who went through the mild variety, with some physical consequences, such as weight loss and irritability.

In the moderate type, they felt anger and helplessness; they were obsessed with the subject, with frequent feelings of anguish, injustice, and loneliness that made them fall into depressive states. Decreased work or academic performance. We found, then, that stress impacted them physically, with various alterations.

In the severe type, it was characteristic that they experienced depression, marked anguish, crying crisis, and suicidal thoughts. They were obsessed with the situation, with almost permanent feelings of anger and helplessness. They presented pronounced insecurity, disorientation, insomnia, chronic physical disorders, both gastrointestinal and cardiac. They had shoddy work and intellectual performance and suffered from nightmares. In general, they were under medical and psychological care, since everything in their lives had gone haywire.

For a father, discovering that a son is the origin of the attacks, insults, and denigrations towards him initially generates a reaction of stupor. After this, the anger to face the objective so sought by his former partner arises, finally becoming frustrated when it is assumed that the fight has been lost.

Many of the parents who are subject to moral, psychological, economic, and practical damage by being deprived of their children, become ill, lose their job, their mental balance, and some, in their despair and helplessness, end up committing prohibited acts of violence.

Actions That Help the Remote Parent

Other aspects investigated were the responses that justice provided to this problem, both those that were positive and those that did not help.

In general, as a practical action that helps the remote parent to mitigate the consequences of the SAP, the family support they have received is highlighted, either from their family of origin or the new couple; The birth of a new child also adds to the relief. These relationships are crucial to lowering the intensity of the affective collapse in which at times they fall, in the face of the powerlessness they feel to modify the estrangement of their children, whom they believe are lost forever, submerging them in an ambiguous loss (physical absence, psychological presence) that makes mourning almost impossible.

Actions That Do Not Help the Remote Parent

In general, the actions taken from the justice system are not very effective in helping to dismantle the behaviors that hinder the bonding of the alienating parent, except in minor cases, where the indications and the weight of the law end up being respected, albeit irregularly. In severe cases, there is no energetic and effective modality in Argentina to protect the rights of the alienated parent. Usually, the alienator does not respect or comply with the judges' sentences, and the actions to reverse them are slow. A false complaint of abuse, including imprisonment, suffered by one of these parents, took five years to resolve. When children refuse to visit the non-cohabiting parent, their wishes are generally respected by the professionals involved in the cause.

In all cases, custody of the alienating parent is maintained. The interviewees have the perception of the lack of training and ignorance of the professionals involved in the problem, from the lawyers, experts, advisers, and judges, to the psychologists, which significantly complicates the consequences of the departure, since when faced with any questions or complaints The first thing that is prevented is Contact, instead of carrying out said departure in a controlled manner, until the actions denounced are verified.

What to Do?

Based on our experience and that of the subjects who participated in our study, we are going to make a series of suggestions to the parents involved in a highly conflictive divorce:

- Always maintain Contact with sons or daughters, however brief or infrequent it may be.
- In the face of the attacks of the sons or daughters, try to recall the relationship established before the separation and do not go into the reply.

155

- Avoid self-fulfilling prophecies, giving arguments that favour criticism.
- In the face of the alienator's attacks, transform into a reed that bends in the wind and stays straight when it stops blowing.
- Always remember that children are sensitive to oral and non-verbal language.
- Take care of the moments of meetings, share news, establish commitments, put on credibility.
- Try to know the tastes, beliefs, and feelings of the children.
- Have patience and persist in contact actions, facing them serenely. Do not force any situation.
- Handle adult problems between adults and not pass them on to children.

Guidance for Professionals

Regarding the professionals who intervene in any stage of the divorce, custody, tenure, etc. process, we could conclude:

As there is a profound lack of knowledge about the nature of SAP, which generates diagnostic errors and subsequent indications, it is advisable that all professionals involved in these cases inform themselves adequately and bear in mind the consequences of the recommendations they make, especially taking Take into account the context in which they are developed and all those involved.

We Could Also Say That

- The recommendation of family therapy or mediation is only possible in mild cases of SAP; in the other types, only judicial and police intervention is feasible.
- The parent should not be deprived of contact with their children; if necessary, the meeting can be carried out under controlled conditions (technical team, supervised visits with a therapeutic companion).
- In the case of severe SAP, the change of custody of children should be considered since inducing a syndrome of parental alienation to a child is a form of abuse, and as such, must proceed.

156

The usurpation of the time of the remote parent allows the denigration campaign to be installed since by preventing Contact, the contrast with the real bond with the other parent is impossible, and the affective relationship is weakened. Time is a weapon in the hands of the alienator since it allows the son to become an active member of this campaign. The hindrance in the regular passing of visits and the various interferences through legal resources are a characteristic feature of SAP. The longer the time of withdrawal, the higher the influence on boys and girls, which is why it is vital not to cut or distance this relationship.

When Your Ex Is Sending Toxic Messages About you

Over time, narcissists will manage your expectations of the relationship in such a way that you will expect less and less of them, to obtain a very high margin of freedom. It is one of the most potent weapons in the narcissistic arsenal and gives the narcissist (male or female) the most rewards. The narcissistic personality shines when he implements this particular strategy because it shows how much patience he has when it comes to using control strategies. The management of a partner's expectations allows the narcissist to never depart from the relational agenda that guides him and will enable him to move freely on this planet without any kind of obstacle. At the same time, you stand aside by scratching your head and gritting your teeth.

The way you manage your expectations shows how much a narcissist can equip himself with all the patience in the world to achieve his goal. The process starts already from the first dispute or from the very first treatment of silence (whichever comes first) and lasts until the final evaluation and the discard. The whole process can take many weeks, months, or even years, and we don't even realize what's going on. It is the narcissist's way of teaching us how to behave and how to react to any type of behavior suddenly decides to experiment on our skin.

The narcissist manipulates your expectations by "training" you to react in a certain way to certain situations—for example, the act of disappearing. If your narcissist acts in a similar way to my ex, he will disappear for days, sometimes for weeks, not answering the phone (or changing his number), refusing to answer the door (or not being found at home for days) and acting as if you didn't exist. It is a behavior that causes horrible anguish and suffering so much so that, in effect, you will do anything to make it stop, including forgiving their disappearances instantly, as soon as they return. Anxiety disappears and feels more relieved, and you will even go as far as not to ask any explanation or ask a single question to create separation. In other words, they get along with what the goal of narcissists (men and women) is in whatever they do: control. Now, to lower your expectations, they will always go further. The next time they disappear, they will be away from a little longer than the previous time, thus lengthening the time spent with new lovers (because that's what they are doing with each treatment of silence, by the way). Eventually, they will have managed your expectations of the relationship to the point of being able to walk away for months, returning with little or no fanfare on your part. They are lengthening the time spent with new lovers (because that's what they're doing with every treatment of silence, by the way). Eventually, they will have managed your expectations of the relationship to the point of being able to walk away for months, returning with little or no fanfare on your part.

Narcissists use this narcissistic ploy to their advantage for many situations, for example for:

- Keep yourself in suspense with the dates: practically they never take you anywhere and therefore learn not to wait any longer for invitations from them;
- do not spend holidays/parties with you: learn that they may have other commitments, or;
- don't shell out anything for your outings/trips.

Your expectations of what's "normal" in a relationship are completely turned upside down, and you start allowing everything and anything to happen right under your nose. It becomes automatic to look the other way just to "forgive" the leaking indiscretions and their unusual behavior. At this point, you are trained not to call a narcissist on his behavior in order not to risk another departure. In other words, you have learned to give everything without ever expecting anything in return: and nothing is what you get!

Everything that narcissists do or say in the course of their interactions is a means of achieving an end, never forget it. Nothing is ever random. Narcissists want to get what they want, whenever they want, with anyone who wants to do it. It doesn't matter at the expense of who it is, the easiest way to achieve this is to lower the expectations of the official partners on the relationship to the point to get them to accept the mere crumbs of attention that they offer as something very natural. In doing this, they can disappear and reappear on the fly without any fear of the consequences. They will count on their suffering to keep them in hand and on the acceptance of their crumbs to prevent them from giving proper weight to their lies.

Think about this when you think about the reasons that led you to endure such treatment. Your concept of a healthy relationship become or was becoming distorted, and now, whether you are still in or out of the link, you have to re-train your brain to understand normalcy.

What we allow will continue to happen, and only we can make the changes that will ultimately lead to our recovery from this type of manipulation.

What Do You Need to Do?

Regardless of what will happen, do not get back in touch. Months after starting Zero Contact, my ex came to say to a mutual friend: "I was the only one who loved her, all she had to do was say yes (marry him!) And things would change between us." Detail: he married a few months later. I kept zero Contact. After a few months, it was my mother who told me that my ex had sent her a chat message explaining that she was going to marry another because I refused to marry him.

I Kept Zero Interaction

After a few more months, he sent me a birthday greeting via e-mail: "May God bless you" and "May all your dreams come true" (with an arrow added later), "although sometimes they may seem high. "

I Kept My Decision

AFTER YEARS when I no longer felt him - since I had blocked him from my email accounts - once again, my mother, on Christmas day, received an email from him describing a personal tragedy in his life. This tragedy, he said, had provoked in him the desire to ask "apologies in general" for "everything he had done or omitted."

No Move on My Part

Then, a few days later, on New Year's Eve, I received a text message from my insurance agent, an acquaintance of his. It was a message forwarded by my ex narcissus asking him to "Greet me" on his behalf.

- Do not answer their calls.
- Do not reply to their text messages.
- Do not reply to their emails.
- Block email, phone numbers, etc.

- Block them from your life.

They Only Want to Extract Narcistic Supply from You

If you think their "sorry" are sincere, if you believe that their promise of change is real and that you are noticing positive changes in them, know that the duration is short. The "changes" last until they are sure of your falling in love. Once you are hooked again, expect the return to their anger-abused, manipulative, and controlling self.

I have made numerous unsuccessful attempts to establish zero Contact during the years of my relationship with the narcissist. I was bombarded with his constant calls, his requests, his efforts to make me feel better, and his apologies. I ALWAYS forgave him. I ALWAYS believed it would change. I had ALWAYS given the advantage of the reservation.

When I broke up with him since of his being physically violent, he promised that he would never hurt me physically again. And, in fact, he never did it again.

However, only later did I realize that his violent being had "refined," transforming into something that I was unable to detect because there were no more physical bruises.

What I felt was permanent anxiety, a feeling of constant worry and guilt.

I suffered from obsessive ruminating thoughts, and I had difficulty sleeping, my body suffered, I was overweight, I felt consistently weak, tired, and run down, I was always short of breath.

Going on, I discovered that he had lied to me, who was manipulating me emotionally, mentally, and psychologically. He abused my trust, told lies about me to others while, likewise, he told lies about others to me.

I decided to no extended be his supply nonetheless of how sweet, sweet, and sincere he was, and despite his "efforts" to "make things work."

Know That It Is Not Your Knight in Sparkling Armor

Zero Contact is particularly challenging in times when you feel emotionally vulnerable, times when you cannot help thinking about him/her, and the "good things" they have done for you.

Be aware that what you are missing is the FICTION side of the thing. It is your desire for a relationship or romantic love invented by an imaginary character.

All they have to give you is a pseudo-love and a pseudo redemption from the unfortunate situation generated by themselves. They do it only to put you back in the merry-go-round of pain to turn with them.

- Don't allow yourself to get sucked in.
- You are not dealing with knights in shining armour.
- They are not your saviours.
- They are the reason why you lived a real hell.

They cannot solve the problems caused by themselves. They can only add other issues to make you temporarily forget the previous ones.

Once Contact has been established, others will be added to the previous pains, which will multiply as many times.

Based on my experience, my ex-narcissus never took responsibility for the injuries he caused or the lies he said when we were together because it was logically impossible for him to be responsible for anything.

Take Note of What You Hear and See/Talk About This/Look for Support

It is easy to doubt yourself when you start Zero Contact. Sometimes you will wonder if everything started only from your head.

You can also consider saving the relationship or meeting your narcissist simply to say "hello" or to remember "the old days."

As long as you recognize that you are invaded by thoughts, write them down.

Record them. Write down all your experiences with the narcissist.

Once done, you will usually see patterns emerge that you were unaware of the situation. You will be able to see clearly how your Achilles' heels push. You can also realize through the schemes identified how they managed to immerse themselves in their network of poison.

Writing helps organize confused thoughts or at least eliminate them from your system.

Also, start a "notebook of gratitude": list the small or big things that makes you grateful every day. Doing this helps to focus your attention on the details that you consider positively significant. It also helps to safeguard your energy by making you look at the brighter side of life.

Start a notebook of gratitude on the first day, from the first moment you decided to leave with Contact Zero. It will keep you focused on maintaining your decision and healing.

It is also better to talk about your experiences with someone who can understand them without judging your experience.

Share your experience: it will help you get rid of your negative feelings as you learn from other people's experiences.

If there is no one you can talk to, go to the narcissism forums. They are places where you will read experiences similar to your experience. You can also learn from them and share your story. Some of these forums are listed below.

Concentrate on Your Healing

Continuing with the Zero Contact becomes more bearable when you are equipped with tools to assist healing and recovery, so as not to make narcissistic attacks even more extreme.

When we become the only architects of our solidity and inner peace, we also learn to detach ourselves. It is exciting to see how narcissists lose importance and can no longer influence or damage our life ".

Cleaning and releasing yourself from the emotional slime of being used/abused/deceived/manipulated is the most important thing. It is the value of the Zero Contact: it gives you breath to allow your evolution and removes any poison from your system; it is the perfect time to empty and fill your soul with pure air.

Focusing on your medicinal and regaining is one of the critical benefits of Zero Contact. Don't take this for granted.

Act on your critical points to avoid the evil influence of narcissists.

Zero Contact is a small step to keeping your Self safe, and it is also a giant step towards love for your Self. Allow yourself to experience authentic

162

freedom and empowerment.

When Your Ex Is Nosy with Contact and Message

Before doing anything, you need to take a step back and understand why your ex-husband looked for you. If you recently broke up, then you must take this episode with a little detachment: your emotions after the break have not yet recovered; you are still not lucid and, therefore, you could make mistakes that could make you feeling sick and repenting later.

So, let's analyze some reasons why your ex-husband may have contacted you. Later on, I will give you some tips that will help you reflect and make the right choice.

He Has Difficulty Overcoming What Has Happened and Moving Forward

When an ex-husband is looking for you for no apparent reason, he may have trouble breaking through and moving forward. It's normal. Since you haven't been in touch for a while, he may have figured out what it means to lose you and be without you. It scares him, and surely, he thought that if he does not go forward, you will find another boy.

In these cases, the no contact period was successful: he understood that he had made a mistake and that the new girl he dated was not right for him. Or he has decided that he doesn't want to go out with another because he wants you.

It can happen even after a breakup caused by a betrayal of the boy. He may have concluded that leaving you was a big mistake on his part. Sometimes, we have to lose someone to realize how important it is for us!

Guys can easily be distracted by women and make bad decisions by thinking with the hormone instead of the heart and head. Therefore, it would not be the first time that a man has given up on a stable relationship to go after an attractive girl he has just met. Then, as soon as he realizes he was wrong, he retraces his steps.

Your Ex Needs to Be Back with You

It could be one of the reasons your ex suddenly contacted you: he is still in love with you and wants to give your relationship a second chance.

Of course, depending on his personality and the causes of your breakup, he may not be as direct and not tell you right away what his intentions are. However, later on, we will also see if and how to respond in these cases and how to behave.

Also, I must point out that an ex-boyfriend who cares about you and who wants to get back together is willing to do anything to solve relationship problems and make constant efforts to put everything in place and make you happy. However, one must be careful when an ex impulsively declares endless love! Better a guy who starts wooing you again than someone who insists on words. Remember!

Your Ex Doesn't Want to Lose His Friendship with You

Some of my friends have remained on good terms with their ex. They are friends. Simple. Nothing more. If we want it, it is possible. So, you shouldn't be too surprised if your ex-husband wanted to have you as a friend even if you broke up. Maybe he can talk to you calmly, and he can tell you practically everything, and he doesn't want to lose this type of relationship.

As you have both noticed, a romantic relationship may not work between you, but it is not said that your friendship should disappear at all costs. It could be difficult for you if you are still in love with him but, if even you think you can always talk to each other, why miss the chance to have a good friend?

He Needs Your Help with Something

It is unlikely, but it is not impossible. Maybe he needs a favour from you. It explains why your ex suddenly contacted you. In this case, the decision is up to you only: if you are not interested in doing him favours or giving him particular help in something, remember to say it with kindness anyway.

On the other hand, if it's been a long time since you last talked to your ex, I can understand how surprised you can be and, at first, you may feel as if the sound of the phone and its name had you only deluded. Therefore, you may have been disappointed to find out that he only contacted you for a favour. Think about it. Maybe I change my mind.

Your Ex Is Curious About You

It is also possible. He may have seen something, someone, or a place that led him to think about you. So, he wanted to contact you to find out how you are and what you are doing.

If your ex contacted you via a message, he might just want to hear from you, without invading your spaces. In any case, however, know that it could even be just an "excuse," but in any case, you should not try to think about it too much: you could deceive yourself and suffer.

Over time, if he gets in touch with you, you will find out what his real intent was, if he just wanted to hear you or if by chance it was an attempt at rapprochement Time would tell you the truth. So, don't overthink.

When Your Ex Is Removing and Changing You

When the relationship ends, people drift away and forget, or at least it is the theory. However, when you loved with all your heart, it is tough to separate. The most often stalker the social networks of his recent and as the saying goes, "he who seeks finds" and view photos or videos of that person with someone else share your soul.

But why does it hurt so much? Science has answers for almost everything, and this issue is no exception. The jealousy is inevitable separation have the time you have and, say the scientists, and we are always in competition with our gender by instinct.

So, when you see your ex with one or the other, your unconscious possessive instinct (or sometimes very conscious) comes to light because you have the idea that they may probably return in the future. Still, when you see that you are enjoying your life with someone, the more, it nullifies the possibilities of your fantasy.

According to a study, 88% of people between 18 and 35 years of age are 'professional stalkers' inquiring on the social networks of their exes, even 80% harass new couples. It is due to the anguish that is felt in a mixture of emotions: impotence, guilt, among others.

If you have already ended your relationship, we advise you not to add more salt to the wound, and you will only put your self-esteem in danger and act irrationally. No one says it is easy and fast, but remember these tips before harassing your ex.

He started with another, while until recently he said he loved you madly and was lost I believe you want to understand the behavior of your ex after breaking up and try to understand why he does what he does! Generally, a boy behaves like this because he does not want to be alone and does not want to "face himself." It is often a choice that women also make.

Regardless of how it ended with the ex, what caused the breakup and had the idea of closing, sides were indeed suffering. You feel lonely, even when you prefer not to show it outside. Jumping into a relationship with another girl can help put pain, thoughts aside and can help you feel appreciated and safeguard or restore your self-esteem. The same can happen to the woman who immediately finds another partner. Usually, we look for these things, even unconsciously. So how do you know if your ex started this makeshift relationship, or is he taken by the girl he's dating?

To understand the truth, you have to look mainly at two things:

- How long did it take you to get with her?
- And how long he has been with you.

If you have been for a long time and were very well together (before the problems) and the other one came soon or shortly after the end of your relationship, the chances of it being a fallback, a spare wheel, or a relationship "Consolation" are very high! If you and your ex have been together for a long time and spent a lot of good times together, it won't be so easy for him to forget you and move on so fast, Believe me, the fact that he is a man does not imply that it is easier for him to go on. Therefore, it is very likely that that poor girl is only a temporary replacement.

If you continue to make these mistakes, it will surely be impossible to win him back.

However, you should know that these types of relationships almost always end after a short period. Because firstly because your ex could only use this story to distract himself and relieve the pain from breaking up. It means that once these needs are met, the new girl will no longer be so fundamental in her daily life. Secondly, it is useful to consider that he is not in the ideal emotional state to enter into a serious relationship: nobody is immediately after a breakup. Also, the new girl may realize that he is using her as a replacement, thus ending the relationship.

So, what are you supposed to do? Well, know that a widespread mistake that women make when they find out that their ex got together with someone immediately after leaving them is to go directly to confront the ex. If your ex already has another, I correctly understand that you feel angry and betrayed, but don't make the same mistake

Instead, let off steam with a friend, but I assure you that to trigger a good reaction from him, what you have to do is not to show that you are jealous, especially in front of him. Also, remember that it's a bad idea even to send someone to talk badly about his new girlfriend. It won't let him leave her, especially if he finds out it was you! Instead, what you have to do is ignore what's going on. You will see that he will do everything to understand why you are so disinterested. It's a perfect start!

Every love break is usually seconded by pain, to a lesser degree, on one side or both. It is not pleasant for anyone to break a relationship that sets expectations and dreams. Well, after the convenient stage of mourning, this does not end here. When you find out that your ex already has a busy heart, it can all fall apart again.

If this happens after the relationship ends, it usually stings even more. Thoughts of all kinds of our minds related to the love he had for us, with the possibility that he has been unfaithful to us or the sadness of considering that, perhaps, he has not loved us as much as we intended to see in his gestures.

When we discover that the person, we once loved has another partner, something is removed from within

After this rain of contrary reasoning, an inner feeling arises from the fear that our ex has found someone, but we have not yet. Suddenly we feel older and desperate at the thought of being alone. He has succeeded, but we are not, however, ready to start a new relationship. It may even be so, but we have decided not to do so in order not to close the door to a possible reconciliation.

I Feel Like It Still Belongs to Me

We have referred to the possibility of feeling bad when we discover that our ex already has a partner, while we still do not. However, what happens if we also have a new partner? Why do we get such jealousy as a result of discovering that this person's heart is busy again?

Even if you want to believe that you have overcome the breakup, sometimes this is not the case. We lie to ourselves by meddling in new relationships when, in reality, we continue to be "hooked" on our former partner. We are not talking about love, but inertia that leads us to believe that the other person still belongs to us.

167

In the society in which we live, relationships still have some meaning of possession. We believe that our partner is our property. It causes us not to see it as a person, but as a territory that must be defended so as not to lose it and not to take it from us.

This slightly distorted conception revives this feeling of belonging when it is all over. There is no love, and there is no more of that. However, we become blind people who are carried away by an uncertain belief that our ex cannot be with anyone else. This fact bothers us; it makes us angry. It is ours, only ours. The person you are with now is a usurper.

My Ex Keeps Hurting Me

Not really. Your ex doesn't keep hurting you, and you're the one doing it to yourself. You feel worried. After all, you have not been chosen because you begin to compare yourself with the person you are with now. You notice your insecurity mixed with anger and pain—a jumble of emotions that confuse you. You need to end this.

- Never compare yourself: «your partner is younger, prettier, smarter. Enough! Comparisons always hurt and don't fix anything. That person will also have her defects, and you have a thousand and one virtues. Stop beating yourself for free.
- Don't be selfish: think about that feeling of possession so deep-rooted and so selfish that it prevents us from truly loving. Now is the time to learn from it and realize that even after love is over, you are coveting your ex's situation.
- "A nail doesn't get another nail": don't think about going out with someone now to feel better about yourself and so that your ex has the same feelings as you. For starters, it's not a good idea to use people for these purposes, and second, you may not be able to make your ex envy your situation and feel angry.

Let go even if you are scared, and your mind tells you otherwise. It is better to contradict all this than to be unhappy for the rest of your days

Remember that love is not what we have been taught. Maybe you are still in love with your ex, but think that when you love someone, all you want is their happiness, even if it is not with you. Turning the page is difficult, but it is also an opportunity to learn and gain security.

Your ex has been an essential part of life. Now he must continue on his way just as you have to keep on yours. Stop being aware of a relationship that has already ended. It is time to look forward. Are you ready to start again?

If you stop to think, logic tells you that what your ex-partner does, now that you are no longer together, should be irrelevant to you.

Logic and all your rationality are left behind when you wake up with a pang in your stomach, remember that now you are sharing with someone else all the things that they shared with you.

Your mind is divided. A part of you does not want to know more about new life, and part is searching the networks for any information about a substitute.

I Can't Stand My Ex Having A Partner

Do you want to get an image of your ex with another person out of head, but you can't?

Would you like to fit better the fact that your ex-partner remakes his life? The truth is that it is tremendously difficult for you.

You are facing a breakup as best you can, but when the possibility that your heart is occupied by another person comes to your mind, the pain becomes unbearable.

Suddenly, jealousy, sadness, frustration, and anger appear. Images of them invade you, causing rejection, disgust, and violence.

You hate feeling this way, and you think that "you shouldn't feel this way," you would give anything to stop feeling this way.

Sometimes you feel silly and guilty for having such a wrong time with this idea when you rationally know that he is no longer your partner and that both of you have the right to remake your life.

You would like to be cold enough to remain indifferent and decide that what your ex lives on no longer belongs to you, nor does it concern you.

People who love you see you suffer and beg you, over and over again, to forget about your ex. Because they noticed by your conversations, behaviors, and absent glances when you lose the thread of a conversation, that even It is too present in your day to day, to such an extent that you begin to obsess.

I'm Getting Obsessed with My Ex

You spend so much time thinking about them that you end up witnessing

169

their stories on all social networks. And with every detail, real or imagined, you feel worse.

In psychology, we speak of obsession when we have a recurring negative thought, which slips insistently into our heads, and from which we do not know how to get rid of, it has become our shadow and persecutes us wherever we go.

I invite you to answer these questions, to begin to become aware of the level of invasion that is causing you to resist accepting that your ex has a partner:

- Do you surprise yourself several times a day, recreating the image of an ex with another person over again?
- Do you have trouble stopping those kinds of thoughts and replacing them with more positive ones?

If your answers are yes, then you know that you are making it very difficult to elaborate on your duel.

Tips to Accept That My Ex Has A Partner

You cannot continue dodging this issue forever, the time has come to face what scares you so much and look at it face to face.

Start believing that you can do something to deal with this more positively. Your duel is going to be much more painful if you stay anchored in rage, attending the movie of your ex as a passive spectator.

Let's talk about it and come up with a little action plan:

Your Pain Is Annoying but Bearable

When you say to yourself, "I can't bear the idea of being with someone else," are you aware that you are posing it dramatically, that you are telling it in agony?

Stop telling yourself, over and over again, that this is unbearable, be careful with the words you choose, because they condition your emotions!

It is not about denying your feelings or forbidding yourself to feel wrong about this. Why would it be good for your ex to be with someone else? Why is this not supposed to affect you? Who says that? Are you cold as an iceberg? Do you have to cancel your emotions? Noooooo, of course not, start by accepting that it bothers you that your ex has a partner. It is annoying, yes, but bearable.

It is painful, yes, but you can feel pain and, at the same time, progress in your life.

Do you appreciate the difference in approach? Your emotion depends on how you tell yourself what is happening. Be realistic, but don't induce yourself into unnecessary drama.

Your pain is a discomfort that will diminish over time, accept it. If you try to pretend that you don't care who he is with, you will deny a lawful reality and emotion. Paradoxically the passion will become more intense for you to pay attention to, like a little child you ignore.

Make It Easy

It is especially challenging to focus on yourself and your process when all your actions, thoughts, and conversations are single-issue.

How do you want to start thinking about yourself if?

- You keep talking to your ex on a daily or weekly basis (you will say that "friends only"), looking in each of his comments for signs that he likes someone, or that he is with someone, etc.
- You dedicate yourself to always seeing their photos, to recreate yourself in the last events that you lived mentally, and immediately afterwards, you imagine that your ex may be living the same with another person.
- You have become a private investigator interviewing mutual friends, family, etc., recovering news and data that can confirm that you are maintaining a relationship with another person.

Stop doing this immediately, and it's like hitting yourself against the wall, what do you want your head not to hurt afterwards?

Do we redirect focus? Start now to focus your attention on other social relationships, other activities, other topics of interest.

Discover yourself talking about the same topic, gossiping their social networks, and with affection, allow yourself to be redirected. Talk about other things, remain receptive to taking care of your social relationships, keep expanding your hard drive with additional content.

Sorry to be so direct, but you're torturing yourself with something secondary. What is relevant is your grief, decision, that of an ex, or that you not to continue together.

The real and concrete problem is that the relationship upset one or both of you. What does it matter what I can do after you, if what you had no longer worked or did not convince you?

The more time you spend directing your thoughts toward your ex's love life, the more you delay accepting the only essential: your relationship is over, it's over, for one or both, there was no reason to continue.

Just Think About Your Horrible Experience

Do not suffer unnecessarily, comparing yourself with your new partner, belittling you, devaluing what you lived. Think of them as two different experiences at two different times. If you let your ex run its course, you are simultaneously allowing yourself to follow yours.

Some people and relationships only occupy time and space in our lives, and that does not mean that they disappear. What they gave us is not cancelled.

Advance one more chapter of life, do not resist staying on the same page, do you no longer want to read more? Are you not curious about what you still have to live? Yes, go ahead!

Yours had its moment, function in each two, and now it is your turn to seek learning from it or to remain stuck in pain and denial.

When Your Ex Is Inspiring Your Kid to Betray Your Belief

You will surely ask yourself: 'Why did this happen to me, have I been an exemplary husband?', 'Why do you pay me in this way for all the unconditional love that I gave you?' 'Why do these happen? things, after so long of marriage? ' Maybe you don't have an answer, and you can't find an explanation and the most challenging job, you can't do anything to change that situation.

The infidelity has already happened; the time cannot return; be brave, the face that moment, don't let this scare you, and change who you are, those qualities and characteristics that make you unique. He is indeed going through a crisis that marks him, do not be filled with grudges and sadness.

You must live the process, the mourning, weigh the pros and cons of your relationship. If you decided to forgive, if you want to save your home, get through this episode and continue, your relationship may be transformed and from now on it will be more durable and more robust.

To take into account, according to the psychologist specializing in Couples Therapy, Rosalba Urrutia, a couple who faces this situation should: The man who has an extramarital son should confess it to his partner. Carry out the DNA test to be sure that the child is your child. A moral and economic responsibility must be assumed towards the child outside of marriage. Seek professional help to overcome the betrayal process. The woman must remain calm, seek therapies that help her overcome this moment, but she must not become the cloth of tears for her partner. The wife should not try to become the mother of that child as a result of infidelity, nor should she approach the child to be in control of the situation. Talk to the extramarital son with the truth, who knows your real location. After accepting the existence of the son, the father must promote, in a measure, a rapprochement between the brothers. The father must tell his children about the presence of the extramarital child. The father must tell his children about the existence of the extramarital child. Before this moment, you should analyze the stage the child is in, whether he is an infant or a teenager if there is a relationship of too much attachment between parent-child. Accompaniment and professional advice must be carried out to avoid psychological problems. When the children are adults, they are more cautious about accepting that new brother, the interest for what he will receive as an inheritance prevails. Still, an approach and reconciliation must be sought.

He decided to forgive infidelity and move on, but it is evident that he has to work hard to overcome not only the betrayal but also the arrival of that new son. Rosalba Urrutia and Luz Elena De la Rosa Puello, psychologists specialized in Couples Therapy, give some guidelines to overcome infidelity and achieve strength as a couple:

- There must be repentance on the part of the one who failed, and if the other person is willing to continue, it is necessary to create some commitments.
- Expose the expectations of the party, make the requests or requests the emotional needs that she presents, and also his.
- Identify the strengths, qualities, and virtues, as well as the weaknesses or defects that could negatively affect the perception of each one.

173

- Analyze if there is emotional distance or withdrawal, lack of communication, monotony, sexual dissatisfaction, and other aspects that can be identified.
- Establish a trial period agreed by her while preparing the grief and acceptance. It is aware that the relationship will go to another stage of greater maturity, less idealization, and conditionally.
- Accept that the couple assumes the economic and moral responsibility of the minor. An extramarital child has the same value as a legitimate child and should be treated the same.
- The couple must decide to give themselves a new opportunity to establish what kind of relationship they are going to have with the mother of the child.

Have you ever thought before divorce that at one terrible time, your children can hate you and instead of respect and love pay you, your parent, inexplicable spite, slander, humiliation, and insult? Will publicly disown you?

In this case, no one will stand up for you and explain to you what is happening, and you will be left alone with these terrible events. No, judges, psychologists, guardianship officers will pretend that they know how to change the situation, how to curb this doomsday, but this is just a game and hollow cheeks. They do not know this and want only one thing - so that you stop bothering them with your "poltergeist" with your children.

Psychologists and psychiatrists do not speak openly about these phenomena. They do not write in Russian, although there are hundreds of monographs and hundreds of English-language sites devoted to this terrible problem. Lawyers and judges are well acquainted with these unusual phenomena. What happens in a severe family conflict involving children and whether you can survive yourself and save the children - I would like to write about these issues. You never thought before the divorce that at one terrible time, your children might hate you and pay you instead of respect and love, to his parent, inexplicable malice, slander, humiliation, and insult? Will publicly disown you?

In this case, no one will stand up for you and explain to you what is happening, and you will be left alone with these terrible events. No, judges, psychologists, guardianship officers will pretend that they know how to change the situation, how to curb this doomsday, but this is just a game and hollow cheeks. They do not know this and want only one thing - so that you stop bothering them with your "poltergeist" (that is, obscure and somehow inhuman, infernal phenomena) with your children.

One of the researchers of this terrible phenomenon very accurately noted - "there is a quiet global epidemic." The Western Internet is full of sites (hundreds of them) devoted to the problem of "rejecting the parent" by the child (that is, renouncing the victim-parent) in a problematic post-divorce conflict of the parents. These sites are maintained by specialists in mental health, researchers of the phenomena of "Parental Alienation" and "Parental Alienation Syndrome," support groups for parents-victims, sites are informing about the problem, sites of stories of the victims themselves. The Russian-language Internet is silent, there are no resources on this issue, but this does not mean that the child does not have the problem of "rejecting the parent" either. The "silent epidemic" does not bypass the Russian-speaking population, I think, on the contrary.

When Your Ex Is Discouragement Your Authority and Development Need in Your Kid

The children of divorce are always the children - a sentence that is not quite right. Indeed, the separation and divorce of his parents is anything but beautiful for a child. But don't children suffer much more when their parents stay together and argue aggressively with each other every day? From this perspective, the separation and divorce of the parents can also be better for the children. The parents must respond to children and above all, give them the feeling that they are there for them despite the separation.

There should never be any interference between your child and your ex, at least not on your part. The reason for your divorce, the best or worst husband that he was, or the defects that, according to you, he should not be pretexts to interfere in the relationship as they need father and son.

A situation that should have started with the healthy preparation of the minor to face, in the best way, the marital separation of his parents, should not continue with discord between the two people he loves most in life.

Play Your Role of Who You Are

You, as the mother of the son, you are one of the main responsible for their well-being, but not the only one.

The father of your son: your ex nowadays, must take care like you of his economic sustenance, his physical and mental health, his education and protection.

If it's your job to get him up every morning, make him breakfast, supervise his grooming and dress and comb his hair, it may be his dad's responsibility to pick him up to take him to school or pick him up after school.

Allow your ex to share the responsibilities he has as the father of your son and, incidentally, let the little one enjoys time with his dad.

You do not want to become the only person who takes care of his education, care, distraction, who gives him affection and spends time with him.

Unless it is about preserving your health, your well-being, your life or your ex is not the best example for the child, you should never put obstacles, but buts, when the two want to be together.

"A child has the right to enjoy a father and a mother who watch over his care, who love him and raise him in the best way and act as the support that gives him security and confidence to get on with life. "

Not because you live in different homes and the marriage you once had is broken. The son you have in common must suffer the physical absence of his father because each child has the right to enjoy his father. Especially, the father who no longer lives with him.

The Way You and Your Ex Should Proceed

"The best way to prevent a child from suffering the consequences of a recently broken marital relationship is to make him feel safe, loved, giving him the attention he needs. "

Even if you and your partner have divorced and who for years was your husband is now only "the father of your child," you have no right to hinder the respectful relationship that must exist between your son and your ex.

For nothing in the world should you aim to hurt, offend, least in front of the minor, whom you loved in the past? Keep in mind that, although they are no longer part of a family nucleus, they have a common goal, a priority that will keep them together throughout life.

Find a way for you and your ex to agree to maintain the child's emotional stability and happiness. These guidelines can help you.

- Both parents will share the responsibilities they have in raising the child.
- They should never be disrespectful, less in front of the minor

176

- Neither will speak ill of the other in the presence of the child
- They will listen to the opinions and feelings of the minor. He is the most important
- You have to let the child know and feel that, although separated, your ex and you love him very much and continue to be the support of his life
- They will never put the child as a judge to decide between any of the disagreements that, as adults, you have
- They will never use the child as an attack weapon to harm each other.

Between Your Son and Your Ex

Between your child and your ex, there should only be love, healthy and open communication, trust, respect, and admiration. Whatever you can do to reinforce this, do it.

FROM PARENTING TOGETHER TO CO-PARENTING APART

Impact of Separation

Loneliness after a divorce or separation can be frequent and even expected. You shared life with your spouse or partner, perhaps raising children and possibly planning a future together. Divorce and separations bring out strong emotions, many of which lead to feelings of loneliness.

What are the causes, and what can you do to manage loneliness after a divorce?

What Makes You Feel Lonely After A Divorce or Separation?

When a relationship ends, many factors can contribute to loneliness after separation:

- Pain, sadness, and anger: Divorce and separations can trigger an emotional turmoil. Emotions such as pain, grief, and even violence can be universal. They can lead you to distance yourself from other people and isolate yourself, which can lead to feelings of loneliness over time.
- Separation from family and friends: When a divorce or separation occurs, it is common to distance yourself from groups of friends and the family circle, especially those close to your ex. Those people were an essential part of your shared life and could completely disappear from your new life. And let's not forget about pets. Many divorces and separations also mean that a beloved family pet will go with one or the other. If you had a close relationship with a pet that is no longer there, this absent "loved one" could also make you feel lonely.
- Child Custody: When there are children involved in a divorce, there are generally custody issues that need to be addressed. If you share custody with a former partner, there may be times when you find yourself alone with no children around to distract you. It can also help you feel lonely after a divorce.
- Nostalgia for the holidays: Many couples and families have regular holiday traditions, usually shared with family and friends. Divorce and separations can change all of that. When

178

those holidays get closer, they can bring with them a feeling of loneliness.

How Can You Handle Loneliness After A Relationship Ends?

- Accept your feelings of loneliness after a separation: You suddenly lost someone important in your life. It is not physically present, nor emotionally. You may also feel disconnected and removed from others. As you overcome the pain and heal of separation, you may experience periods of loneliness that can be a regular part of the process of moving on.
- Avoid having a relationship out of spite: Don't let the loneliness after your separation or divorce push you into another relationship too soon. If you are using a link out of spite to avoid loneliness or the emotions of a departure, you may need to reconsider. Instead, try spending a little time with yourself to recover before you start dating again.
- Join a support group for divorced people: You are not alone. Therapy groups offer the opportunity to gain help, understanding, and perspective from others who are going through a similar experience. Loneliness after a divorce is widespread, and you will likely find others in your same situation who are willing to speak, listen, and offer advice.
- Start a new routine: Losing a relationship can also mean that your lifestyle has changed dramatically. If you lived with your spouse or partner, you possibly had a daily routine. The longer that relationship or marriage has been, the more accustomed you would be to that daily routine. A separation can change all of that, and, as a result, you become disoriented and aimless. Methods such as feeding, sleeping, and even exercise routines are set aside, affecting your health and well-being. If you exercised regularly, do it again. Exercising can help stimulate endorphins, which could make you feel happier. So, tries to plan a new routine for yourself to see if it enables you to counteract some of the factors that contributed to loneliness after separation.
- Get Involved: Whether as a volunteer or joining a club, interacting with other people can stimulate endorphins in the brain two and help make you a happier person. Find volunteer options or clubs for people who share the same interests and stay open to new friends and support networks.

179

- Be kind to yourself: Find special activities that give you satisfaction. Try to enjoy some pleasant moments every day. Maybe you enjoy a walk, a foam bath, yoga, reading a good book, or listening to your favourite music. Whatever it is that brings you immediate happiness, spend time doing it. Developing good habits like these can help you manage the feeling of loneliness when you end a relationship.

How Long Can You Feel Lonely After A Divorce or Separation?

The length of feelings of loneliness after a divorce or separation depends on the factors you are dealing with the situation. The opinions of social isolation and disconnection from others may not be constant; a particular case can cause them, or they can appear and disappear. For example, holidays can bring periods of loneliness that then go.

For most people, loneliness after a divorce or separation is temporary and part of the grieving and healing process. If loneliness lingers and doesn't seem to end, it may be time to talk to your doctor, therapist, or other health care provider about chronic loneliness. They can help.

Impact on Children

It is essential to define some concepts to start our journey. Divorce is the act of dissolving or separating the marriage by sentence, with the effective cessation of conjugal coexistence or separating people who lived in a close relationship.

In Colombia, in the first seven months of 2016, the city with the most divorces reported by the Superintendence of Notaries and Registry was Bogotá with 2,923, followed by Cali with 1,238 and thirdly Medellín with 824.

Among the most frequent causes of divorce, infidelity is reported first, followed by financial problems, then the lack of balance in the time spent in the family, marital violence, and the lack of definition in the execution of the work. Domestic.

A divorce is then an event that occurs within the dynamics of the couple, which is a large percentage of families that do not happen at any given time but is part of a sequence of conflicts in which children are immersed both actively as passive.

180

Divorce Is Characterized by Three Stages

- Pre divorce stage: in turn, composed of two sub-phases, the phase of manifest conflict: in which the typical problems of the couple's life are maximized. There is dissatisfaction, discomfort, disappointment, emotional and physical withdrawal begins, but they may exist reconquest attempts. Then comes the second phase of emotional divorce, in which the positive effects are overridden by the negative ones, and a series of verbal and physical confrontations and attacks begin, in which attempts are made to place the children against the other parent.
- Trans divorce stage: legal, economic divorce and problems of custody and parental relationship begin, where on many occasions, the benefit of the children does not matter, which are used in the conflict trying to "earn them" through emotional blackmail, gifts, and privileges.
- Post-divorce stage: social or community divorce is involved, there is a conflict of loyalties in the children. But, at the same time, it is a critical stage because the preparation of mourning begins. There are new friendships and routines with the children, and a final psychological elaboration phase, with acceptance of the loss.

The Effects of Divorce

Depending on gender, children have different reactions to this event.

Children seem to have more significant difficulties in going through the crisis, in the intensity of their feelings and their duration. It is more frequent than they present more school problems than the girls, becoming much more irritable, and that some violent behaviors appear.

As for the girls, they will show their feelings with less violence, and they tend to withdraw and speak little; on some occasions, they become anxious or, on the contrary, they behave excessively well and present a better social, school, and emotional development.

In addition to gender differences, we have different ways of assuming parents' divorce according to age. In the first year of life, children do not understand the concept of separation but begin to notice changes in the environment, in the caregiver and routines.

Regarding development, in the stage of essential confidence vs Basic mistrust, which is why in this phase. The child must be given appropriate support, and their basic needs must be met by their caregivers, to stimulate

181

the development of confidence. If this accompaniment is not provided, it can manifest itself as an insecure attachment, with whims, irritability, sadness, changes in sleep and appetite patterns, and delay in meeting developmental milestones, constituting a response to maternal stress and depression.

Between 1 and 2 years, according to Erikson, the stage of autonomy vs shame and doubt. May manifest with excessive crying, difficulty being away from the mother, even for a moment. It is why she can use maternal substitutes, such as blankets and stuffed animals, and will also have difficulty sleeping or staying asleep.

From 3 to 5 years old, the stage of autonomy vs shame and doubt and the start of the initiative stage vs guilt. It could manifest as regressions to achievements obtained in previous stages of development, possessiveness, excessively good behavior, and on some occasions, aggressiveness.

In schoolchildren, those who go through the industry stage vs inferiority. There are more significant cognitive growth and a better understanding of the concept and the permanence of divorce. There may be a decrease in school performance. Also, they can develop feelings of loss, rejection, and guilt. There is a conflict of loyalties concerning their parents, for which they present concern about losing the father who does not live with them and being replaced, propensity to blame themselves for the dissolution of the marriage of their parents and even may develop reunion fantasies.

Adolescents are in the identity vs stage. Diffusion of identity; They may feel very anxious, highly concerned about their future, or present intense anger, in addition to outsourcing problems that can lead to drug, alcohol, and even rule violations.

Strategies to Improve Coping

We will focus on strategy according to the age and stage of development that the child is going through.

In infants, we must ensure early secure attachment with a trusted caregiver, consistency in routines, increased interaction time with primary caregivers, and reinforce positive social interactions.

In preschoolers, we must continue with consistency in routines; the child must have quality time with her parents, and they must understand that the child is full of doubts. So, she will ask repetitive questions that will help her in the processing of the information; Besides, your caregivers must provide accurate and appropriate information about the divorce process and explain that it will affect daily life.

The students need reminders that the divorce is final and that they are not to blame because at this stage tend to blame themselves for the separation of their parents. Additionally, they must maintain relationships with both parents, who must allow them to express their feelings openly.

As for teens, it is important to have quiet conversations about the reaction to divorce, and teens should not be held accountable for legal and financial issues, which should be apparent from the start; They may also need individual or group therapy.

Recommendations for Pediatricians

Pediatricians should spend time talking to the child alone during consultations, at the beginning and during the divorce, and after the process.

Dialogue with parents so as not to involve the child in the conflict; Besides, they should talk to them about essential sources of support.

The pediatrician should avoid taking sides or identifying with one parent and going against the other.

Bear in mind the possibility of suspected abuse or neglect and always make the proper notification.

Determine according to each case if the support of any other specialist is needed.

Recommendations for Parents

Always be careful with what they say and how they say it. Find the best way to tell children that parents separate; ideally, both parents should be present at that time. How you want to communicate it to the child will depend on the age, sometimes the use of drawings or stories can be useful.

Clarify to the children that they are not responsible for the separation and that it is not in their hands to recompose the marriage. Reaffirm that both parents will continue to love them the same after the separation.

Talk to all the children at the same time, regardless of whether they are of different ages, this way they can help each other. Prepare answers to the following questions: Who am I going to live with between my parents? Will

I have to move?

Clearly explain what will and will not change in your life. Avoid putting children as spies, messengers, or judges, and don't argue in front of them. Assure the child that he will be visited by the father who does not live with him and fulfil his promises.

Ensure that the visits are pleasant and that the child expresses when he gets home how well he spent with the other parent.

Conclusions

A divorce is an event within the couple dynamics in which conflicts occur; the children are going to be immersed. Children's feelings dissolution of the couple may be expressed in different ways, age the stage of development in they are. It must be taken into account early to intervene if necessary.

Children must always be accompanied in this process, clearly explaining what is happening and the changes that will come. Clarify to the children that they are not guilty of the moment the couple is going through and that it is not their function or their duty to unite their parents again. Children and their parents must have regular support and observations from health personnel.

Co-parenting Goals

One of the most challenging things for parents is to tell the children that father and mother are separating. Since this is a significant cut in children's lives, they should only be discussed with them once the separation has been firmly and finally decided. Parents' considerations as to whether a separation or divorce should take place with the children should never be discussed with the children. It would only unnecessarily burden the children, who, depending on their age, for example, because of school or puberty. Conversely, it should still be talked about a decided separation that is again delayed (for example, because one parent is always looking for a flat). Because the children inevitably notice when the parents are distant due to the final and upcoming separation. Here the children should not be left in the dark and thereby disturbed, but specific conditions created are.

Another question is how to convey to the later children of divorce that the parents no longer love each other. Only younger schoolchildren who go to primary school can understand from their thinking that the parents no longer understand each other and therefore have the opportunity to separate. It is much more difficult for smaller children. If they were told, for example, that the separation was due to constant arguments, the answer from their way of thinking would be rough: "But why then, I also quarreled with Linda from kindergarten and now we're friends again." Smaller children are therefore best told that father and mother no longer want to live together and that everyone wants to live their own life.

The reasons for the separation disputes should depend on age, be explained to the children briefly and only in a few sentences. Detailed justifications should be avoided since they regularly contain "adult issues" with which the children are entirely overwhelmed. In a way, this applies to adolescents who, because of puberty, are primarily concerned with cutting off parents and developing personalities. Conflicts of loyalty among children should be avoided at all costs to evoke. If, for example, one parent was left because the other had fallen in love with a new partner, the children would quickly say: "Papa doesn't want to live with me anymore, he fell in love with another woman." It awakens the feeling of the children that they have to stick to the abandoned parent and should no longer love the other one. Responsible parents should spare their children with this emotional balancing act.

Children Want to Know How to Proceed

Once the children understand that the parents are separating, especially smaller children and younger school children ask very pragmatic questions. These are, for example: "Where do I sleep (if we move out)?", "Is there enough space for my toys?" Or "Who will drive me to kindergarten?" Parents talk to children for the first time about the decided separation should have thought of an answer to all questions in advance. It also presupposes that the parents have at least roughly agreed on what future togetherness with the children should look. Also, the children should be involved in all questions relating to the future. If the mother is looking for a new apartment for herself and the children, she can Take children to the viewing appointment and say that these could be your rooms, and so we could furnish the apartment. If the new studio is renovated itself, the children can help. In this way, the children know how to proceed and experience a certain amount of security that takes away their fear.

How Parents Should Deal with It

Children have significant problems when the father and mother finally separate. When one parent moves out, the previous world collapses for

185

future children of divorces. From the perspective of the children, the family's security ceases to exist, they are initially completely disoriented and first have to learn to deal with the new situation. Even if every child reacts differently: Almost every child shows specific age-typical reactions, whereby the transitions are fluid.

- Babies and toddlers also notice when a parent moves out and thus separates with the toddler. The helplessness of the children often shows up in tantrums and aggressive behavior. Others are afraid and do not leave the remaining parent alone for a moment. Because according to the children's thinking, this parent could also leave them. Finally, some children go backwards: they wet themselves again or want the pacifier back; all of this was already a thing of the past. The parent with whom the babies and toddlers live should have patience and be there for the children despite their separation problems. Regular contacts or visits to the parent who has moved out should take place, even if only for a few hours. The children's fear of loss can be gradually reduced. It will take some time until the future children of divorce have security again, especially since there is no sense of time yet.

- Children of kindergarten age react in a similar way to babies and toddlers, albeit much more clearly. So, it can happen that they beat other children in the daycare centre, not lunch, eat like it, or refuse to go to the toilet. At this age, they are not aware that other people can perceive the world differently than they. Relationship and affection are developed through concrete "doing something together," in which the children see themselves as the focus. If a parent is less available due to move out, the children perceive as a love deprivation due to way of thinking. The children look for the reasons for this and believe that they are to blame for the separation.

- A typical example of this is that a child tends to tidy up his room after a long time, which he never did despite the parents' ranting, and now thinks: "Now I've cleaned up, my parents don't need to argue about me anymore. " Clear structures and relative orientation of what will be in the future are essential for children of kindergarten age. Both parents - especially the one with whom the children live - are required to give the children security and fear despite the separation. The reliability of the parents is the top priority here. Also, everything that is important for the children should be integrated into the new ways of life of the parents and the people to whom the children have a fixed relationship.

186

- When the children go to primary school, they can already partially understand what is happening in the family and how they are separated from children. The later children of divorce recognize that other people perceive the world differently than they do. The children think, however, that the others are expressing their actual intentions through their actions. The children cannot yet recognize the hidden intentions of other people. For the first time, children can understand the changes affecting them themselves through the separation of parents, as well as express feelings such as sadness and the desire for the parent to return. Even so, the children are helpless, sad, and angry. Sometimes school performance deteriorates and dealing with friends and classmates suffer. Also, there are the first conflicts of loyalty.
- On the one hand, some children would like to assist the "abandoned," "lonelier" parent who needs support, for example, by doing household chores. On the other hand, the children themselves need help from what they believe is the healthier parent. Most of the time, the children, therefore, want the parents to get together again, and there is no divorce with the children - which expresses the children's desire to avoid the conflict of loyalty. Parents need to be aware of this phase of their children. The parent grieving for the end of the relationship should not continuously burden the children with their problems. But the parent who ended the association should also handle it sensitively in the presence of the children. A piece of normality in the changed living conditions is desirable here. Also, recently, schooled children need a large part of their strength and energy to find their way in the new environment they are unfamiliar with. Parents should also take this into account when separating children.
- Older schoolchildren up to around 12 years of age recognize that the actions and intentions of other people can fall apart, whereby behind "unpleasant" effects can also be good intentions. Love and closeness between children and parents are no longer shaped by action, but by mutual feelings. It means concern for the well-being of others, combined with the recognition of goodwill. If the child recognizes the good intentions and beliefs of the parents, positive emotions are evoked. Conversely, there can now also be conflicts between children and parents come because of different attitudes and opinions - and no longer exclusively because of behavior that is perceived as unpleasant. Due to development, there may be strong solidarity between the children and one parent due to the separation or divorce. The children ally with the parent

187

injured by the separation and sometimes even assume the role of the missing partner, which the parent unconsciously accepts. It inevitably leads to alienation from the other parent. If this is recognized by the parent with whom the children ally, they can be manipulated extremely (so-called Parental Alienation Syndrome- PAS). Unfortunately, there are always cases in practice in which mothers abandoned by their husbands influence the children against the father in this way, which sometimes leads to the children breaking off contact. Other possible reactions from children of this age are that they lose all respect due to the constant arguments between parents about them. Because the parents fail their authority over the children, massive educational problems often arise. Again, the children should not be burdened too much with parental difficulties. The separation, the children, need the support of parents, in turn, have to seek help other than children because of problems. Also, the function of partner replacement overwhelms the children in the long run, since they deal with conflicts that are not age-appropriate. Due to the associated impairment of the ability to concentrate, the children's performance can drop. The future children of divorce must have fun in life, at school, in hobbies, with friends, with the support of their parents, so that in the event of separation despite having a child, they can again approach both parents with ease and joy.

- At the latest from around 15 years of age, the children can view things in a higher-level way, that is, to see and generalize their point of view and that of others from a "third person's point of view." At the same time, due to puberty, the children are busy separating from their parents and developing into their personality. Conversely, parents often seek consolation and support from their children because of the separation, which disrupts their development. The results are sometimes very violent reactions from young people, ranging from "zero bocks" to drug or alcohol consumption to the search for support from friends. However, some young people also take sides with a parent and are almost hostile to the other. And some young people want to have contact with both parents but are afraid that this will injure the "weaker" parent. If adolescents are older, it can also happen that they completely withdraw from the home where they want to move out or flee to friends. As a result, separation with children often leads to adolescents growing up faster than is right for them. One of the biggest problems for young people, when their parents are separated, is that the general support breaks down in the awkward phase of personal development. Even though adolescents are "rebellious" during puberty and often behave negatively towards their parents, they know that the parents are ultimately there for them. Despite the separation, the parents should therefore clearly reduce their problems vis-à-vis the young people. Young people are allowed to have their own experiences. However, the parents should convey to their children that they are there for them despite the separation with help and advice, if the young people want it. This Support should be offered to children even if they misbehave towards their parents. At the same time, clear rules are essential. Ideally, the parents talk about this and exchange ideas about the jointly observed development of adolescents.

These Are the Legal Conditions for Separation with Children

After the separation, other questions related to children are essential. It includes custody, the right to determine residence, the power of access, the right to information about the personal circumstances of the child, and maintenance for the children. In the context of the child, subsistence is regulated, the parent receives the child support in separation or the child support in a divorce.

Both Parents Have Custody

If the parents were married to each other (or have each issued declarations of care for the children), they have joint custody of the children, Section 1626 of the German Civil Code (BGB). It also applies to the period after separation or divorce.

A total of three areas of shared parental care in separation and divorce can be distinguished, § 1687 BGB:

- The decisions in matters of everyday life are made by the parent with whom the child is habitually resident. These include decisions about school tuition, the treatment of minor illnesses, or the specific stay with relatives.
- In matters of actual childcare, the parent who is authorized to handle decides when the child is with him. It includes the type of diet or bedtime.
- Decisions on matters of significant importance can only be made by parents together. Such choices include the choice of

school or vocational training, approval of operations (except in urgent cases), or fundamental decisions about where to live.

- A parent receives sole custody only if this is applied for at the family court. Child welfare is crucial. Only if this is endangered or impaired, can the court wholly or partially withdraw parental responsibility, § 1666 BGB? For example, there are dangers or impairments to the child's well-being if the children are at risk of being neglected or if urgently required healing treatments are not given. Another case that can lead to a complete deprivation of custody is the parents' unwillingness to communicate. For example, if the parents stop talking to each other after a bitter divorce war, this can lead to the custody of the person with whom the children of divorce are not habitually resident.

Right of Residence for Divorced Children

The question of whom the children should live with after the separation is of considerable importance in practice. For this purpose, the parents as an outflow of personal care - must agree on whom the child should have his permanent residence with, 1627 BGB. If this is not possible, the family court decides on the right of residence, § 1628 BGB. However, custody and power of residence determination must be separated. For example, the mother may have the right to determine home, but both parents have care.

Right of Access: The Parents Are Obliged and Entitled

The child has the right to deal with each parent, whereby each parent is obliged and entitled to deal with the child, Section 1684 (1) BGB. The child has its right to deal with parents, from which the parents can, in turn, derive their power to deal with the child. Conversely, the parent who is entitled to access should not forego dealing with the child for reasons of child welfare.

So that the handling is not impaired, the so-called ethical conduct clause applies to both parents according to § 1684 (2) BGB. According to regulation, parents "must refrain from, which affects the relationship of the child to the other parent or complicates the upbringing." It means that the parents are mutually prohibited from negatively influencing the child compared to the other parent. Also, grandparents, siblings, step-parents, and other vital caregivers have a right to deal with the children of divorce if this serves the child's best interests, Section 1685 (1) and (2) BGB.

If there are disputes about the handling or if this should be restricted or excluded for reasons of child welfare, the family court decides, §§ 1684 Abs. 3, 1685 Abs. 3 BGB. It also includes the cases in which the court orders "accompanied" ("sheltered") handling in the presence of a willing third party (e.g., from the German Child Protection Association) to rule out a risk to the well-being of the child or to initiate initial contact between father and child.

The Children Can Have A Say

Depending on how old they are, the children are allowed to have a say in custody, the determination of residence, and handling. For example, when dealing with the wish of even a six- to the seven-year-old child, the family court must take into account. For example, the withdrawal of custody from a parent against the will of a 14-year-old child is almost impossible. To exercise their rights, the children also receive from the court a method counsel assigned (known lawyer of the child), § 158 Act on Proceedings in Family Matters and Matters of Voluntary Jurisdiction (FamFG).

In practice, however, it is difficult for young children, especially small children, to have a permanent stay with the father, if the father works full-time while the mother is a housewife.

The Right to Information About the Circumstances of The Child

In practice, the right to information about the child's circumstances is rarely used following § 1686 BGB. The judicial officer decides on this claim, which is treated somewhat "neglected" by some family courts. According to this, the parents are obliged, if there is a legitimate interest, to provide the other parent with information about the child's circumstances unless this contradicts the best interests of the child.

This claim is significant if, for example, one of the parents has no dealings with the child. Here, this parent can request - usually every six months - two photos of the child, a copy of the school report, and a report on the development, interests, and health status of the child. It does not matter that the child does not want this information to be released. The claim is only excluded if there is a risk that this information will be misused.

Children Are Entitled to Maintenance

Maintenance is one of the questions that need to be dealt with when separating children or divorcing children.

Where to Find Help and Advice on Out-of-court Conflict Resolution

Even if many parents are willing to compromise after separation for the benefit of the children, a friendly solution cannot always be found. The local youth welfare offices offer help and advice, and they also provide information on the advice provided by other local bodies and institutions.

If no agreement is reached in this way either, the only option left is the way to the family court. Since laypersons cannot understand the matter, it makes sense to consult a specialist lawyer for family law. In difficult financial circumstances, legal aid can obtain. The lawyer will also be happy to advise you on this.

Core Concepts of Positive Parenting

The positive parenting style is a parenting style that is based on respect for children, raised with love, and, above all, doing so through non-violent behavior. Currently, there is a will of many parents for non-violent parenting. Still, on many occasions, parents need support, advice, and tools to manage the challenges and conflicts of family life daily in a positive and non-positive way. Violent.

What Is Positive Parenting and What Is It?

It is not easy to find a definition of positive parenting. Still, it does not matter the language in which it is spoken or where you are. In positive parenting, you work with the same objectives, and parents share a shared vision: use affection as a basis of education.

Positive parenting fosters the relationship between parents and children based on mutual respect, helping children to develop properly, and children to grow up so that they know how to relate to others in a non-violent and constructive way.

It is important to praise good behavior, setting clear rules, really listening to children, working as a team, and of course, using positive discipline instead of physical or psychological punishment.

Therefore, positive parenting is parenting that recognizes children as individuals with rights that must be respected.

192

How to Get Positive Parenting at Home?

Although below you will read some tips to achieve a positive upbringing at home, you must remember that it is a lifestyle, beliefs that must be had and respected in the family, and above all, you will have to forget about negative discipline in your home.

- Be a good example. Children need the case of their parents. If your child witnesses loving and respectful relationships at home, they will be more likely to adopt those same values.
- Understand your child's personality. Every child is dissimilar and may need unlike kinds of guidance to suit their personality. For example, a very active and stubborn child will need a different approach to positive discipline than a calmer and more reserved child.
- Think about the needs behind the behavior. If your child is jumping on the couch, it is because he will need to burn energy or maybe because you have been working too hard, and he wants to get your attention or simply because he is bored.
- Help your child express his feelings. Communication needs to work in a family that everyone knows and is taught to express feelings and also to share them before they are challenging to control.

Parenting Guidelines

Parenting as an educational process aims to guide children and adolescents to live well in the adventure of life, through intelligent and affectionate accompaniment by parents or significant adults.

The parenting guidelines are not recipes with which a good child is prepared, and they are diverse according to the culture, the family trait, the social content. Despite this, here are some that should be taken into account:

- Know and assume the rights of children and adolescents as responsibilities that adults have to guarantee their sound development.
- The masculine presence is essential in the development of the children and the family coexistence. Therefore, it is not only the mother's task to educate and raise.
- The proper treatment is having joy, availability of time and space to share with the children and the couple, the game, the

193

care, the accompaniment in work, and the strengthening of the emotional bond. It implies maintaining excellent communication and respect for the other from the difference, establishing agreements in the couple in terms of authority mediated by dialogue.

- Accompaniment at different stages of development, a 6-month-old baby is not the same as a 6-year-old, each has different needs; each step of the child is important and deserves attention and stimulation.
- Use the game as a learning tool where it is possible to develop a recreational way to feed the spirit, improve other functions, exercise the body, and finally be happy. Play should be a way of implementing values and generating creativity.
- Authority, rather than a way of giving orders, is expressing discipline with love. For them, the couple must establish clear rules since the child is young. When the norm is not complied with, create dialogue and define if it deserves a sanction, if this happens, it must be met, each time we give up oblivion and remain in the promise, we subtract points from the authority. In the same way that a sanction is applied, it is essential to establish recognition for the right actions. In creating power, it is necessary to forget that this traumatized the child, and that will be the way to achieve obedience in the other person.

Growth Development Goals

The upbringing in itself must bet to some development goals, that is to say, to some purposes that facilitate the effectiveness of the achievements and become a motivating force, these are:

- Self-esteem: judgment about oneself, is the ability to consider being capable of doing. The concept of self-esteem is mediated by self-recognition (recognizing corporality and the use of tools), self-concept (ideas around body parts) and self-definition (who thinks of himself in terms of virtue, competence, and power)
- Autonomy: Ability to develop and determine one's will against the norm.
- Creativity is the ability to create in the personal, the familiar, the artistic, the scientific, and the social, achieving superior well-being.
- Happiness: state of vital affirmation, the ability to make plans, or choices that are enjoyed.

194

- Solidarity: it is the promotion of the collective before any particular consideration; it is giving confidence.
- Health: it is the complete physical, mental and social well-being, and not only the absence of the disease.
- Resilience is the ability to cope after or during failure.

THE JOURNEY THROUGH SEPARATION FOR KIDS
Effects of Divorce on Kids

Divorces are very hard for couples, but more so for the children, they have in common. The numbers of couple's break-ups increase little by little every year, and the effects this has on children is very evident, in addition to be the majority.

For children, divorcing their parents involves many things on an emotional, social, and influential level. First of all, one of the figures, mostly the father, usually 'disappears' from the child's daily life to only visit him when appropriate, for example, weekends or weekdays.

It means that this person no longer directly influences the child's day-to-day life and their most common problems, only promptly. Also, if there are not many visits arranged, the parent can choose to be more benevolent and not correct the child as much, since he sees little.

The child may also experience forced coexistence with other people in his family with whom he has not chosen to live or is not accustomed. Sometimes, the time he spends with the father must be paid in a house that is not his own, but that of a relative, where he does not feel so comfortable.

Or perhaps, if he stays with the mother, he must also live with grandparents or uncles who are helping the new family nucleus to get ahead, probably against the wishes of the child.

Divorce can, in turn, mean a change of residence, city, school, and, therefore, friends and familiar environment with the disorder that this implies and with the impact it has on their development.

Sometimes, if the divorce has taken place because the father or mother has a new partner, a new person is also introduced into the child's life, which radically changes the relationship and perception of the child and the parent.

If the divorce has been traumatic, in turn, the child may be living with a depressed, sad, hostile, and angry person at the separation. This bad environment can also be reflected in the parents' relationship, with discussions and disagreements, with problems in sharing custody or in agreeing on essential issues in the child's life.

In a longitudinal study of 60 divorced couples whose children were

196

between 3 and 18 years of age at the time of separation, six particular tasks emerged as vital to the adjustment of the children.

Recognize the reality of marital breakdown. Often young children do not understand what is happening, and many older children initially deny separation. Others feel overwhelmed by fear of total abandonment or take refuge in fantasies of reconciliation. Most children face the facts towards the end of the first year of separation.

Separate parental conflict and tension and regain habitual goals. At first, children may feel so worried that they cannot play, do any homework, or participate in activities that were common to them. They need to put a distance between themselves and their parents to continue living their own lives. Most children do it a year and a half after separation.

Resolve the loss. Absorbing all the damages a divorce causes can be the most challenging job to do. Children need to adjust to the loss of the father who no longer lives with them, the loss of the security of feeling cared for and loved by both parents, the loss of daily family routines and traditions of the family: the loss of a whole Lifestyle. Some children need years to cope with these losses, and some never make it, bringing a feeling of rejection, contempt, and heartbreak to adulthood.

Resolve anger and guilt. Children understand that divorce, unlike death, is voluntary, and very often, they are furious for years against the father (or parents) for doing something so terrible to them. They look for the cause of the divorce is something they did or did not do. When they forgive their parents and themselves, if they do, they feel more empowered and more in control of their lives.

Accept the permanence of the divorce. Some children maintain for years the fantasy that their parents will rejoin, even after having remarried some accept the stability of the situation only after the psychology separation from their parents is reached in adolescence or early adulthood.

Achieve realistic hope regarding relationships. Some children who have adjusted well to other aspects of divorce fear the opportunity to establish intimate relationships for fear that they may fail themselves as their parents did. They can become depressing cynics or simply always doubt the possibility of finding lasting love.

Many children successfully overcome all of these situations and go through a divorce with their ego intact. The ability to do so seems to be related, partly to the child's adaptability and, in part, to the way parents handle issues related to separation and the challenge of raising their children alone.

In general, children of divorce have more social, academic, and behavioral problems than children from united households. It is particularly true in the case of boys. However, several factors influence how children adapt to this situation.

Long-term Effects of Divorce on Children

Today one in two marriages ends in divorce, and many divorced couples have children. Parents who are divorcing worry about the effect that divorce will have on their children. During this challenging period, parents are primarily concerned with their problems but are also aware that they are the most important people in their children's lives.

While parents may well feel heartbroken or happy about their divorce, children invariably feel frightened and confused by the threat to their safety. Some parents are hurt or overwhelmed by the divorce that they seek the help and comfort of their children. Separation can be misinterpreted by children unless parents tell them what is happening to them, how it affects them, and what their fate will be.

Children often believe they are the cause of the conflict between their father and mother. Many children take responsibility for reconciling their parents and sometimes sacrifice themselves in the process. In the shocking loss of one or both maternities due to divorce, children can become vulnerable to both physical and mental illness.

With great care and attention, however, a family can make use of its strength or positive factors during divorce, thus helping children to deal constructively with the solution to their parents' conflict.

Parents should be aware of persistent signs of stress in their child or children. Young children can react to divorce by becoming more aggressive, refusing to cooperate, or withdrawing into themselves. Older children may feel very sad or experience a sense of loss. Behavioral problems are widespread among these children, and their work at school can be negatively affected. Whether as teens or as adults, children of divorced couples often struggle with relationships and self-esteem.

Disorders Associated with Divorce in The Child

Divorce is a traumatic factor for both spouses and children, but it should not be dysfunctional. The dissolution of a significant relationship can produce emotional disorder, anguish, and suffering in the person who experiences it—even leading to depression, suicide attempts, psychosomatic illnesses.

Currently, divorce is socially accepted thanks to factors like the loss of the influence of religion or the rest of the family, the agility of divorce laws, etc.

Most people who get divorced experience depressive feelings, ambivalence and also mood swings. Recovery usually lasts approximately two years, during which psychotherapy would be necessary in many cases, to cope with these symptoms and the favourable improvement of the person and her environment, which can be of vital support in therapy.

Alternative Solutions

Children will have fewer problems if they know that their mom and dad will continue to act as parents and that they will continue to help them even when the marriage ends and the father and mother do not live together. Prolonged disputes about child custody or coercion of children to side with mom or dad can hurt the kids a lot and can add to the damage divorce does. Research shows that children develop best when parents can cooperate for their well-being.

Parents' continued obligation to achieve the well-being of their children is vital. If the child shows signs of stress, parents should consult their family doctor or paediatrician for a referral to a child and adolescent psychiatrist for evaluation and treatment. Additionally, the child and adolescent psychiatrist can meet with parents to help the family learn to minimize stress. Psychotherapy for the children of a divorced couple and divorced parents can be of great benefit.

Things Parents Should Avoid

When a relationship stops working, it's often better to part ways. But couples who have one or more children make this decision not only for themselves but also for their offspring—ten things you shouldn't do for your child when they break up.

1. Blaspheme About the Ex-partner In Front of Your Child

It is human to take revenge on a high emotional pain like disappointment, sadness, and anger. To endure what the separation does to you, you start by making the ex-partner wrong, pulling him over him, and getting some relief in the stressful separation period and afterwards. This behavior can be dubbed "broken heart syndrome."

But if children are affected by the separation, the rule is: stop! Your child is not the right recipient of your pain because it has to struggle with the situation and needs more support. It is essential to convey to your child that they are not alone, even if mom or dad has moved out.

No matter how deep the pain or how big the anger about the ex-partner is, don't let that out with your child. Since a separation or divorce of the parents affects the child anyway, it is essential to keep the adult problems away from your child as far as possible. It includes the resentment of the ex-partner because, for the child, it remains the beloved father (or mother) despite the separation.

If parents make the other parent terrible in front of the child, they deprive the child of access to his second parent. It doesn't matter who or whether someone is to blame for the separation. The child has a right to have a relationship with the separated parent and must not be forced to live the parents' resentment. Children want to be proud of both parents. If you curse about dad (or mom), children experience a devaluation of themselves.

2. Use the Child as A Messenger

After a breakup, preferably not wanting to speak a word to the ex-partner is an understandable wish. The disappointments are often too high; the emotional wounds too fresh. However, using the son or daughter as the bearer of messages in separation with a child is no alternative to talking to the former partner. "Ask dad if he gives you something for the school trip. He can still pay something!" Sentences like this one, which may even have an accusatory or angry connotation, do not belong here but should be clarified directly between the parents. The child is neither a messenger nor a judge. If it is misused for this role, the parents often unwittingly unload ballast on the shoulders of their child, who they are currently carrying.

One or more children keep you connected even after a divorce. Children together have a shared responsibility that is greater than the pain of the individual. It is essential to communicate and learn to bridge differences despite your situation.

3. Arguing in Front of The Child

As far as communication is concerned, it also says here: keep the problems between you and your ex-partner to yourself. The child will still notice that the mood is not right; even small children have highly sensitive antennas for the atmosphere in the room. Conversations that have the potential for disputes are best avoided in the presence of the child. If the parent's quarrel, it further increases the fear of loss of the child is insecure because of the separation.

If there is an actual friendly conversation in front of the child, you should pass the phone on: "Mom is on the phone, do you like to talk to her?" it conveys a feeling of togetherness instead of working against each other. A child needs to experience this in order not to get into loyalty conflicts between mom and dad.

4. Start A Competition for The Child's Love with The Ex-partner

"With dad, everything is always great, and I'm always the bad guy because you have to learn from me." Anyone who has agreed to a weekend arrangement with the partner will only know this problem too well. Understandably, one wants to make up for the lack of time together with the children with extra great excursions, restaurant visits, TV evenings, or the most generous Christmas. Forget it but not that of the child, the time together is one, because the knowledge a dad to have - despite separation - is the decisive factor. Therefore, a little everyday life does not spoil the precious weekend - on the contrary: Especially in everyday life, the parent who moves out of the shared apartment and only sees the child at certain times of visit is particularly missed. Rituals such as the bedtime story disappear overnight. It is all the more important to experience both parents as a regular part of everyday life despite separation by doing the homework together or going shopping together.

It's not about offering the kid the better program, because that's not what divorced children crave. A child needs the certainty that they have not lost either parent and, above all, that they can love both.

5. Pull the Child to Your Side

Unfortunately, children often become a game ball between parents who no longer understand each other. The supposedly only common denominator is the child. It doesn't justify conflicts carried out on the back of the child, but disputes are resolved precisely because of this common denominator by the parents. If the parents demonize each other, the child inevitably gets between the fronts and has to decide: Am I for Team Mama or Team Papa?

Children tend to side with the parent who suffers more. According to

201

children's logic, the child compensates for the lack of love of the other through his loyalty to this parent - which, of course, is not valid.

Always keep in mind that you and your partner have separated, not the child. Your child needs and loves both parents, and you should grant your child this right despite your differences.

6. Be Silent About the Reasons for The Separation

Children have no worries and quickly forget - one of the greatest mistakes of humanity. What is going on in the small minds and how suffering on the young shoulders should never be underestimated. Therefore, every child, even if it is very young, deserves an explanation if the parents separate. If descriptive words are omitted, the child finds its version of the account, and this usually does not work in his favour. Kids often reason that it is their fault that mom and dad no longer understand each other. They conclude that they could have prevented the separation with the right behavior. You should take this conviction from your child. Talk to your child and make it clear that the divorce has nothing to do with the child's behavior.

If the kids are a bit older, they often assume more responsibility when they are separated than their age. They worry about the parents and put their problems back when they see how bad the mother or father is. Here, too, an honest and open approach is essential to create glassy conditions. Separating parents is, of course, a burden for a child, but it should not give up its role as a child and take care of all worries.

Many children of divorce, especially children of primary school age, are ashamed of the problematic family situation. They compare themselves to the other seemingly perfect families and are embarrassed about their job. You can also help your child with conversations here. For example, ask your child whether they still know a child with separate parents (sure!) And whether this child now has two children's rooms? Take away the taboo your child may have imposed on itself because different parents are no longer uncommon these days.

7. Cancel Visits Too Often

The fear of losing one parent is very significant among children. Another aspect to reassuring your child comes to open, informative conversations: Keep appointments. All kind words are of no use if, in practice, dad visits are omitted continuously. Your child must be able to rely on you to have the separation heal the vibration. It means a lot to children if some things do not change despite the divorce. As a dad, have you always been at Sunday football tournaments? Keep trying to set it up. It shows the child that nothing has changed in the parents' love for him even after the divorce.

8. Want to Do Everything Alone

Separation is a time of crisis for everyone involved. A significant upheaval for parents and children demands all nervous resources. It is not possible to keep the children away from his anger about the ex-partner or to hide his pain. And practical changes such as moving, sharing property, or dealing with the authorities also require a lot of time, strength, and nerves. Get help during this time and accept support! Spending the kids, a weekend with grandma lets you breathe deeply and gives you space to deal with the situation. Impartial helpers, who are not one or the other faction, help your child through this stressful time and give you a breather.

9. Underestimate the Child's Injury

If the family situation changes drastically, children react to it very differently. In principle, a child should always have the feeling that it can express its feelings. Sudden tantrums, an obvious need to cuddle, or grief need not be a sign of a developmental disorder but are how your child adjusts to the changed family situation. Your child's behavior shows you what it needs. Find it more often than usual, react to it and respond to these needs. If it suddenly becomes conspicuously aggressive, talk to your child about what interests them.

10. Use the Child as A Pressure Medium

Unfortunately, it is not uncommon for parents to abuse their children as a means of pressure. If these or those conditions are not met, the other parent simply cannot see the child. Such threats are entirely inappropriate because blackmail with the greatest fear - of not being able to see the child anymore - also affects the child. Exploiting the other's fear poisons the atmosphere and disrupts a healthy relationship between parent and child.

Outstanding maintenance payments and other highly explosive and challenging issues are very, very difficult to solve - no question. But the child should never have to suffer for it because that is the least it can do for it. Treat it that way too, because, despite all the arguments, there is one thing that all moms and dads, divorced or not, agree on: love for their child.

Protect Kids from Parental Conflict

Today, out of every two marriages, one ends in divorce, and many of the divorced couples have children. Parents who are divorcing worry about the effect that divorce will have on their children. During this challenging period, parents may worry about their problems, but they continue to be the most important people in their children's lives.

While parents may well feel heartbroken or happy about their divorce, children invariably feel frightened and confused by the threat to their safety. Some parents are so hurt or overwhelmed by the divorce they seek the help and comfort of their children. Separation can be misinterpreted by children unless parents tell them what is happening to them, how it affects them, and what their fate will be.

Children often believe they are the cause of the conflict between their father and mother. Many children take responsibility for reconciling their parents and sometimes sacrifice themselves in the process. In the traumatic loss of one and both parents due to divorce, children can become vulnerable to both physical and mental illness. With great care and attention, however, a family can make use of its strength or positive factors during divorce, thus helping children to deal constructively with the solution to their parents' conflict.

Talking to children about divorce is difficult. The following tips can help children and parents with the challenge and stress of these conversations:

- Don't keep it a secret or wait until the last minute
- Tell your child along with spouse
- Keep things simple and direct
- Tell him/her that the divorce is not his / her fault
- Admit this will be painful and perplexing for everyone
- Reassure your child that they both still love him and that they will always be his parents
- Do not discuss with the child the faults and problems of each one of you

Parents should be aware of persistent signs of stress in their child or children. Young children can react to divorce by becoming more aggressive, refusing to cooperate, or withdrawing into themselves. Older children may feel very sad or experience a sense of loss. Behavioral problems are widespread among these children, and their work at school can be negatively affected. Whether as teens or as adults, children of divorced couples often struggle with relationships and self-esteem.

204

Children will have fewer problems if they know that their mom and dad will continue to act as parents and that they will continue to help them even when the marriage ends and the father and mother do not live together. Prolonged disputes about child custody or coercion of children to side with mom or dad can hurt the kids a lot and can add to the damage divorce does. Research shows that kids do better when their parents can cooperate for their well-being.

Parents' continued obligation to achieve the well-being of their children is vital. If the child shows signs of stress, parents should consult their family doctor or paediatrician for a referral to a child and adolescent psychiatrist for evaluation and treatment. Also, the child and adolescent psychiatrist can meet with parents to help them learn what to do to make the stress of divorce easier for the whole family. Psychotherapy for the children of a divorced couple and divorced parents can be of great benefit.

Although occasional arguments between parents are expected in any family, living in a battlefield of constant hostility and unresolved conflicts represents a significant emotional burden for any child. Screaming, fighting, arguing, or violence in domestic life foster fear and apprehensive reactions in children.

Having a child witness conflicts between his parents is an inappropriate role model for a person who is still learning to relate to others. Children whose parents have relationships full of hostility and resentment are more likely to have emotional and behavioral difficulties that will last beyond childhood.

Talking to a mediator or divorce psychologist can help couples air their recriminations and mutual resentments in a way that is not harmful to their child. Although it can be difficult, if the two parents make an effort to collaborate in this way, they will avoid the child the pain caused by a couple of relationships full of bitterness and resentment.

How to Reduce Conflict with Your Child?

Parents who are divorcing (divorced) must sit down to talk to their children and encourage them to say what they are thinking and what they are feeling. But be sure not to mix this with your feelings. Reassure your children that their opinions are important, valid, and healthy. Let them know that you can handle a conversation about feelings that can be even difficult or painful.

During these conversations, avoid trying to solve problems and change how your child feels. Instead, focus on listening and thanking your children for their honesty. Almost always, children feel a loss of family, and they may blame you or the other parent for what is happening in their lives. Therefore, you will need to be prepared to answer questions that your children may ask or address your concerns.

Turn conversations about divorce and how it's affecting your children into one continuous process. As they grow and mature more, your children may have questions or concerns that have not occurred to them before. Even though it seems like you've already talked about the same topics before, keep the dialogue open. If possible, sit down with the other parent, plan together how you are going to talk about what is happening.

If you think you will be very distressed, ask someone else (maybe a relative) to talk to your children. It is okay and healthy for children who see their parents sad or distressed, but if their emotions are too intense, they may feel responsible for their parents' feelings.

If your children see you dealing with a complicated emotion, try dealing with it in the healthiest way possible to set a good example for them.

- Make it clear that you know that it is reasonable to feel this way sometimes ("It's okay and it's normal for me to feel sad").
- Talk about how you will deal with this feeling ("Something that always helps me feel better when I'm sad is cooking cookies with you and playing outside. How about we do it?").

It is usual for children to have a lot of emotions about a divorce. Perhaps they feel guilty and imagine that they "caused" the problem. It is especially true if children heard their parents arguing many times for them. Children and teens may feel angry, scared, or worried about their future. If they express these emotions, reassure them that this is not the case and remind them that this is a normal feeling.

While children can suffer from divorce for quite a long time, the real impact is often felt over about 2 to 3 years. During this time, some may express their feelings. But depending on age and development, other children won't have the words to do it. So, they may act out emotions or be depressed. For school-age children, this may mean their grades drop, or they lose interest in activities. Look out for the "sleeping effect" in young children: They may take significant changes easy at first, but years later, they may have disruptive behaviors or challenging emotions. Communicating openly with children and setting an example for dealing with feelings healthily, even when they seem to be okay with the changes, can reduce problems later.

You may be tempted to tell a child not to feel a certain way, but children (and even adults) have a right to have their feelings. And if you force them to have a "happy face," your children are less likely to share their real emotions with you.

Group programs for children going through divorce that take place in schools or religious organizations are an excellent resource for children and families who need help getting through the early stages.

The Correct Road

- It is one of the most challenging things to do. But it's important never to say bad things about your ex in front of your children or in a place where they can hear you. Children pay special attention to these things. Research shows that the most critical factor in the long-term adjustment of children with divorced parents is the level of conflict they see between their parents. It puts children in a difficult place if they have to choose a side or hear negative comments about a parent. Just as important is recognizing real events. For example, if a parent moves or abandons the family, acknowledge what has happened. It is not your responsibility to explain the behavior of your ex-partner. But if your children ask you questions, you must answer them with as much neutrality and sincerity as possible.
- As tempting as it may be, don't use your children as messengers. There are many other ways to communicate with your ex-partner. Also, resist the temptation to ask your child what happened in the other house. Children are offended when they feel they are being asked to "spy" on the other parent. Whenever possible, contact your ex-partner directly about things like schedules, visits, health, or school problems.
- New relationships, assembled families, and new marriages are among one of the most complex parts of the divorce process. A newly constructed family may add more stress for a time and require another adjustment period. Keep communication open, allow children to spend time alone with parents, and watch for signs of stress to help prevent problems.

To Look for Help

Think about how to reduce stress in your life to help your family. The support of your friends, family, religious groups, and organizations like Parents Without Partners can help parents and children adjust to separation and divorce. Children can meet other children who developed excellent relationships with their separated parents and can tell their secrets.

Whenever possible, you should encourage children to have as positive a view of both parents as possible. Even in the best of circumstances, separation and divorce can be painful and frustrating for children.

Parents should also remember to take care of themselves. Try to keep some of the old family traditions while building new memories to share. Showing children how to take good care of their minds and bodies in difficult times can help them become more resilient in their lives. Remember that honesty, sensitivity, self-control, and time will help in the healing process.

SETTLING INTO A TWO-HOME FAMILY
Guideline for Managing Your Residential Schedule

It is a protection for the dependent sons and daughters of their parents that has the effect of preventing the sale of the home when they divorce or separate (in the case of not having been legally married).

When Does It Apply?

It applies when requested by the custodian and so the Court declares it and only while the sons or daughters are minors, or while their disability lasts, in the case of children who have a disability.

For purposes of a safe home, the minority of the sons and daughters can be extended to 25 years for study reasons. When custody is shared, the Court will have the discretion to choose which of the homes will be designated as a safe home, seeking the best welfare of the minors.

How Long Does the Right to Safe Home last?

The person will have the right to keep the designated safe home until:

- The son or daughter turns 21
- Until the son or daughter finishes studying (until the age of 25)
- The duration of the disability of the sons or daughters, even in their custody.

About Residence That Will Be Safe Home

- It is the home in which the couple lived with their sons or daughters as the main house. It can be a house or an apartment that the couple bought together, for example.
- It does not matter that the property belongs to only one of the parties (even who will not live it as a safe home).
- It also does not matter if the house was purchased during the validity of the marriage or the relationship. What the law seeks is to protect the minor or dependent and guarantee a home.
- This property may not be divided as long as the right to a secure home last.

209

- It does not matter that there are marital capitulations in cases where there is marriage. What matters is the best welfare of the minors, not to whom the property belongs.
- The right to a safe home does not end because the person who has it has a new partner. The reliable home is a protection for sons and daughters.

When Can You Claim the Right to A Safe Home?

At any time that is necessary during or after a Divorce or Custody procedure, one can claim the right.

Who Has to Pay the Rent or Mortgage?

It will depend on what the Court has or the stipulations (or agreements) reached by the parties included in the divorce decree. It is important to remember that this amount (and who pays it) will be taken into account when establishing alimony.

Co-Parenting in Long-Distance

The parenting plan consists of an agreement between parents who are committed to satisfying the needs of their children in the new condition of the co-parenting relationship.

The goals of a parenting plan are as follows:

- Provide for the physical care of the child
- Maintain the emotional stability of the child
- Provide for the needs of the child, constantly changing
- Explain the authority and responsibilities of each parent
- Minimize the child's exposure to harmful parental conflict
- Protect the best interests of the child

If it is well designed:

- will reduce disagreements;
- will lower the battle;
- will help the family understand and accept the change;

- guide parenting behavior and co-parenting relationship;

Parenting plans can be divided into four models according to the needs and characteristics of the parenting couple and the family unit: basic parenting plans, long-distance parenting plans, safety-focused parenting plans, highly structured parenting plans.

The married couple transforms with the arrival of a child; it also becomes a parental couple: a system that sees two individuals cooperate for the growth of a third, but which in turn evolves into a triad. Spouses and children thus become a "small group" of a multi personal type, such not only for the presence of multiple individuals but for the two internal development lines that come into being in terms of processes of regulation and internalization of relationships.

The relationship regulation process offers us a measure of how a given behavior can have a regulatory or deregulatory effect on the other. Together with the relationship internalization process which can contain all those personal, emotional and profound meanings, with which we "read" that specific bond that binds us to the other.

Let's look at these processes in concrete terms: a child's expression of anger is welcomed by parents, listening. The son is taught to "normalize" emotion anger through words, thus seeking a connection between feeling and the cause of it. The parents allow in this listening a regulation of the emotional state of the child. They are starting a process of rationalization that helps the child to understand his anger without acting negatively. At the same time, the child internalizes an open and empathic mode of relationship, capable of offering containment even to negative emotional states (internalization).

It is in the face of anger events, requests for autonomy, the definition of rules, exploratory requests that a parent "becomes" such: he experiments, tries, makes mistakes, and repairs, thus defining his parenting function. This function includes all those practices that the parent puts in place to bring up their children that are accompanied by ideas, beliefs, and expectations that the parent has, as well as emotional, therefore emotional factors.

The union of the parenting function of both parents allowed researchers and scholars to study the family group no longer through the dyadic model (mother-child; father-child; parents-parent). It was considering the triangle, as that relational configuration that forms the basis of the emotional system of the family, whether nuclear or extended. The use of the new setting, analysis and evaluation of family dynamics, allows the whole system to be supported in parenting paths with a view that defines the complexity of the triad as a valuable tool, avoiding the risk of "fragmentation of the system and a loss of the total sense of the relationship. ".

This change allows us today to speak of "co-parenting," which is the union of the practices that the parenting couple puts in place to support their child in healthy personal development. Co-parenting can be observed concretely through specific indices, such as solidarity, antagonism, division of labour, and mutual commitment.

Solidarity is configured as a form of inter-managerial cooperation whereby there is an action by the parent that is exercised and validated by each other, contributing to a climate of family integrity.

On the other hand, the antagonism on family conflicts is configured, which appears unhealthier for the health and adaptation of the child, those concerning the management of the child himself, compared to those adequately married. The antagonism is configured an action opposite to the index of solidarity, the parent validates, supports the operation of the other parent. In the opposition are noted: mutual devaluations, competitiveness, and a distance between parenting ideas. The latter indicates the presence of different beliefs and, therefore, various practices that tend to generate disharmony.

The division of labour appears to be a crucial task to which both parents must carry out, especially in the transition to parenting phase, in particular for all those "practical" tasks performed for the physical subsistence of the unborn child.

Last but not least, mutual commitment is considered as a "needle of the balance" in the dynamics of entanglement, engagement, and emotional disengagement. In the case of involvement, the parent tends to be intrusive towards the child, seeking emotional support in him, even before the spouse or entrusting the child with inadequate decision-making power. At the opposite extreme lies the emotional disengagement in which the co-parent disagreement generates a communicative fracture between the spouses a withdrawal from a need for shared need. Ultimately a failure to respond to the problem raised.

Parents, like architects and heads of the family, create relationships jointly. (JP McHale, 2010)

In the triadic relationship, the parent, therefore, establishes a connection, responding to needs, behaviors, and requests that become increasingly structured. It is in this complex construction that the parent experiences:

212

- the ability to exercise a practical function or to experience, over time, an educational self-efficacy, first detectable in the ability to solve the problem, secondly in preventing it;
- parental competence, that is, the set of choices and acts which presuppose at the base a transversal ability which is that of carrying out the care of children;
- satisfaction, or that subjective dimension of parental experience;
- the attribution is the ability and the tendency the parent has to trace "causes" and "events" with an internal or external locus, concerning himself and the child.

The whole and the parts are complementary and indispensable to each other. (Spiegel, 1971)

Although there is, therefore, individuality and a dyadic relationship that generates a necessary degree of separation, healthy co-parenting will always work for the establishment of a heterogeneous but at the same time integrated triangle.

Co-parenting Tool

The Court of Civitavecchia is proving to be at the forefront in the care of conflictual separations. It proposes the parental plan tool, borrowed from the parental coordination of Debra Carter, able to articulate and define almost all aspects of parenting, thus offering parental couples a solid structure to refer to for the management of minors.

These are the basic rules of the parenting plan.

Both Parents

- Maintain functional communication with the children
- Maintain regular contact with the other parent and be collaborative with each other
- Strictly follow the parenting plan
- Contact the other parent immediately in the event of an emergency involving their children

The Placing Parent

- Share all information about the child with the other parent (e.g., school, teachers, activities, friends, etc.)

213

- Be flexible and support the child's relationship with the other parent. It must not disqualify the other parent, nor control or interfere in the communication between the parent and the child

The Transition for Your Child

The couple breaks down, and the family structure changes: one is no longer "spouses," but remains forever parents how to accompany and support children in this transition.

Happy families all look alike; unhappy families are each in their way.

No couple lightly decide to separate, especially if there are children. When it comes to determining in this sense, usually, the crisis has been going on for some time, and the situation is no longer recoverable. If everything has been tried to save the relationship, but to no avail, separating may be the only possible solution, even in the interest of the children, for whom it is devastating to live in a climate of perpetual conflict or hostility.

Beyond those who have made the final decision to separate, the couple's crisis never has a single "culprit," even if the partners, overwhelmed by sadness, anger, and resentment, can mutually bear responsibility and make heavy accusations.

But how do children live all this? And how to protect them in such an awkward moment?

Children First of All

All parents, when it comes to separation or divorce, are concerned first of all about the well - being of children. Still, unfortunately, it is not so easy to always act adequately, in an affair that first of all affects us as people, which destroys such a great life project.

Many, despite good intentions, fail to put aside mutual grudges and face conflicts in a " separate home, "so children often become real emotional hostages in the struggle between ex-parents.

In the Shoes of The Little Ones

A separation or a divorce can put even the most reliable people in crisis. It is painful to live to mourn for the end of love, a life plan, face detachment,

214

lose our reassuring habits and have to rebuild a new life, completely different from what we were used to it. However difficult it is to separate, in this significant change of life, as in all variations, there is always the possibility of a rebirth, of redemption, of future happiness, which the adult can glimpse and desire.

The condition of children is different: the family is all they know, their existential dimension, therefore they feel threatened at an intense level, in their inner security and identity. In addition, adults have an all-round view of what is happening and, for better or for worse, they are the protagonists: they know the situation well, they can confide in friends, ask for the help of a trusted person or a professional, talk to lawyers, so somehow be " active " in this painful process. Children, on the other hand, passively undergo something that most of the time, they don't understand, and often they do not have the words to express their doubts and all their suffering. For this reason, both parents must make an effort to identify themselves with their children, trying to put themselves in their shoes.

To Manage Children's Emotions, One Must First Manage One's Own

In the complicated process of separation, we often focus on the practical aspects and seek support concerning the real difficulties of management and organization. It is crucial, but it is even more essential to take care of the emotional element, which is the cause of most difficulties, both for adults and children.

In this challenging moment, children have an extreme need to be supported and helped, even if they don't show it. First, you need to oversee them and make an effort to understand what they think and what they feel. Then you have to listen to them, let them express them, help them identify their emotions, answer their questions. The goal is to " filter " the earthquake that separation entails and manage the situation in a way that protects serenity and interests as much as possible.

Parents must first be able to understand and manage their emotions, which is by no means easy or obvious. When a plane loses altitude, we know that first, you have to wear his oxygen mask, only after you can help children and people in need. Why do parents who part ways forget it so often?

Bright Minds: Clear Agreements, Confused Minds: Impossible Solutions

First of all, it is necessary to distinguish the problems deriving from the separation from the issues that led to the departure. The first category includes all the organizational issues related to the new family structure, but often, behind the impossibility of finding satisfactory solutions to the practical questions, they conceal all past emotional problems. Thus conflictual, mutual distrust, grudges, desire for revenge, or emotional blackmail (and not only), affect the already difficult path of family reorganization.

Frequently, partners need the neutral ground to negotiate the agreements that will govern their future relationships. But often they need even more to work on their destructive emotions and be able to establish a "peaceful" climate to continue exercising parental function together.

Clear thoughts and emotions are even more important than clear agreements because the latter is a direct consequence of the former. Separating "physically" is not enough if all the tensions and grudges remain alive, and in the first place, the minds and hearts of the ex-spouses are not pacified.

When Love Ends, The Parent Couple Remain

If it is clear that separation is the consequence, certainly not the cause of the couple's problems, it is equally evident that this "solution" certainly cannot solve everything as a " magic wand. " The problems remain and must be addressed, both personally and together, as an "ex-couple." If you can separate from your spouse, you do not divorce your children. When the marital relationship ends, an indissoluble entity remains to be taken into account: the parental couple.

Children have the right to have a mom and dad to take care of them, even if separated. Partners must necessarily continue to exercise their parental role together, agree on a joint educational line, and make shared decisions. Otherwise, the divorce will turn into a family and educational disaster.

What to Say to Children?

In comparing children with the decision to separate, you must first keep against their age, as well as their personality and maturity.

216

However, hurt and confused you may be, when you talk to them, you have to be precise. Avoid ambiguous messages and reassure them. Even if mom and dad are no longer together, you are still a family, and they will always have two parents who love them and protect them. The relationships between parents and children will not change, even if some practical arrangements will change: for example, Dad will no longer live here, but you will feel every day and see you regularly. Or, we will move house, but you would always have your bedroom where you can bring all your things, and we will always be close to you.

Of course, the proper concepts and words depend on the age and maturity of the child. The point is to be sincere, not to lie, but to transmit trust and hope, even in this challenging situation. Make the children understand that your parents are doing your best to manage the problems, and you will always take care of them, so they have nothing to fear.

Avoid The "Traps" Of Childhood Thinking

Children have a childish mentality, so we must not take anything for granted: what is visible to us may not be for them. At the same time, they can be convinced of things that, in an adult perspective, appear absurd and unreasonable.

Giving clear messages will help the little ones, who live in a "magical" world, not to hope too much for a miraculous reconciliation (even if they secretly do so) and to accept what is going on. It must be made clear that the separation is due to issues that concern only the parents. To appease any feelings of guilt due to infantile egocentrism, that is, to the way of thinking, typical of children, whereby everything that happens has in some way dealing with them. Being guilty can also be a defence against the experience of impotence because if a problem is due to us. We can do something to change it, and perhaps by behaving better, if it is not expected to us, we cannot do anything about it. It is why we need to be clear, avoiding both that they feel responsible for what happened and that they are under the illusion that they can change things.

To prevent them from making the fantasy of being children of a "mistake," make it clear that when you got married, you fell in love, but things changed later, and now you don't get along anymore: they were born because they have been desired and are children of their parents' love.

No to Confusion, Yes to Fixed Points

Hesitations, sudden changes of direction, and wrangling continue to

217

confuse and destabilize the children, who instead need certainties: understand what is happening and what will happen in the future helps them to deal with the situation in a more serene. They also need material safety: knowing where their things are, keeping their habits, having regular schedules, and life patterns.

The smaller a child is, the more aspects related to habits and routines are fundamental, because they are his "safe bases": recognizing the environment that surrounds him means mastering him, feeling adequate and competent. For this reason, it would be advisable to avoid, where possible, the removals and organize themselves so that the children remain in the marital home together with the cohabiting parent. But soon have own space at the home of the non-cohabiting parent, also to stay in bed, according to the agreements made. The ideal is a joint or, in case, shared custody, in which both parents divide, and ideally share, the management of children and all responsibilities regarding their growth.

Avoid Manipulation and Deployment

How do children experience the pain and inevitable conflicts that accompany every separation? It depends on the age and personality of the children, but above all, on the attitude of the adults.

If the youngest children experience the situation mainly as a reflection of their parents' mood, the older ones will develop their ideas, which will be all the more independent and autonomous the higher their age and maturity. The problem is that all children, due to affective and cognitive immaturity, are particularly vulnerable to manipulation, even the most subtle ones, which are indeed particularly harmful because they are less evident and more "subtle." If the young child risks to live in an adhesive and unmediated way the suffering of the parents, the older one risks entering a game of sides, intrigue, and manipulation, of which he is ultimately the only real victim. Unfortunately, many parents, even unconsciously, frame their children in their dynamics, so strong is the emotional charge of the situation.

Always Safeguard the Image of The Other Parent

Each parent must protect the image of the other in the child's mind: however inadequate he/she may have been as a spouse; everything must be done to put him in a position to be a good father or a good mother. It is not to be generous towards him, but because our mind is founded on two pillars: the maternal and the paternal. Destroying one of these supports, which are relational but also internal, means undermining a developing mind at the base and, in fact, boycotting our child's mental balance. Devalue or demonize the other parent is like detonating explosive charges in the foundations of a building: we don't know exactly how, but surely sooner or later, this will crack or collapse.

In addition to never speaking ill of the ex-spouse in the presence of children, special attention must be paid to indirect or subliminal messages. One should be calm when they go to the other parent, welcome them with a smile when they return, do not interrogate them, do not use them to "spy" the former, not to use them as an emotional "crutch" or "substitute" for the absent spouse.

Consequences and Risks of Separation for Children

Unprocessed separation can have severe consequences for the psychic development of children. First of all, a child who is not serene from an emotional point of view does not have a "free mind." Therefore, he cannot "invest" adequately on a cognitive level, with the risk of developing school and learning problems. Furthermore, he has more chances of being involved in an "entangled" bond with the cohabiting parent, especially if perceived as unhappy and alone. It triggers those "role reversal" dynamics" So the child takes care of the parent, while it should be the other way around. Often the "adultized" child is happy because he feels useful and essential, while the parent is reassured by the pseudo-maturity of the child and gratified by this "special" relationship. Still, all this has severe consequences for the development of the child, also on an emotional and social level.

The children of separated or unhappy couples, once they grow up, can fall into the unconscious trap of " repetition compulsion, ". The divorce will lead them to build complicated relationships, reliving the family drama, but transforming it from passive into active, as a defensive way to face pain and fear of relationships.

Ask for Help

Our whole life is made of detachments, and children must be helped to metabolize this separation, painful and premature for them, by adults who, in turn, have (or are) metabolizing it. In this sense, external help, such as psychological counselling with the parent couple or the whole family, can be invaluable. Until even one of the parents, however unconsciously, accepts the separation, this mathematically cannot be accepted by the children.

In the complicated process of restructuring family life, we need to help them express emotions, which otherwise can channel themselves into psychophysical symptoms: agitation, insomnia, nightmares, school problems, eating disorders, aggression, anxiety, depression. All expressive channels can be used in this sense, also based on the age and personality of the child: in addition to words, there are drawings, role-playing, and symbolic games, stories, and tales to share or invent. These channels, to the function of expressing emotions, have an even more critical purpose of organizing them, giving order and meaning to one's inner experience.

Finally, asking for help from an expert, but also from a trusted person, in addition to ensuring immediate support. Also, transmits an essential message to our children: in difficulties, there is always someone who can help us, there are resources to be activated and solutions to search for it. Suffering is part of life, and it must be accepted, but, above all, it can be transformed into positive strength and energy for the future.

Parenthood After Divorce

Divorce is a very complex event to be faced within a family. There are as many "types" of divorce as there are families, and each family has its particular representation of separation.

It is how James Lehman, an expert on youth discomfort and problematic teenagers, begins to talk about it, specifying that he does not want to overlap with psychologists and professionals in the field, but only to make some observations that arise from his long experience with the boys.

For some families, observes the expert, divorce originates from the inability of adults to continue to get along, to solve problems, or communicate with each other effectively. In other families, divorce is the acknowledgement that things are not working for the good of all family members. In still other families, divorce is a way to end an abusive or destructive relationship, in which case the boys gain a psychological advantage, even if they still face fear and confrontation with the abusive parent.

The reason why a divorce is a traumatic experience for the guys involved is that things are changing entirely for them, and the future now looks full of unknowns in their eyes. The most influential people in their lives have decided to go on different paths. The boys, especially if still very young, use their parents to manage their fear of the unknown.

When young people become anxious about the future, they have an unconscious mechanism that tells them that their parents will take care of whatever is disturbing them. They do it often and almost without thinking about it. Divorce is, therefore, traumatic in that it overwhelms young people, who do not have the tools or experience to manage the feelings and changes that are upsetting their lives.

Each boy faces them differently, depending on his character or nature.

"Fear" is often the prevailing feeling, as they fear that they will lose what they have and that they will not be able to have what they want. In one case, you will see a boy making a commitment and doing well in school. In another, you will see one giving up and stopping his commitment.

These two very different reactions can also occur in the same family. It means that a boy faces his fear and insecurity by isolating himself, while his brother focuses on external things like school or sports.

Some kids deal with their fear and anger by projecting them out and hitting others. One locks himself in his fortress, and the other comes out to challenge the enemy.

The primary emotions involved in a divorce are fear, anger, and pain. The general concern for kids is that things are changing, and they don't know what they are turning. Passion stems from having no control or power over the situation. And the pain from the real fact that the family they knew is gone. It is as if she were dead, and over time they must mourn her.

Parents see these signs. Anger manifests itself verbally or physically, through greater oppositionality and defiant attitudes, inappropriate behavior at school, or is directed towards other siblings or the cohabiting parent.

Fear also manifests itself through a closure process. The boys isolate themselves emotionally and physically, spend more time in their rooms or outside the home. They may seem more mysterious. Instinct drives them to believe that withdrawing into themselves is the best way to protect themselves.

Other boys will show different stages of pain. They can "bargain" with their parents trying to understand how to keep them together, and they will deny the sense of divorce. They will get angry at what it means to them and, eventually, if it is a normal process of working out the separation, they will come to accept it, but this takes period and effort.

No matter how the kids "handle" the divorce, they generally don't want to

221

talk to any of the parents about it, which creates problems for those parents who desperately want their children to understand what's going on from their point of view.

Children derive energy from different sources, but above all, from their parents and their family system. When they are mainly young, parents and family are their only source of strength.

So, the first object parents need to recognize is that when divorce is announced to them, kids will experience a lot of insecurity about what their future holds. Parents may also feel insecure but are unable to handle this insecurity. The boys, on the other hand, are entirely dependent.

It is a sad but frequent fact, Lehman points out, that many boys end up in poverty after the divorce because the money that was once intended to support one family must now support two. The leading cause of poverty among single-parent families in the United States is divorce. It scares the kids. They ask themselves; Will we have enough food? Will I have the clothes I need? Will I still be able to go to the mall to shop? Will we be able to do the similar belongings?"

These queries go through the boys' heads. Some worries have to do with the happiness of parents and family, and some are self-centered. Parents will do well to attend these belongings when they conversation to the kids about the divorce.

Develop A Culture of Responsibility in Your Home

Both parents must develop a culture of responsibility in their home once the separation or divorce has taken place.

A "culture of responsibility" position is one that tells kids: "You are still responsible for your behaviour here at home." So, it doesn't matter what is going on the home of the feelings, the boy is experiencing, including obvious and legitimate ones, the boy is responsible for his behavior.

It is necessary, stresses Lehman, to be structured and transparent after a divorce. This behavior is more useful for children rather than "letting down" their guard and altering their values for the difficult time the kids are going through. It must be remembered that it is precise during difficult times that we need a structure that is as reliable as possible.

Limits, responsibilities, parental support, external support when necessary: these factors are all part of a culture of accountability within the family. Boys experience a whole range of emotions when separation and divorce occur. "Divorce" and "separation" are only formal terms. Once a parent leaves, the adverse emotional experience begins, regardless of how it is labelled.

They had a structure in family life that clearly defines each child's responsibilities defines how they should treat each other and how they should treat the parent. The limits must be clear.

Problems occur at the time of return, the use of the telephone, the time spent on the computer and TV. The expectations regarding school commitments and other commitments should be kept very clearly, holding young people always responsible for not respecting their responsibilities, preventing them from flying over things that are wrong because of their divorce.

This without being punitive, but consistent. Always staying available if the children want to talk about divorce or any other topic, making them feel they are available for comparison without specifically mentioning divorce.

When necessary, of course, external support can be sought. Some types of counselling can be beneficial for those kids who are experiencing feelings of particular pain.

Furthermore, if the kids are already old and test the limits set physically, or in a threatening way, one should not avoid turning to the police officers.

There are many situations in which children perceive a power vacuum and try to fill it if the parent does not. It can be particularly problematic in families where there is a teenager, or in families where children no longer live with the parent who most represented authority and kept the limits.

What to Do and What Not to Do After A Divorce

Many things should be done or avoided after a divorce. Lehman points to some crucial for him.

Don't force kids to talk about divorce if they don't want to. Being available but not demanding, letting them know that there are other resources available outside the family for this.

Hold kids accountable for their behavior. If they are misbehaving, they must be explicit, letting them know that even if kids act in a certain way because of the divorce, they will still be held responsible for their behaviour.

223

Don't talk negatively about the other parent. It is never a good idea.

Don't jump into another relationship by expecting the kids to accept the new person. A new relationship can soothe the sense of loss for the adult, but for children, it is often just confusing and frustrating.

Don't try to have deep and meaningful conversations with your children about divorce. They can act as "adults," although still particularly young, they are not small adults.

Recognize that things have changed.

Don't share all your terror, anxiety, irritation, resentment, or pain with them. They are not at a level of development where they can manage it. Often, it makes them feel like they should take care of the parent, which is not a good condition for them.

Plan and structure the family organization without emotions, letting the children know what roles will change. You don't have to be "democratic" in this: you don't have to ask for their opinion or put it to the vote. It is not helpful for kids to put this responsibility on their shoulders.

"Daddy or Mom Allows Me to Do It at His House"

Each parent must develop a culture of responsibility in their home. What happens in the other's house is none of his business, except in cases where the safety of the child goes away. There is no need to leave room for the child to create an alibi for breaking the established rules.

If a son says, "Dad allows me to do it at his house," we simply have to tell him that he will have to wait to be back to the father to do it again because, in this other chaos, there are consequences for that behavior instead.

The way your ex exercises his parenting can be frustrating. However, you should avoid trying to control what is happening in your home. It would be a dead-end street. There are many situations where parents cooperate after separation or divorce. Still, people get divorced because they don't love each other anymore, so cooperation can't go that far.

Another problem is that many ex-spouses tell their children details of the marriage that they would prefer not to know. It is a common occurrence, and parents must "work" in order not to give them power over their behavior with their children.

First of all, if you show a child that this information has power over

224

himself, he will use it in certain situations. So, it's better to say something like, "Whatever your mother says at home, discuss it with her. It isn't a place to talk about it."

Personally, Lehman continues, I believe that details of divorce should not be discussed. Better to say, "This is Mum's opinion. Talk to her. At my house, I don't blame your mother for anything, and I won't let her blame me."

Separation and divorce usually do not occur in a peaceful and accommodating marital situation. The couple often happens after quarrels, clashes, blame, insults, and bad feelings. For better or for worse, the children witnessed what happened and know the truth.

Parents who pursue the "culture of responsibility" teach their children using apologies, and blaming others do not justify their inappropriate or irresponsible behavior.

If a child is taught not to make excuses and not to try to justify inappropriate behavior, they will be more prepared to understand when the other parent is using excuses and justifications to explain their behavior.

When Do You Need A Family Counseling Service?

Family counselling is a compassionate issue. Some therapists argue that it shouldn't include both parents because this creates an "artificial" situation and leads children to develop the fantasy that their parents will get back together.

On the other hand, some therapists believe the family should face divorce as a unitary system.

Many variables come into play when deciding which path to take with a therapist. However, one thing is clear: the boy should have the opportunity to see someone but should not be forced to do so if the parents manage the divorce effectively. If a child has behavioral problems that result from, or are intensified by, a divorce, help should focus on him or how he can learn how to handle the difficulties and feelings behind his behavior.

Therapy, Lehman concludes, should be flexible enough to involve everyone in various combinations, while avoiding sessions that include both parents with their children at the same time, unless necessary. Before these sessions, strict basic rules and a precise "agenda" must be agreed upon by both parents.

Probably, the differences in perception, interpretation, and behaviors that led first to divorce can be reproduced within that artificial situation. In some cases, children will not want to participate in this kind of therapeutic activity.

In my experience, Lehman concludes, if kids manage divorce well and other areas of commitment in their lives, they shouldn't be pushed to get involved. On the other hand, if they have behavioral problems or academic performance, behavior management therapy is needed.

Divorce carries an inherent risk of harm to the kids involved. The faster adults who face divorce take responsibility for being parents rather than spouses, and the more likely children will have to adapt to the new reality of their lives.

How to Work on Blended Family

Since many second marriages include children from previous relationships, "mixed" or "adoptive," families are more common than ever.

When families "mix," however, things rarely progress smoothly. Some children can resist changes while you, as a parent, can feel frustrated when your new family isn't working the same way as your previous one.

While merging families requires adjustment for everyone involved, these guidelines can help your new family work through the growing "pains" or difficulties. No matter how tense or stressful things seem at first, with open communication, mutual respect, and a lot of love and patience, you can develop a close bond with your new stepchildren and form a loving and successful family.

What Is A "Blended" Family?

An established family or family is formed when the two partners build a life with the children from one or both of the previous relationships, recomposed or "mixed." The process of creating a new mixed family can be a rewarding and challenging experience. While parents have the opportunity to approach modern weddings and a new family with great joy and expectation, their children or the children of the new spouse may not be as enthusiastic. They will likely feel uncertain about upcoming changes and how they will affect relationships with their natural parents. They will also be concerned about living with new brothers and sisters, who may not know well, or worse, those who may not like them. Last but not least, the concern of future brothers who might arise from this relationship.

226

Tips to Make Your Blended Family A Successful Family

Trying to turn a mixed family into a copy of one's first family or ideal family often causes confusion, frustration, and disappointment and is the antechamber of failure. Instead, it is essential to welcome the differences and consider them the starting point for your blended family to be a success.

- Solid marriage. Without marriage, there is no family. It is more challenging to take care of marriage in a mixed family because you don't have much time for yourself as a couple, as is the case in most first marriages. The spouses will have to grow and mature in marriage while you are parents.
- I was civil. If family members can be public with each other frequently, without fuss or excess, but also without ignoring each other, intentionally trying to injure or completely withdraw from each other, you are already on track.
- Respect first of all. It does not only refer to children's behavior toward adults. Respect should be given not only based on age but also because everyone is now also a member of the new family.
- Members of your mixed family may be in various stages of life and have different needs (for example, boys and young children). They may also be at dissimilar phases in accepting this new family. All family members need to understand and have respect, understanding, and patience for these differences.
- Leave mental space for the growth of the new family. After a few years of living together, it is hoped that the family will grow and that the members will choose to spend more time together and feel closer to each other.
- In order to have the best chance of success in creating a mixed family, it is essential to start thinking and planning how the new family will and will function before the wedding takes place. Clarity and predictive ability are always a necessary key to the proper functioning and future harmony.
- Knowing how to wait is the keyword. Often when you have survived a painful divorce or a separation and have finally managed to find a new love relationship, the temptation can be to hurry in second marriages and a mixed family without first laying a solid foundation. Instead, you need to take the right time to give yourself and everyone the opportunity to get used to each other, to the idea of marriage, and the formation of a new family. Too many changes simultaneously can

227

destabilize children. Mixed families have the highest success rate if the couple waits two years or more after a divorce to remarry, instead of using the new family as a "nail drive away."

Tips for Managing Your Children and Your Partner's

- Find ways to live "real life" together before marriage. Taking the kids from both and taking them to a theme park every time you meet can be a lot of fun, but it doesn't reflect everyday life. Better to get children used to their partner and their children in everyday situations.
- Decide on parenting roles before getting married and tell the children. Decide with your new partner how you intend to parent together, then make the necessary changes to your parenting styles before you get married again. With a smoother transition, children will not be angry with their new spouse. Children often feel unimportant or invisible when it comes to making decisions in the new mixed family. For this reason, recognizing them a role in the new family when making important decisions, calms them and makes them feel an essential part of the new project, dispelling fears of being abandoned, forgotten, set aside. Kids of all ages respond well to positive comments about their behavior, encouragement, and love to feel appreciated
- Never make preferences. It seems obvious, but it is good to say it. Your children or those of the new partner may put you in a situation where you feel you have to choose between them. Always remind everyone that you love everyone because they are all part of your life.
- Teach respect and affection. Children must treat the children of their parent's partner and also the new spouse always with respect because love is a cake to which slices are added, they are not taken away if someone new arrives. But this should be explained to children because they don't know it and they can become jealous, irritated, oppositional and even rude. Children like to feel affection, but it should be a gradual process that also involves processing the loss of the family from before and from the mom or dad who stayed to live elsewhere and whom they see less often.
- Have patience and the right support. It can give a lot of time, energy, love, and affection to your partner's children, who will not be returned immediately. Make small gestures and have daily, thoughtful, heartfelt, constant attention that can arouse

228

interest and desire to reciprocate. Children need to love and be returned. Given the right support, children should gradually adapt to the prospect of marriage and be part of a new family. It's your job to communicate openly, meet their security needs, and give them all the time they need to make a successful transition. Kids want to be talented to count on parents and stepfathers,

- Consolidate ties with "new" children—the chances of a positive bond with your new daughter increase by thinking about what they need. Age, gender, and nature are not irrelevant, but all kids have some basic needs and desires that, once met, can help you establish a rewarding new relationship. Creating an honest and open environment, free from judgments, will help children feel heard and emotionally connected to a new parent. It is essential to show them that the new partner can see or try to understand the situation also from their point of view, enhancing them.

- Establish clear boundaries and limits. Discuss the role that each parent will learn in raising their children, as well as changes in family rules. Children may not know or think they need limits in the new family, but a lack of boundaries sends a signal that the child is unworthy of the parents' time, care, and attention.

- As a new passing parent, you should not intervene as before but work with your spouse to establish what are the physical and mental spaces and the limits to be placed on their own and partner's children, according to principles of equality and justice while respecting diversity and everyone's needs. Clear rules help you get along.

- Find support in the routine. Creating family routines and rituals can help build bonds with your new children and unite the family as a whole. Invent at least one new special family ritual, such as going to the beach on Sunday, a weekly evening where everyone plays together or unusual ways to celebrate a family birthday. Regular family meals are vital, especially in the evening or at lunchtime on holidays, offering an excellent opportunity to talk and bond as well as encourage healthy eating habits.

- Keep all parents present in children's lives. Children are best suited to the mixed family if they have access to both biological parents. It is vital if all parents are involved and work for a parenting partnership. To let children know that mom and dad will continue to love them and be there for them for life is an essential thing for children. It is crucial to explain to the children that your new spouse will not be a "replacement" mom or dad, but another person to love and support. On the other hand, a separating couple no longer has a "conjugal" role but will always maintain a "parental" position towards their children.

Challenges Common To "New Families"

- Age differences. In mixed families, there may be children with birthdays closer than those with natural siblings, or the new parent may be only a few years older than the eldest child.
- The inexperience of parents. A "step" parent may never have been a parent before, and therefore may not have experienced the different stages children go through.
- Changes in family relationships. If both parents marry the parents of existing families, it can mean that the children suddenly find themselves with different roles in two mixed families. For example, a child may be the firstborn in an evolutionary family, but the youngest in the other. Mixed families can also mean that a child loses his uniqueness as the only boy or girl in the family.
- Mourning. In some children of one of the two members of the couple or both may no longer have a parent or have never had one. Create an atmosphere of serenity; it is essential to talk about it, discuss, tell, remember or always open a narrative about how the parent who is no longer there was, about the life of before and the life of now. Because only in this way can mourning be worked out and no longer interfere in the lives of children, spouses and the life of the new family. To be able to separate and move forward, in fact, one must first feel that he/she has always found within himself, in his / her heart and mind, the parent who has disappeared but lives in memory. But for two people who love each other, all these situations can be faced and overcome, all together, newlyweds and children of previous relationships, who will still have their natural parents by their side. If children see love, respect, and open communication between spouses and with their parents, who, in turn, may have responded, they will feel more confident and are more likely to shape those qualities.

COMMUNICATION PROTOCOLS
Modes of Communication

Let's face it: communicating with an ex-husband, ex-wife, or ex-partner is not always easy. Talking is often easier said than done. Feelings like anger, confusion, or nerves can make it difficult to say what you want or need to say. Although your relationship may have ended, communicating with a former spouse or former partner may be necessary on occasions such as when children are involved. By doing the good of giving your children a happier and healthier childhood with both parents involved, applying effective communication techniques to your conversations with your ex will be of benefit to you.

The constructive modules of effective communication after divorce begin with a commitment to raising your children together and creating the best possible environment for them to thrive. Remembering your commitment to them can help you and your former partner to continue a goal for what you hope to accomplish in your parenting collaboration. With your focus always in mind, you can turn your attention to creating different modules of effective communication.

Language

Effective communication depends mostly on the choice of language and words. Saying the wrong things in conversion at the wrong time can quickly change the course to where you would not have wished to have chosen. Sometimes the words can be misinterpreted, and the listener can give it a different meaning. So, it is essential to choose wisely. Choose the appropriate words to convey what you need to say adequately. Avoid language that has no other function than to hurt the other person. It may include an insult or different vulgar language.

Way of talking

Like word choice, how those words are conveyed is as essential to building effective communication. Your method of transmission, tone of voice, and timing are all aspects to consider when communicating. Choose a manner that allows you to deliver your message accurately. Depending on what you are talking about and how well you communicate verbally with your ex-spouse or ex-partner, face-to-face or over the phone conversations may not always be the best way to transmit individual messages. Written communication may work best for some former couples since it allows

231

long-distance conversation. It can give you the confidence to convey what you want to say more clearly. Even when written communication is used as your preferred method of communication, the tone still carries a lot of weight. The sound in written communication is not entirely based on the choice of words. Punctuations express volume, the use of capital letters, quotation marks, underlining. Other punctuation marks can change the tone of your written voice in a way that perhaps did not intend to do so. Avoid excessive use of dramatic punctuation. Finally, time can have a significant impact on how a person receives a message. While negotiating a parenting time exchange, it is probably not the time to touch on sensitive issues with your ex-spouse or ex-partner. Keep the more severe conversations reserved for times when you and your ex-partner can adequately focus on the issue at hand without putting your children in the middle of the conflict.

Listening

There are moments to speak, and there are moments to listen. It is often true that the moments of listening are just as, if not more, crucial to building effective communication after divorce. When I don't hear what the other person had to say correctly, how am I supposed to make a proper response? Be attentive during conversations with your former spouse or partner, listening carefully, or thoroughly reading the messages you receive. Don't jump to reply, take a moment to understand what you've heard, and then write your reply. If you don't know what to say or feel like you're about to explode, it's okay to say you need to talk about this later. However, don't forget the conversation, come back to it when you once feel ready to focus and give a smooth and effective response.

Consistency

A saying goes: 'Practice makes perfect.' Although 'a teacher' may be a bit of a stretch when it comes to how well you communicate with your ex-spouse or ex-partner, putting these building modules into practice will help you achieve and maintain effective communication over time. Commit to regularly consult with your former spouse or ex-partner about things that have to do with your children. Plan these conversations ahead of time so you can better focus on the topic at hand. Be consistent in sharing any concerns you have right away rather than allowing something that bothers you to become something more significant. Having open channels of communication will help you and your former spouse or ex-partner better overcome the needs of your children as a team,

As long as they are dedicated to creating a better life for their children, the modules for building effective communication after divorce are easy to implement. Language, speaking, listening, and consistency is elements that can help improve the way you and your former spouse or ex-partner communicate, which will also help you build a stronger relationship as peers in parenting.

Kids and Communication

In many cases of divorces with children, the parents often refer to the good of the children as essential and based on innumerable actions and efforts, failing instead to carry out different activities necessary for communication with the other parent, which in the opinion of our law firm. It is one of the important causes of child injury in cases of divorced parents since multiple conflicts occur as a result of this lack of communication, which ultimately harms ordinary children.

After the divorce, the spouses should make an effort to communicate in the simplest and most friendly way possible and otherwise seek solutions such as family mediation, since in many cases, both spouses have reasons in their conflicting foundations and their hostile actions. They create hostile reactions in the counterpart, in many cases producing chains of disagreements that could be arranged with communication and mutual will since, as a general rule, the lack of communication in divorces is the responsibility of both.

When parents get divorced, some parents never want to talk to each other again. Or parents agree to communicate only when necessary. They can do this to avoid arguments and conversations that can cause more pain.

However, children have very different needs when it comes to communicating with parents after divorce. Having frequent and continuous access to every parent can benefit children. As such, it is essential to create and discuss ways to preserve definite boundaries when it comes to communication between parents and children after divorce.

Decide What Is Necessary

Finding useful and beneficial communication limits will usually depend on the child's age and needs.

Younger children may need more frequent and constant communication with each parent; Older children may need more guidance on when to contact a non-custodial parent or how to be responsible when it comes to text messages, email, or communication with each parent.

Think about how a child can benefit from discussions with another parent and what that may entail.

For example, it may be a good idea to let your toddler call the other parent to say good night as he or she adjusts to spending time away from the other parent. But if you have a teenager who is more likely to use communication as a means of manipulation or avoidance, it may be best to set time limits and frequency of interactions with the other parent.

Having these limits can protect each parent's time with the child and also allows the child to maintain healthy and safe relationships with each parent.

Establish A Plan

Rules for communication can be part of a comprehensive parenting plan. Parents can dictate a call time and communication rules when the child is with the other parent. The policy may include guidance for parents if a child is calling or getting in much contact with a parent.

It is easier than ever for people to communicate, through a phone call, text, direct message, or video chat. Many children are more tech-savvy than their parents, and as such, the rules and limits of communication can be critical elements of any modern parenting plan.

Importance of Good Communication

With time the children arrive, they are no longer just two, and they are a family whose interests and needs must be watched, the road brings with it many changes, ups, and downs, changes that when love and desire are still there, together, they can face.

However, things don't always happen that way. There are couples that, over time, routines, and among other things, end up realizing that perhaps they are not that ideal couple they dreamed of so much and that maybe it is better to go their separate way.

But, when it comes to that point, whereas a couple they understand that they no longer work. The question always arises of what to do or how to do with the children. Should we stay together for them? How can we make them not suffer? Should I be friends with my ex? And countless other questions often arise at those times.

234

Although each family is different and each person has a different style of coping too, there are certain things that we must know and put into practice before and after making this decision. But instead of alleviating suffering, which in a way will be inevitable, to make the process a little smoother and easier.

Although we do not believe it that way or do not see it that way, many times children prefer to have separated parents, to live with parents who are still together but who no longer love each other, or among whom the fights are constant.

Often the suffering is less when the parents separate than when they decide to stay together for the "good of the children." What is important is that whatever the decision is made and the terms in which the parents have been left, communication between parents exists and is excellent.

Perhaps it is something challenging to think about when the relationship has not ended in the best terms; however, if we analyze it thoroughly, we will understand that maintaining excellent communication with the other parent will be a decision for the "good of the children."

We must recall that parents are the primary example figures of children. Therefore, most of the things they learn are given by the attitudes and behaviors of their parents.

The fact that as a couple, they can no longer understand each other does not mean that as parents, they cannot, by understanding and maintaining excellent communication beyond couple problems. They will be teaching their children adequate problem-solving strategies, and they will be able to learn to be empathetic, assertive and respectful of others' differences.

On the other hand, when there is inadequate or non-existent communication between divorced parents, children are usually the most affected, regardless of age.

Sometimes we tend to think that when they are older, they can better understand why mom and dad no longer speak to each other, and yes. However, they may interpret it better, and this does not mean that it does not affect them in the same way, because no child or adolescent in the world, kids would like their parents to live in conflict. Whatever their age, adolescents or preschool age, they will always need both parents for their proper development.

Remember that both mom and dad play fundamental roles in the growth process of children and the formation of their personality, so it is essential that both can be present and on good terms.

Now, when the communication between divorced parents is excellent, perhaps at first it will be difficult for the children to accept it and adapt to the new life with separated parents. The process will be much easier for them because they will feel the security that both parents, despite the differences, they will be there to support and care for you. In addition to this, not only do children benefit when there is excellent communication between divorced parents, the whole family will.

As parents, even if they are no longer a couple, they will be able to continue supporting each other in the upbringing process, which eases the work a little. Being a single mother or father is not the same as having the support of another person when raising children.

Like people, they will feel much better knowing that despite the differences, they can put them aside and work for the common good. It will not only bring peace to children, but it will also bring peace and tranquility to parents Because a person who lives with grudges or bitterness because of another, but it is too difficult to be calm.

DECISION MAKING

When I talk to parents about children and divorce, the first thing they usually want to discuss is how they can protect their children during the process as a lawyer. I am proud that most of the time, it is.

The most valuable advice as a lawyer and as a parent is that I can give is to minimize conflict and ensure that children are not placed amid battle. Children should not feel that they need to choose between their parents or that they are responsible for protecting them emotionally.

While this is the most important thing parents can do for them during divorce, there are other ways parents can put their children's needs first:

Make a Parenting Schedule

Managing schedules can be stimulating for married couples, and separation only exacerbates those challenges. The development of a manageable and realistic parenting program must take into account the child's developmental stage and unique personality. It's easy to recognize that a parenting plan for a 15-month-old and a 15-year-old look different.

A 15-month-old child is likely to have an early bedtime and nap schedule, so any transition should recognize those physical needs. In contrast, a 15-year-old boy's program has less to do with her physical needs and more to do with activities like school, extracurricular trials, and social interactions. The structure around your kid's developmental stage will reduce her physical and emotional stress by meeting her unique needs.

The other layer to consider is the child's temperament and personality. For example, some children thrive on routine; These children need to know their schedule and may have difficulties with transitions (especially younger children with special needs). They will need more bodily and expressive support to ensure that the changes are not disruptive.

Create A Decision-making Process

Parents who share decision-making on issues like medical treatment, religion, extracurricular activities, and education need to have a process to resolve disagreements as they will occur. For example, you have both been on the same page about medical issues, but one of you wants your child to go to therapy, while the other does not see the need.

As an attorney, when I work with couples to write parenting plans, we create a process that involves multiple steps. For example: First, parents have a discussion, they can go to a consultation for more information (e.g., medical provider, teacher), and then meet with a neutral third party (e.g., mediator, divorce coach) before going to the court. The creation of these steps provided a structure that minimizes post-decree litigation.

Check Your Personality Regarding Your Kids and Separation

It is the most challenging step to take because you are often not conscious. It requires the hard work of digging deep, to be honest with yourself about your motivations. For example, if you have been primarily a parent who has stayed home, sharing the shared upbringing may be a loss to your identity. It would not be unusual to say that children need to be with me more often because they have always been with me more often.

Separation is an opportunity for the other parent to become more involved and take on more responsibilities as a parent. We know from the literature on separation that one of the best forecasters of a child doing well after the divorce is having a positive connection with both parents.

On the other hand, a parent who journeys Monday through Friday needs to be honest with himself when requesting 50% custody time. Getting out of your comfort zone, being open to new ways of parenting, and accepting your limitations is an essential part of adjusting to a modern parenting dynamic.

These steps can be complicated and may require professional assistance from an attorney.

- Being in therapy during the separation process can allow you to sort through painful feelings so you can make decisions that are good for your future, as well as for your children and divorce priorities.
- Using a divorce coach or child specialist during the process can ensure that the needs of the children come to the fore. While all of these things can be emotionally and financially challenging at times, they will be worth it in terms of protecting children.

Timesharing

Divorce generally has a severe impact on children; with this in mind,

238

courts can order provisions to ensure that children are not harmed by the separation. Our Miami Gallardo Law Office always makes sure that children continue to develop in a good environment. We want children to maintain a healthy connection with the non-custodial parent. To do this, parents must present the Miami timeshare schedule to the court. In the case of parents who share joint custody of the children, they can resolve this issue out of court.

The Purpose of Timeshare

- Minimize loss: When parents get a divorce, children feel uprooted by the damage or loss of one of their parents. Studies show that divorce has a profound bad effect on kids and their future adult life. The timeshare minimizes the damage acquired after the separation.
- Maximize Relationship: As long as timeshare is involved, it's important to reinforce all the old relationships the child had before the divorce. It includes contact with the rest of the non-custodial parent's family. Parents should remember that they can never make their children feel guilty about enjoying their times with the non-custodial parent. They should also reassure the child that they are not to blame for the breakup. Parents should also avoid blaming each other for the breakup. You should try to prevent the details of why the separation, since the child may decide to be on your side to ease her pain.
- Increased safety: Parents must live near schools. It will prevent the disruption of the child's school life. It will also help maintain the old structure and stability of your life before the divorce.
- Avoid conflict: Parents should avoid arguing in front of children. When parents meet during child visits, they should limit themselves to cordial topics. They have to avoid all the problems that used to infuriate them in the past. Recall, quarreling in front of children does them no good. They should also try to keep up appearances at events that require both parents to be present. It will prevent the child from feeling embarrassed in front of her peers. If the parents cannot avoid fighting when they are close, they should meet in a neutral zone, where they can exchange custody of the child. The neutral zone can be with a grandfather or a friend.
- Age Needs: At each age, a child has different needs. They should arrange things in a way that is according to the age of the child. Older children may have more flexible hours. However, babies need special attention. It is up to the

239

safeguarding parent to provide the non-custodial parent with the baby car seat for the car and all the toys the baby may need.

- Right of Preference: Parents should discuss vacation dates as well as holidays. If the custodial parent plans to leave their child with a babysitter, the non-custodial parent should be given the option to fulfil that role.
- Parent Reintroduction: Parents can maintain a healthy relationship with their child. Sometimes it happens that the non-custodial parent had a hard time seeing his son for years. When this occurs, the custodial parent in Miami should make an alternative visitation plan that allows the child to get used to her father again.
- Cancellations: If one of the parents decides to cancel the timeshare, it must be done at least 14 days in advance. Cancellations lasting more than 72 days should be made only with the consent of both parents. If they disagree, the non-custodial parent must pay for childcare.
- Mediation Before Litigation: Parents should discuss visitation issues before presenting them to court.
- The new home should be large enough to give free rein to the comfort of children.
- Have flexibility in developing changes in the new plan for children's education.

Timeshare Statutes

Florida's timeshare statute requires that children spend enough time with their two parents. They must decide on important issues together unless a court order has ordered the waiver of all legal rights of one parent. Both parents deserve to see the kid's medical, dental, and school records. The custodial parental cannot deny this data to the non-custodial parent.

Timeshare schedules have three main objectives:

- Children are expected to develop in a meaningful time relationship with their parents after divorce.
- Parents have a significant time with their children.
- It also serves as a guide to what is expected of each parent.

Basic Needs to Take into Account Regarding Children

- Let the child know that he is not guilty that his parents live apart.
- Encourage and sustain a separate relationship with each of the parents, maintaining teaching and continuous guardianship of them.
- They had a pleasant coexistence with each of their parents, without pitting them against each other.
- Children have to enjoy regular and consistent time with each of their parents.
- Have financial help and support from parents, regardless of the amount of time each of them spends with the minor
- Have physical and mental security when you are with one of the children
- Having a relationship with close relatives as long as these relationships do not prevent or replace the child's bond with one of his parents

Regulations That Apply to Parental Custody Time

- Parents need to update their contact information. Share any topic regarding the kid. The kid should not be used as a tool for swapping data between parents
- The minor must maintain fluid communication with the parents without the interference of either party. Educate the child to love her father or mother equally. Do not verbally attack the other in the presence of the child
- Maintain privacy in communications either by any means (Fax, Telephone, E-mail) of the minor concerning each parent
- Leave detailed information in case the minor goes on a trip with one of the parents (Ex: Itinerary, dates, telephone number where it is located)

Timeshare Compliance

Concerning the timeshare calculated at our Gallardo law offices in Miami, we can highlight some of the sanctions that are issued when the children's timeshare is not correctly followed, such as:

241

- Contempt Sanctions. The parents have to abide by the orders ordered by the Court, strictly complying with the times stipulated by it.
- Powers of Equity. If the custodial parent denies the timeshare parent, the non-custodial parent who regularly pays the child's child support may file a request to obtain this timeshare by law.
- Criminal sanctions. Interference with custody or visitation rights can be a crime.

Development of The Timeshare Plan

The timeshare plan must be prepared by both parents, complying with the child's requirements and, in turn, theirs. Taking into account that one of them has primary custody, both must be directly related to the child and must be prepared and empowered to care for the minor. Each being responsible for providing adequate food and health. Maintaining a connection between the parent and the child is of utmost importance so that there is no distance between them. Create particular parenting schedules with irregular work schedules, allowing your child to have his / her proper time.

Decisive Steps and Children

A separation with children means that family life, as we knew it, is broken. It will be necessary to do two duels at the same time: the loss of the partner and the failure of the family.

Also, the breakup not only affects the couple but also affects the children, children who have not decided on it, but who must accept the new scenario. The break will generate a change in habits and daily routines, in addition to receiving that they will have two houses and their things distributed and that they will see their parents separately, and 50% of the time in most cases (joint custody).

So, what do we do when they tell us to leave home after several years of relationship? The writer Nicholas Lezard has lived, in the first person, the experience and has wanted to share his experiences.

1. Curb Emotions

The most important thing, he says, is not to make radical or far-reaching decisions right after the separation, since the thirst for revenge may appear. Therefore, it is best to wait a bit to manage the papers, and when the time is right, try to negotiate and find an agreement between the two parties. We have to wait for the emotions to calm down, get in place, and we can make decisions from the most rational part.

2. Don't Rush into Relationships

Social life has to be promoted but recommends that no couple relationship be started. During the phase of mourning, one becomes very sad and unmotivated and meeting new people helps to recover from the blow and not to be locked up thinking about everything that happened, but to disconnect and distract the mind, apart from looking for friends to occupy that time that was dedicated to the couple.

Once the grief phase overcome, one tends to fall into the error of turning in the first relationship that appears due to the desire to regain the life of a couple. It can involve making hasty decisions. Therefore, you have to be patient, learn from experience, and spend time with yourself and know how to manage loneliness.

3. Create New Bonds with Children

Children become the most important thing. The shock caused by the separation helps to focus much more on the children and not on work and day today as it used to be. It leads to an improvement in the emotional bond with them and in the quality of the timeshare. We must create a new relationship, generate a new dynamic, and know-how to listen to the needs of the children. We must not forget that the family does not break; the couple breaks. Therefore, to continue educating the children, it is essential to communicate with the former couple and achieve the highest well-being towards them, coordinate and show them that the part Family continues with a new format.

4. Accept the New Reality

It is time to accept the financial limitations and value the day today. A new stage has to be assumed with different conditions. You have to try not to think about what you had, but how to live in the current moment, look for solutions, tools to be able to face the expenses.

5. Learn from Experience

It is essential to reflect and learn about what has happened. It is customary to change the way of living and to see things. There is personal growth, and you learn that there is no point in trying to change people. Every experience is an apprenticeship, and the good thing is to take advantage of the discomfort and the painful experience.

6. Enjoy Yourself

The tastes are again similar to those of youth. The majority of hobbies shared with the couple tend to be eliminated with the separation. They recover their hobbies before the relationship. It is a moment where one tends to find oneself again. It offers a space where you can connect with yourself, know what you want, think about needs, fears, insecurities. And if you take advantage of it, it can be a great source of well - being and growth.

FINANCE DECISIONS

Getting divorced is a roller coaster of emotions, but it can also be a real threat to your finances. You must have clear accounts, or you will risk not being able to pay the commitments of your new life.

We give you some tips to get your finances intact after taking separate paths.

1. Fair Agreements

It may seem impossible amid the emotions of a divorce. Yet, it is essential to remember that making the best financial decisions for both parties will benefit you in the long run.

2. Advice from An Expert

Nothing healthier than a good agreement under the recommendations of an expert. If there are joint debts, mortgages, or any other type of financial commitments that are paid between the two, we suggest you find a personal financial advisor to help you establish fair agreements.

This professional will be able to help them understand the new financial panorama of each one and make recommendations to them not to become economically unbalanced.

3. Close Shared Accounts

Once you have filed for divorce, it is essential to stop accumulating debt together. It is a risk factor for each person's credit history in case the opponent spends more than she can pay.

4. Create A Budget

Moving from a two-income home to one is a significant transition. If you're not used to budgeting, a divorce is a compelling reason to start doing it. Be sure to record all your daily and monthly expenses, including child support and alimony payments. It will help you avoid overspending as you adjust to your new financial life.

5. Learn to Manage Your Finances

In many marriages, a spouse acts as a financial manager. That means that he is in charge of paying the services and debts, establishing the budget, filing annual tax returns, etc.

It is time to take control of your finances and develop the habit of planning.

6. Update Documents

Check the documentation to which you must change personal data and postal address: account statements, insurance policy contracts, subscriptions, and other correspondence.

7. Ensure Your Health and The Rest of The Family

If one of the spouses is the owner of the policy in the health insurance coverage, establish the grace period so that individual plans are contracted. At this point, they must also analyze with which system the children will be insured, trying to choose the oldest and best price.

8. Establish Your Credit

If they handled the same credit cards as a couple, it was time to open accounts separately. Although it is not advisable to accumulate a lot of new debts, it is advisable to establish new credit, open a bank account and credit card in your name.

Remember that if you need an immediate personal loan, Kubo Financiero offers alternatives for the amount, term, and periodicity of payment.

9. Update Wills and Beneficiaries

It is common for the spouse to play a beneficiary role in credits, assets, retirement plans, or insurance. Update all of this to establish who the new person you would like to appoint to fill these roles is.

10. What About Savings?

Saving money may seem counterintuitive at a time when your financial situation changed significantly. You never know when unexpected expenses may arise and need a little more. Divorce is something that is not planned, and it can feel completely overwhelming to face all the decisions and details that need to be resolved. But the faster you take control, the adaptation to this life change will come peacefully.

Determine Financial Reality

The first guideline to consider, after undergoing a separation process is to determine the current financial reality. Because it is the starting point for any readjustment action that you want to implement. Current Financial Reality

It displays the relevant aspects that influence consumer decision-making. In other words, it is the x-ray of contemporary financial management; and for this, the preparation of the budget is necessary.

For this, the following questions must be answered:

- To whom and how much do I owe?
- How much is available in stock?
- What are the fixed costs?

The answer to three questions represents the financial x-ray of what's going on in managing money with the person right now. But at the same time, it offers a global overview of how this new reality of life should be addressed. Since to the extent that there is a clarity of what the commitments are and the availability to meet them, then there will be a better economic performance. Budget

It is for this reason that the ideal tool to develop all this is the budget.

The budget is the backbone of finance. And its use, within financial management, is critical. It is used as part of the planning and is the benchmark against which to compare business performance.

It consists of three parts:

- Income
- Expenses
- Savings

And its elaboration consists of three necessary steps:

- 1st. List sources of income

247

- 2nd. Make an inventory of costs, taking into account those of lesser amounts. For this, it is suggested to do a 30-day exercise where all transactions are recorded.
- 3rd. Develop a savings system based on surpluses. It is identifying which are for contingency and which for the materialization of previous planning.

In other words, the budget provides an opportunity for the person who implements it to have a useful and reference tool for planning money management and making adjustments to place.

Prioritize

The second guideline for financial restructuring after going through a separation process is to prioritize. It is perhaps one of the most critical points, since, to the extent that it is prioritized, there will be a scale that will define what is most important within this new stage of life that is beginning.

In this sense, prioritizing is defining what goes first and what goes next. In other words, establish a differentiation of primary, secondary, tertiary needs, etc. and to develop them, it is necessary to be clear about what is dispensable and what is not. By then, discriminate the level of importance of each of them.

Save

The third guideline has to do with the creation of contingency funds. Because, now more than ever, it is necessary to have available resources to solve the different commitments that can be assumed. Save money

In this sense, there are several alternatives to savings systems that can be implemented:

- Piggy banks
- Percentage
- Permanent
- Staggered

Each of these systems involves an adaptation process in which the person assumes the discipline and culture of saving. The important thing in all this is knowing that divorce represents a reality that must be faced, and to the extent that you have the necessary tools, you can cope more suitably.

248

PLANNING KID'S HOLIDAYS

In these times of rapid change, where few traditions have managed to preserve a prominent place, the Holidays continue to hold many wishes and hopes in society all over the world.

The manger that appears armed in many places accompanying the little tree, beyond the belief that we profess or the scepticism that we defend, is a symbol of the mother-father-child triangle and, therefore, a direct association to the most primitive family plot. Consequently, it emphasizes the functions of the couple, whatever their gender, and the child as the initial nucleus of what is called "family group."

The Classic Divorce

A divorce usually brings with it a conflict that rests UNFAIR and generally on children and adolescents that have nothing to do with the decisions their parents have made regarding separation.

The family as a cell continues, despite enthusiastic attempts to destabilize it, playing a protective and structuring role that has been sustained over time and sets fire to the identity and social belonging of its members.

Thus, divorce will generate an inevitable process of mourning for a lost project that will settle on the individual and family-historical bases that have preceded this event of separation. Again, it is necessary to emphasize that children do not have to do with this and that parents should keep in mind that in this role, they are united for life.

It is worth waiting then, instead of harmony, disagreements, power fights, threats, projection of sadness transformed into a narcissistic rage, lack of rationality, eternal discussions. Questions divide the boys without breaking them so that they can spend the holidays as a whole, with the family (although not "all") and happy.

Ideally, adults should make life easy for children, but without overprotecting or "compensating" them with excessive gifts and pampering since divorce is painful but not necessarily dramatic. Sometimes it avoids worse evils.

Cultural Imperatives

The festive atmosphere, in general, implies an imperative: "Love your

249

family and your neighbor, in peace, eating and drinking (in moderation?), Forgiving family and friends, even the horrible ones, be happy!" Dominant discourse aims at joy without limit, to fill what is empty - without first thinking if it is necessary to fill it -, to quickly cover what we suffer at any cost without stopping to think about what it is about.

It is better to do as Seneca said: "When you cannot correct something, the best thing is to know how to suffer it." Here we are with people who suffer and get very angry at parties, with the consequent feeling of guilt that haunts them for not being able to sing Christmas carols out loud and make a religious or loving feeling so that the world hurts less.

The new forms of families: single parents, same-gender fathers, and mothers, extended groups, fractured groups, single people, people who have lost a loved one, deserve that we try to create flexible processes to include these forms of social bonding. Always consider that it is essentially a function that authorizes, decides, and, if necessary, sanctions to transmit a limit that acts as a loving containment of the little ones in the full constitution of their person.

Trends for Peace

- If parents cannot agree to decide with whom their children will spend the holidays, they may consider using the services of a mediator to help them resolve BEFORE communicating the decision to the children what will be taken for granted for the holidays and vacations.
- The advisable thing, if it is in the possibilities of the couple, is to alternate each year the two periods:
- Christmas Eve and Christmas, you can choose one night with one and lunch in the other if you are in the same city.
- New Year's Eve and Kings.
- Seriously try not to make the children feel guilty for not being with a parent on those specific dates. Parents, separated or not, will be in charge of caring for and protecting them and NEVER the opposite. Although it may be difficult for the adult to accept separating from the children on these emotional dates, the stability of the children is the fundamental thing, and this should imply the capacity of procrastination in the parents. The best Christmas gift for a child or teenager is to think about everyone's well-being and adjust to the situation as responsible parents.
- If there is a new partner of one of the parents, the parties will be handled with care to protect the children, especially if the relationship is too recent to present it as definitive.

- The reality of a new couple means losing hope that parents get together, and children often believe that it is the fault of this situation that reconciliation does not occur. Keep in mind that no one will replace or take the place of mom or dad, which is non-transferable and forever, with its defects and virtues.
- Speak to children with transparency. Take times. Sometimes a year that is considered "lost" in terms of vacations is a future "earned" in attitudes of maturity and respect for the other.
- Maintain a definite and firm opinion about the other spouse in front of the children and do not be tempted to criticize them and find out gossip through the children.

Little Gifts

Life is a gift. Existence itself, friendship, the privilege of having a family, shelter, shelter, and good health are the best presents we can find at the foot of the tree. Let us know how to show solidarity and recognize ourselves. It is good to share the food, the excellent bread, the good wine, and some very salty tears. It doesn't matter what we give. It matters what we can provide.

CO-PARENTING IN PUBLIC SPACES

Who is looking for alternative family models, mostly because the classic model did not work, and the despair is great; because you might not want to do it at all, or for whatever reason, you end up with co-parenting or co-parenting? That's why you ended up here. Welcome first, it starts immediately.

Co-parenting

I will use the term co-parenting because the new German co-parenting describes two very different approaches. First, the family model presented here, 'Friends have a child together,' but also a type of parenting or an upbringing style between couples and couples whoever is interested in it, here or entirely scientifically and in English with Mark Feinberg. This article is only about the former, friends as parents.

Why Co-parenting as A Family Model

That sums it up pretty well, I think, but it goes beyond not wanting to live in a partnership, but often merely enough because the right partner has not yet found one, but the biological clock is ticking. Or you want to become a mother or father promptly, for example, because you have taken a lot of time and soon it will no longer be possible.

For me, the dream man is also considerably late, which is why I simply took away his role as the father of the child of choice. Who is new, and so Because how can I find him in peace when my ovaries and uterus hysterically announce their wishes in the brain? Nobody can concentrate when tears come to your eyes at the sight of every baby because you are so jealous and longing.

Desire to Have A Partner, What Now?

I can put it in my own words, but restrict myself here to the constellation of single woman and co-father from the woman's point of view, because I know my way around: the prerequisite is a strong desire to have children, which should be fulfilled. And by that, I mean stable! About as strong. In this situation, women can choose between several scenarios.

252

How Did It Go with Me?

How did the mind game go with me? Have a look at Where do the babies come? To Points 1-4 fell away for me, a child without a man, so only sperm, mostly Danish, was difficult for me since my job as a flight attendant requires childcare for several days. How this can be done elegantly and relaxed with the donor child can be read very well by Hanna von Solomamapluseins and Kathrin von Solomamaherz. So, for me, co-parenting remained.

Details

Women and men come together, but not on a romantic level, but only to be a parent. How the details work is up to each pair of coulters. You can find all details about our agreement, our claims and our reality here. The parents usually live in separate apartments, the child commutes, like a different couple. It's just that all the emotional ballast is gone. No separation, no disappointment, no hurt egos, no hate. Ideally. Of course, many couples also get a clean and dignified divorce, but the child's wellbeing above everything else, get along well and are also co-parents in the end. Still, most of the time, you hear more about rose wars, mud fights and strenuous separations for everyone involved.

Since co-parents were never in love with the sky, the deathly sadness also disappears. Of course, there are sometimes differences of opinion, but just among friends, it usually doesn't get that ugly. Or at least it shouldn't. It works pretty well for us; we had no arguments exactly once, because of some nonsense. Co-parenting also has some advantages in everyday life.

Our Agreement

- We are both alone with the child for several days, but by no means single parent, you are rather bobbed on a long lifeline than swimming alone in the ocean. (How exhausting, demanding, and beautiful life as a single parent is, that describes the pearl mom in a very charming and vivid way.)
- Yes, at 02:00 at night, if the child wants to play and he / I don't have to, he / I have to go through it, but in case of doubt, he / I can sleep in the next day because she will be with me. If all else fails, he / I can come around and jump in at night. If you know from the start that only I have to take care of myself at night, then at least I didn't find it that stressful. It's just like

253

that, and then it works. You don't have this mental relief as a single parent. We also have shared responsibility, and nothing is more substantial on our shoulders than sole responsibility for a child. We make big decisions together because we are partners in crime.

- Financially it is an entirely different story for two. I get maintenance (voluntarily) as wage compensation, we share the running costs. Papa is also responsible for the pony, first own car and condominium, maybe I'll tell him in advance.
- In the first year, the little girl was complete with me, we decided that because of breastfeeding, etc., but you can do it very differently. It was a fantastic year for me, I have a very intense relationship with my daughter, she doesn't have to share me with anyone, and I don't have to split my time between several. I have a lot of fewer roles: I am I, I am her mother, and that's it. If she wanted to go to bed at 6:00 p.m., I could relax with me because nobody was waiting for me anyway and was disappointed because Quality time was neglected as a couple. We lived into the day together, and of course, that was only possible because we have a great, flexible dad who fits in where it fits. He was visiting almost every day and got to know his daughter intensely, but I didn't have to be there, I could do the housework, shower, sleep. In short, for me, the whole pair work ceased, the realignment as parents (couple), the arrival of three is certainly a lot of work.
- One point that mums understand best: I have child-free days! Regularly. In my apartment, to do things, relax, go to work. Or just to sleep, read, do nothing, just not to be a mom. Does it sound mean? Ask every mom around the world how nice it is, how much it charges the batteries, and how great it is to see your little one again after two days of relaxing and missing. How much patience you have with childish anger/slowness/disorder/stubbornness/repetition and noise if you could do without it two days beforehand.

Aren't You Selfish?

Wait, the inclined reader is screaming, what about the child? We treated selfish parents, but what about the children? How are they? I can't ask mine yet, but I can see how much she loves her dad, how much she loves being with him, and how effortlessly she moves from one parent to another. She only knows it that way, and it seems to be good for her. I can only guess what she's going to say in a few years.

The most important thing for me: she is an absolute dream child, from both of us. So much wanted, showered with love from both parents and two happy grandparents. What more could a child want? You learn love from being loved, not because you see that the parents love each other. Otherwise, very many people in the past could not have liked, because the model of a family of father and mother who really loves each other and therefore has a child is not particularly old. My parents got married out of love, and my grandparents didn't. They were married.

The Importance of Co-parenting for Children

Other researchers have investigated more how co-parenting affected the adaptation of children at various stages of life. It has been seen how parental cooperation a protective factor for the child's adjustment is. How the collaboration perceived by one of the two parents can be a loser of the child's social skills and how, instead, co-parent conflict may predict a negative parenting relationship and the appearance of antisocial behavior in adolescents. However, other studies surprisingly found an absence of a link between co-parent cooperation and the life satisfaction of adolescents (Teubert and Pinquart, 2011).

In essence, the co-parenting relationship is also fundamental for its results, in particular as regards the adaptation of children. As explained, the co-parenting relationship can have a powerful influence on aspects of family life and, therefore, also on the adaptation of the child. Co-parent conflict has been shown to predict parental negativity and antisocial behavior in children and, in general, to externalizing or internalizing symptoms. Some factors can moderate the influence of co-parent conflict. These are the characteristics of the child (gender, birth order, etc.) and the characteristics of the family (divorced or otherwise divorced) and the context. On the other hand, it has been shown that the positive influence of co-parenting cooperation improves parenting of mothers and fathers. Consequently, perceptions of the level of co-operation within the co-parenting relationship independently predict an increase in children's social skills.

The Co-Parents, especially in recent years, was discovered to be a central hub, as regards family relationships, and can also be defined as a parental alliance. The use of the term alliance is, in fact, significant: real allies are those who not only agree publicly on an action plan but who then continue to support that plan both when they exercise parenting with their partner and when they exercise it alone.

This bond is of central importance acts as a mediator in family ties, as the relationship between partners, the parenting relationship, and, consequently, for the well-being of the offspring. Finally, co-parenting turns out to be a relatively new study object whose forms change and adapt to changes in society and its needs. For this reason, in addition to its importance for family well-being and secondly for social welfare, we must expect it to become more and more an object of study and evaluation.

RISING WELL-ADJUSTED AND RESILIENT KIDS IN A TWO-HOME FAMILY

A few weeks ago, the director of the Senate declared that the residences where thousands of children are interned to be protected, "are not the hell that some have wanted to show." For the psychologist, Matías Marchant, the official's opinion ignores the hard experience that children live from the moment they are separated from their families. In this text, he reviews the bad psychological skills that are omitted and where sexual abuse is only one of the problems.

Rolando Melo, director Sename recently stated: " The residences are not the hell that some have wanted to show. " His words, without a doubt, do not help us adequately address how the State must take charge of the protection of children who have been effectively violated in their rights.

Since the affirmation is a metaphor that does not allow to be contrasted, I propose to carry out an exercise that will enable us to get closer to the experience that the child has within the residences. Only in this way, the reader will be able to find the figures, the images, or the words that account for the experience that children live when they need to live in a home:

From the moment a child enters a home, he is confronted with one of the most considerable anxieties that a person can experience, whatever their age. The child must be separated from his parents and enter a home that is entirely unknown to him. Regardless of the experience of violation of rights, the child joins a system or a network of people that is alien to him and does not have, at first, good reasons to trust this. One of the first childhood anxieties is to lose oneself; well, this is the real experience that a child who has been hospitalized goes through. A fear is updated that most have had, but that some, unfortunately, have to live personally.

It is an adult who, in the name of his protection, invites the child to live in a new home. At other times they are taken by policemen who tell him that it is only a short walk. In other cases, they say children that their parents are "working" and, therefore, must live in a home while they cannot care for them.

They are removed from their homes and do not take more than their clothes with them, no objects, no belongings accompany them (for example, a photograph), since the house will provide them with everything that is strictly necessary. Thus, they are made from the place where they lived without any object, no memory of their previous existence. The child feels lost because, on infrequent occasions, there are adults who explain to him, at the time, the separation occurs and many times during the hospitalization period, the reasons why he will have to live in a new home. Words are usually fewer than the child needs to understand her situation.

The child meets a multitude of adults whose mission is to protect him, but it turns out that the person who receives him at home with this intention will no longer be at night or the first weekend, due to the usual system of shifts that households have. The child, on his first night, as in those that follow, will wake up alarmed, anxious to know where he is and not to know why those who took care of him during the day are not there. Now he has adults in front of him he doesn't recognize.

Childhood fears of loneliness and helplessness are actualized in the child's everyday experience.

The next day and in the ones that follow, the child will look for clothes to wear and will see how difficult it will be to find their clothing. Your bedroom will be shared with ten or more children, in case they are small, who at night can wake you up with their cries or their calls for help as a result of the situation of psychic helplessness. In the case of older children, they must sleep in a bedroom with other children they do not know.

Care must be distributed to four to eight children per caregiver. It necessarily implies that the child will experience affective deficiency and, as common-sense shows, affection for a child is as important as food. It is relevant to keep this in mind since, if it is intended to close the homes and install the children in foster families in this same number, the problem will not be solved at all, it will merely now occur elsewhere.

While young, children often suffer from skin diseases and respiratory problems inside homes. In periods of physical weakness, does the child who feels even more helpless have enough concern and care from a caregiver who is still in charge of four or more children? How can the child name the experience of being sick, and most of the time alone?

A child who lives in an institution runs the severe risk of losing the records and traces of his personal history. Without this memory, your identity becomes more challenging to constitute, since you cannot integrate into it the different moments and objects that have been important in your history. The main reason why this biographical memory can be lost is related to the usual institutional structure. To do a job, a correct fragmentation of the different roles and functions that adults fulfil in a disciplined family environment is implemented. In very concrete terms, this can be seen in the fact that the child receives the care of numerous caregivers. They are distributed according to the shift system that the institution installed, which even occurs within the same day.

258

By multiplying the efforts that one, two, or three people typically make, day by day, within a family, not only can the coherence and continuity of the dealings be lost, but also - and more importantly - the child's memory.

Households promote a religious experience in children, regardless of the child or his or her family of origin has their own, have not decided, or even do not have it.

Usually, living inside an institution deprives the child of the possibility of having belongings that become objects that remain in time and that accompany him in the transformations and changes lived in the period that he remains in it. Although specific practices seek for a child to have some objects of their own, it is tough for them to keep them for too long. Institutions generally do not have places to store the child's belongings. The toys he receives practically never become a possession. Not even her bed is entirely her.

Little by little, the child will have an experience of loss of all possibility of intimacy. What happens to him will no longer be a domain of private experience; from now on, almost no experience will be personally lived. You will get used to living in common spaces because private spaces in homes are usually closed. Officials often have keys so that only they can open and close the doors. The bathrooms are collective, the dining rooms, the rooms for watching TV, and even the place of visits are shared. The child stops having an individual experience; now, most of her experiences are collective: homogeneous and uniform.

When parents go to visit, they must overcome a series of previous tests. The encounter with the child will no longer be an intimate experience: it will be watched or supervised by someone from home. The child may be visited in places specially equipped for this purpose: the visiting room or patio. Parents or relatives, whatever their characteristics, will no longer be able to visit their bedroom. They will no longer be able to accompany them to the bathroom and cleaning, and they will be prohibited from giving them or attending them to eat (although they manage most of the time to fill them with candy and sweets). Subjects of mistrust, children will see their parents being questioned in their behavior before him.

Usually, no one worries that the child who enters the home can prolong the care experiences that were satisfactory for him before entering. Few cares about keeping the objects - which are so crucial to children - that have been part of their daily experience. No parent is asked about the type of successful care they had before their entry, because in life, these parents, however negligent they were, had the opportunity to learn about some of the child's particularities that allowed them to accommodate their needs and preferences. There is no experience of continuity because you want to break with the child's past. And everything is put in the same bag of the violation of rights.

Children will often see that their parents will be forbidden to take photos with them, even though most of them ignore a ban as absurd as that. Visiting hours will be frankly limited, and during holiday periods (Christmas, September 18, holidays, vacations), many homes are closed to visits due to lack of staff or due to their activities. They will be excluded from the rites even though they will celebrate it in the previous days.

Households promote in children a religious experience regardless of whether the child or his / her family of origin have their own, have not decided or even do not have it. Sometimes the periods of hospitalization crossed by religious rights where both the children and the parents have consulted for it.

In short, a child's average experience is similar to what we see through a kaleidoscope: multiple fragments collected at random. Memory is threatened; the notion of intimacy is lost. The child makes the experience of affective deprivation flesh, his affections to the skin are testimony to the helplessness, the lack of communication is reflected in a language that comes late and reduced concerning children of his age.

If, unfortunately, the child was to meet an adult who, instead of exercising care, attacked, threatened and violently, the experience will confirm that the adults who have promised to care for him, have again failed to speak. It is evident that for the child, it will not be an easy task to denounce the aggressor since he will see in them complicity. Sometimes they will have to come from outside the institution to ask if they have suffered any type of violation of rights. Still, it becomes evident that whatever the methodology. It is challenging for the child to trust this third group of people who say they want to protect him, even more. If there is a fourth group of people (society) that in many cases, ignores even the complaints made by the children, claiming that they have not understood correctly. Your questions or that you have not been able to express yourself accurately.

It is frequent that when the child grows up, he "escapes" from home because crossing the doors will stop being a simple exit and will now be a prohibited exit. In their "escapes," children usually go to their parents' house, which does not fail to attract attention since the hospitalization experience has been unable to show that it is better than that lived with their parents. Otherwise, the children would not return home. In other cases, they simply go for a walk around the city, go to malls, to "Happyland" (sic), squares, game centres, experiences that they are most often deprived of it. We see some of them on weekends wandering around the city.

Many of the difficulties mentioned above have to do with a problem as fundamental as financing. The systems are forced to introduce a series of corrupt practices in their operation because they lack the resources to have the qualified personnel and the necessary infrastructure to take in the children who require our protection.

Incredibly, the State believes that it is legitimate and even valid that to maintain the system of protection of children, one can resort to public charity and charity

It is known that the State does not give enough money to households, not even for the maintenance of basic needs. Anyone who is in charge of his family and who lacks the money to feed, clothe, educate and protect his members, would not hesitate to call it "hell," and submit to the humiliation of resorting to the charity of the others it is a situation that redoubles this condition.

Incredibly, the State believes that it is legitimate and even valid that public charity and charity can be used to maintain the child protection system. It is unacceptable that the State - knowing this - do little or nothing so that children who need to be separated from their parents receive quality care with the corresponding resources!

Indeed, the residences cannot be the hell that many have wanted to make-believe. The experience that I have strictly described is not called that in sociology called the "Total Institutions," an experience characterized by the loss of the distinction between the public and the private, intrusion of the institution in all areas of life, depriving it of a space of freedom and minimal dignity.

It is also true that there are good residences where most of these vices typical of total systems have been overcome, but we can assure that they are the least and that it is done at the cost of great efforts. The truth is that the State cannot demand good practices, because with what moral authority can it request home to protect children if it does not provide the minimum to care for them?

The State does not provide the minimum in a bidding system, as if it were a service company. It imposes the logic of the child attended by day an organization destined for objectives goes further. They aim at the restitution of rights and the repair they violated. Those goals can't be paid for the number of nights a child sleeps in residence!

The experience described above does not mean that there do not have to

261

be residential systems, on the contrary. There must be both short-stay institutions and specialized foster families dedicated to caring for children who require a more specific and sensitive type of care regarding any other child who has not had an experience of violation of rights. Both systems are necessary for the care and protection of children, and a serious technical discussion is required to clearly define the conditions and characteristics that they must have to protect children.

The worrying thing about the Senate director's statement is that it is not accompanied by an unrestricted defence of children's rights, a situation that must start, first of all, by listening to what the children say, whatever the methodology by which they are makes talk

The discussion in Chile seems to end in the child returning to a family that gives him the care and protection he deserves. But that is only part of the job; the other, the most important, the one that is long-term oriented, is the one that asks the reasons, the conditions that led to the children being left unprotected and no longer being listened to it.

Not only are economic resources required for residences, but it also requires an ideological and political discussion about childhood and what society expects of it. A severe technical analysis is also necessary to face the problems already known in a vast bibliography on the subject.

What is worrying about the affirmation of the director of Sename is that his denial is not accompanied by an unrestricted defence of children's rights. This situation must start, first of all, by listening to what children say, whatever the methodology by the that makes them talk. And also, because Sename's challenge is to demand that the public administration and society as a whole provide them with the resources that are necessary to give the children a quality, protective, and therapeutic experience. It is expected of those who are in charge of precisely the most valuable and fragile part of our society, their childhood.